WESTMAR COLLEGE L
W9-BVH-215

The Study of Religion in Colleges and Universities

GEORGE F. THOMAS

THE STUDY OF RELIGION IN COLLEGES AND UNIVERSITIES

Edited by Paul Ramsey and John F. Wilson

WITH CHAPTERS BY

William A. Clebsch
Malcolm L. Diamond
Tom F. Driver
James M. Gustafson
Paul M. Harrison
David Little
Arthur C. McGill
Jacob Neusner
Victor Preller
Krister Stendahl
H. P. Sullivan
A. Richard Turner
John F. Wilson

PRINCETON UNIVERSITY PRESS
1970

207.73
S933

BL
41
.S78

Copyright © 1970 by Princeton University Press
All Rights Reserved
L.C. Card: 70-90957
ISBN: 0-691-07161-6

This book has been composed in Linotype Caledonia

Printed in the United States of America
by Princeton University Press, Princeton, New Jersey

80555

Preface

THE ESSAYS brought together in this volume were originally prepared for a conference held at Princeton University in the spring of 1968. The conference was occasioned by the retirement of George F. Thomas from the University. Appointed Professor of Religious Thought in 1940, Professor Thomas had become Chairman of the University's Department of Religion when it was established in 1946. Beginning in 1955, the Department, under his thoughtful leadership, developed a Ph.D. degree program while continuing to expand its undergraduate offerings. During the last decade of his teaching career George F. Thomas was Moses Taylor Pyne Professor at Princeton.

As it was projected, the conference assumed a particular complexion. There seemed to be a need for serious discussion of the study of religion in American colleges and universities. It seemed equally clear that religion study, probably for contingent as well as inherent reasons, is manifold in composition at the present time and gives every indication of continuing to be so in the foreseeable future. Accordingly, the attempt was made to identify traditional disciplines and subject matters within departments of religion and to seek out a distinguished representative of each who might discuss its present character. It was also decided that certain approaches to the study of religion which, in some sense, are newer and may be more problematic should be reviewed. In these instances as well, appropriate authors were invited to contribute essays.

Each of the participants was asked to discuss his subject in whatever fashion seemed most appropriate to it, without prescription of a common form or a general thesis. Some authors elected to cast their chapters in terms of critical reviews of recent literature. Others chose an essentially philosophical mode of argument in exploring assumptions, definitions, and commitments. At least one individual sought to address his topic through contributing to the ongoing work of the field, in this way exemplifying the manner as well as the constitutive materials of his type of inquiry. In certain respects the decision to foster such pluralism of approaches among the different authors was a deliberate gamble that excellence or virtue in each essay would contribute to a livelier and more useful whole.

In these terms the multiplicity of forms or the diversity of modes renders all the more impressive the emphasis which falls upon certain shared assumptions. All participants took for granted, as not requiring discussion, that the study of religion is entirely appropriate to the arts and sciences curriculum. Furthermore, it was commonly assumed at the conference that purposes underlying the study of religion within liberal arts programs are discrete from, and not to be identified with, work at professional schools engaged in directly serving the religious subcommunities of our society. Indeed, differentiation between the study of religion in the context of liberal arts and the study of religion in the seminaries seems to have proceeded very far—it was even argued during the conference that at the present time the former is significantly less problematic than the latter. In addition, the conferees seemed to agree that the study of religion would require departmental or programmatic status. Finally, the participants appeared generally to think that increasingly the organization of departments or programs within colleges and universities would be grounded upon certain basic families of methodologies.

Accordingly, a twofold intention underlies publication of *The Study of Religion in Colleges and Universities.* First, attention is directed toward the study of religion, the basic intellectual activities appropriate to liberal arts colleges and university arts and sciences faculties, rather than toward questions of curriculum or teaching methods. This is to stress fundamental or primary issues and searchingly review them, assuming that consideration of secondary matters (which are frequently discussed) will profit therefrom. Second, there is a concern that these essays anticipate the future not so much to predict it as to explore, in the light of recent experience, the range of developments now possible for the study of religion over the course of the coming decades.

At the conference the consensus seemed to hold that this twofold intention had been realized. The essays, arranged in appropriate pairings, were delivered as abbreviated papers at general sessions. Discussion followed at each meeting. The authors benefited from these exchanges, and some significant revisions of the original essays have been undertaken for this volume. Thus while the proceedings of the conference are represented through the printing of the following chapters, each contribution appears in a fuller and more substantial form in the published version. An Introduction sketches both the extended background and the more immediate context of present deliberations about the study of religion, especially for the benefit of any readers who may not be acquainted with them. A general conclusion to the volume is provided by an address delivered at the conference banquet. It assesses the current state of the study of religion and provides a forecast of some relevant developments which may be expected. In this sense, the concluding chapter suggests certain practical considerations which are not discussed in the more theoretical chapters in the main part of the volume.

The conference was made possible through the generosity of numerous friends and former students of George F. Thomas. It was organized by Franklin W. Young, who was at the time the Chairman of the Department of Religion at Princeton University. The publication of this book will, we trust, signalize the contribution made by George F. Thomas during recent decades to the development of the study of religion in colleges and universities.

Princeton, New Jersey
April 1, 1970

Paul Ramsey
John F. Wilson

Contents

Preface v

Introduction: The Background and Present Context of the Study of Religion in Colleges and Universities — JOHN F. WILSON 3

Biblical Studies in the University — KRISTER STENDAHL 23

History and Salvation: An Essay in Distinctions — WILLIAM A. CLEBSCH 40

Student Concerns and Philosophical Analysis: Unscrambling Theological Uses of "Contingent" — MALCOLM L. DIAMOND 73

The Ambiguous Position of Christian Theology — ARTHUR C. MCGILL 105

Catholic Studies in the University — VICTOR PRELLER 139

Modes of Jewish Studies in the University — JACOB NEUSNER 159

The Character and Contribution of the Sociology of Religion — PAUL M. HARRISON 190

Comparative Religious Ethics — DAVID LITTLE 216

The History of Religions: Some Problems and Prospects — H. P. SULLIVAN 246

The Religious as it Appears in Art — A. RICHARD TURNER 281

The Study of Religion and Literature: Siblings in the Academic House — TOM F. DRIVER 304

The Study of Religion in Colleges and Universities: A Practical Commentary — JAMES M. GUSTAFSON 330

Selected Bibliography 347

Contributors 353

The Study of Religion in Colleges and Universities

Introduction: The Background and Present Context of the Study of Religion in Colleges and Universities

JOHN F. WILSON

DURING THE last twenty years in the United States increasing attention has been given to the study of religion and the claims which that activity might make upon the resources of higher education. This growth of interest in the subject since the Second World War can be traced in part to intellectual currents and institutional patterns already laid down in previous decades. Obviously, too, the social pressures generated during the period of the war and its aftermath, as well as those originating in the 1950's and 1960's, have directly contributed to shaping developments in this area. In brief, the study of religion in colleges and universities as a problematic has been thoroughly a part of American higher education throughout recent decades. This introductory chapter will sketch the historical and cultural context within which present discussions of religious studies, represented by this volume, take place. For that reason it will be useful to distinguish between patterns for the study of religion common before the Second World War and the specific kinds of innovation during the last decades which constitute the immediate matrix of current trends.[1]

Pre-war Patterns

One condition affecting the study of religion in the past has been the rather pronounced threefold division between

[1] The distinction between pre-war and post-war patterns is appropriate on general grounds, as well as on grounds more directly related to the study of religion. The Second World War interrupted or intruded upon the routines of most colleges and universities which were not simply reinstituted following its conclusion. Specifically with reference to the study of religion, a different generation of leaders became prominent during the late 1940's and 1950's, and pronounced changes in attitudes and programs during that period may be charted.

attitudes and practices identified with publicly supported institutions, those characteristic of nonsectarian private universities and colleges, and finally those associated with institutions (primarily colleges) under the direct control and influence of religious sponsors. In schools coming under the first two headings the subject matter of religion was not entirely absent from the curriculum before the Second World War, although its presence was realized in several modes which ambiguously served to fulfill different kinds of intention. In the latter class, despite marked formal and structural variation from one institution to another, the significance of the study was explicit and manifest. Each of these educational subcultures within our society requires brief attention.

In schools of this third kind, especially in those colleges directly sponsored and possibly controlled by religious institutions, the study of religion was generally required and thus made an integral part of the curriculum. Furthermore, understandably, the bias of the study typically favored the specific heritage—both immediate and extended—identified with the religious community that sponsored and controlled the school. Thus Roman Catholic doctrine and tradition, amplified in apologetics and ethics, was central to the study of religion in Catholic institutions.[2] Comparable assumptions and arrangements certainly held sway in the few explicitly Jewish schools. And a variety of Protestant institutions clearly exemplified the same principle, albeit in ways appropriate to the individual schools, fundamentalistic or conservative ones identifying the study of religion with congenial creedal positions and historical in-

[2] Two surveys published during the early 1950's (both originally doctoral dissertations) report rather fully upon the characteristics of "religious instruction" in Catholic colleges during the early years of the post-war period, when pre-war assumptions were still reflected to some degree. (Sister) Mary Maher, *The Organization of Religious Instruction in Catholic Colleges for Women* (Washington, D.C.: The Catholic University of America Press, 1951), and (Reverend) Roland G. Simonitsch, *Religious Instruction in Catholic Colleges for Men* (Washington, D.C.: The Catholic University of America Press, 1952).

terests, less evangelical colleges construing their "traditions" as normative in the determination of religious subject matter. The specific shape this general pattern assumed differed from one institution to another. In some schools, for example, required academic study of religion was substantively linked with chapel programs. In such cases, chaplains were frequently responsible for instruction within the curriculum, and academic appointments in any department of religion were made with at least informal assessment of the likelihood that an individual would contribute to the "religious life" of the campus.

These broadly descriptive statements about the study of religion in sectarian institutions do not exhaustively cover the variety of forms this preoccupation with religion took within these institutions. In numerous ways an interest in religion was frequently more widely manifested. For one thing, often more attention within the curriculum was focused on certain aspects of religion in the classical world than on the classical world itself in departments of classics or history. As a matter of fact, courses on the religions of the East were probably as common as offerings in the history departments on Eastern cultures and civilizations. It remains true, nevertheless, that apologetic concerns frequently underlay such study and that with unusual regularity these explorations worked toward ultimately invidious comparisons with the sponsoring traditions. Still, the study of religion in religiously controlled institutions before the Second World War often did make room for at least partial consideration of other religions than those normatively informing the central offerings in the curriculum. In another way "religion" may also have been more widely studied in the sense that religious subject matter at times made up a great part of the content of courses in such areas as literature, history, and the arts. Then, too, the extracurricular life was also suffused with religious values. On this point the range of practices varied immensely, but especially prior to the Second World War many schools undertook to nourish directly and self-consciously some species of

Protestant, Jewish, or Roman Catholic culture within the society. In conceptual terms, education was ultimately religious nurture—however imperfectly the goal was theoretically articulated or however ineffective it proved to be in practice.[3]

The contrast between this pattern and the place of religious studies in some of the nonsectarian private universities and colleges was dramatic. Many presently nonsectarian private institutions had developed from denominational origins and had continued for many years under ecclesiastical sponsorship. Part of that development had been achievement of a religiously plural constituency. In the eyes of such a clientele, study of particular religious traditions as normative was considered in poor taste, if not an embarrassment, and study of religion as a general phenomenon was thought to be intellectually demeaning. If expressed in academic and curricular terms, concern with religion was often joined to value study or other philosophical currents. Thus in numerous instances uneasy links with "liberal" Protestantism were sustained. Generally, however, attention to religion was most frequently peripheral to the curriculum, although extra-academic provision might be made for its presence.[4]

Significantly different from both kinds of private institution were schools under public auspices. On the whole, these did not provide for extensive study of religion within the college curriculum per se. Because of concern over church-state separation, such devices as "bible chairs" and parallel "schools of religion" were resorted to in some places. As important as the strictly legal issue was one of public policy, namely, the evolution of the public institutions from practical (and often land-grant) beginnings, as well as the obvious difficulty of serving religiously plural

[3] Merrimon Cuninggim discussed pre-war "attitudes toward religion" which were characteristic of church-related colleges in his *The College Seeks Religion* (New Haven: Yale University Press, 1947), 49-63.

[4] See "Attitudes Toward Religion: The Independent College," *ibid.*, 64-78.

student bodies and state constituencies. If some public institutions did allow privately sponsored and voluntary religious instruction at the edge of their campuses, that very location said much about its status. On the whole, programs of this kind were not integrated into the universities or colleges in terms of either curriculum or appointments, although in some instances "academic credit" was granted to them.[5]

The foregoing comments on the general absence of formal academic programs or curricular offerings in the study of religion within both public and nonsectarian private institutions before the Second World War provide background for a review of the striking changes that have taken place during the last twenty years. Within the broad framework outlined above, one can distinguish at least four factors at work in the private nonsectarian colleges and universities (taken as a class, not singly) that have proved to be significant for development of the study of religion, one of which was also to be found in certain public institutions. It is necessary to identify these factors in order to understand how the remarkable innovations of the last twenty years have come about.

One crucial factor in several of the larger and more prestigious private universities was the existence of Protestant "divinity schools" or "theological seminaries." Most of these schools were interdenominational in fact, if not in theory, and thus were neither narrowly provincial nor parochial in character. Having been strongly influenced by Protestant liberalism earlier in the century, they had come to embody the "neo-orthodox" impulse during the late thirties and forties. For all of their concern over "correct faith," those who were neo-orthodox viewed the tradi-

[5] Merrimon Cuninggim also discussed attitudes in "The Tax-supported Institution," *ibid.*, 79-95. Clarence P. Shedd summarized the place of "religion in the state university" in an article with that title, published as Number Sixteen of The Hazen Pamphlets (New Haven: The Edward W. Hazen Foundation, 1946). See also an earlier prewar discussion of his, "Religion in State Universities," in *The Journal of Higher Education* XII/18 (Nov. 1941), 408-417.

tion within a cosmopolitan framework and sought to study it in a rigorously academic manner. By the presence of these schools and seminaries in major independent universities, the significance of religious concerns was represented. The intellectual vitality associated with neo-orthodoxy demonstrated that study of religious materials might stimulate students without necessarily working to convert them. In brief, within such important university centers of graduate training as Chicago, Columbia, and Yale, study of Western religious life and thought was powerfully represented and frequently influential, albeit specifically located in separate schools or faculties.

Another factor was the continuing presence in private schools of college or university chapels and chaplains.[6] Especially with the advent of the war, and owing to the influence emanating from the neo-orthodox seminaries, the claims for attention to religion were publicized and pressed with renewed vigor and in an effective manner. Following the war, this pattern continued as an important influence, perhaps particularly in the independent colleges.

A third factor, most prominent in the private colleges, was the development of the often vestigial "bible chair" or "department." Israel of antiquity and its literature was self-evidently an appropriate subject matter, and within Western culture it was logical that emphasis might also be given to early Christian traditions. Since the ancient Near East was not, normally, the province of other college departments, and since the materials presented a valid claim to be studied as history and literature, courses in the Old and usually the New Testament, too, were frequently offered within the liberal arts curriculum at many of these schools. In recent decades the bible chair or department has often proved to be the institutional locus around which a broader program of study of religion has evolved.

[6] Cuninggim devoted a short chapter of his study to the "Chapel" (*The College Seeks Religion*, 131-141). See also his chapter on "Official Leadership," where he points to the variety of religious leadership roles which had been developed (*ibid.*, 152-166).

The fourth factor, characteristic of several public and many private schools, was the secondary interest in religious materials displayed in some departments. Sociological study of religion, for instance, which had flourished for a short period earlier in the century, was often surveyed in a sociology course. At one time a strand of psychology proved to be fascinated with religious behavior. Numerous departments of English, especially in schools where "bible chairs" had not been established, gave courses in "The Bible as English Literature." Philosophical study of religion was a subject holding perennial interest, and philosophical idealism as the reigning tradition easily made a place for review of the pertinent materials.

In summary, by the late 1940's instruction in religion within American colleges and universities exhibited considerable variety.[7] In religiously sponsored institutions traditional study of the appropriate faith constituted the main focus of concern, often affecting the quality and content of additional areas of the curriculum as well as of extracurricular life. By contrast, public institutions generally failed to emphasize the strictly academic study of religion, except in peripheral ways. Although private nonsectarian colleges appear to have provided only limited opportunities for the formal and direct study of religion, in fact a more hospitable environment existed in those institutions than anywhere else. The significant developments of the post-war decades found initial expression in this latter kind of context. Rather dramatic and more recent changes in both public and religiously sponsored institutions, however, have resulted in basically similar approaches to the study of re-

[7] Some empirical data from the pre-war period are available in Gould Wickey and Ruth A. Eckhart's "A National Survey of Courses in Bible and Religion in American Universities and Colleges," *Christian Education* xx/1 (Oct. 1936), 9-45 (also separately printed at Bloomington, Ind.). Cuninggim very briefly reviewed "Instruction in Religion" (Chap. X, *The College Seeks Religion*, 142-151). More useful, perhaps, is his review of nine "Significant Programs" in different types of institution (Chap. XIII, *ibid.*, 183-218). Juxtaposition of these chapters indicates the ambiguous status of the academic study of religion at the beginning of the post-war era.

ligion in all three types of setting. Broadly described, the pattern is one of responsible attention to the extended Judaeo-Christian tradition with additional interest directed toward study of extra-Western forms of religious life. It is important to explore the sources of this common pattern, as well as some of the variations upon it.

Post-war Developments

During the last two decades departments of religion have been established in a significant proportion of the private nonsectarian liberal arts colleges in this country. In some institutions this development represented expansion of the province assigned to "bible chairs" or "departments." In other institutions "teaching chaplains" received additional colleagues until a department came into being. In still other institutions departments were created *de novo.* Where divinity schools or theological seminaries were affiliated with universities, they often served as parent or host for the instruction of undergraduates. Far more important than the variety of structural arrangements, however, was the largely common approach to the program of study. At this point the direct and indirect contributions made by pan-Protestant neo-orthodoxy must be recognized. In general, the departments of religion in nonsectarian schools instituted a curriculum or program of offerings resembling that which had currency at the seminary or theological training centers from which, necessarily, faculty members were recruited.

Basic to the programs were, first, courses in the Old and New Testaments—that is, the literatures of ancient Israel and of the early Christian community studied in the frame of reference or context provided by current, and responsible, Protestant theological scholarship. Additional historical offerings usually traced the intellectual tradition of Western Christianity through Augustine, Aquinas, the Protestant Reformers, and more recent "religious thought" —the acknowledged lineage of neo-orthodoxy. Frequently these programs made room for treatment of ethical and moral questions, expanding the horizons within which political and social life was perceived by the students. Thus departments of religion effectively tutored the consciences of several generations. Often philosophical study of religion adopted the modality of existentialist philosophy, thereby pitting itself more or less directly against the analytic cast which increasingly characterized the approach of departments of philosophy. Beyond this core the curriculum in most departments included some study of Eastern religions. In this particular alone the dependence upon the pan-Protestant neo-orthodoxy seminary curriculum was not direct and obvious.[8]

While departments of religion or programs in the study of religion were proliferating among private nonsectarian colleges during the last twenty years, significant changes were also occurring in religiously sponsored institutions. Within many Protestant schools, even those having strong ties to conservative traditions, the courses made available in the departments of religion came to resemble more closely the curriculum described above. In most of these schools this process entailed a distinct broadening of subject matter and a more strictly academic orientation toward it, even though ties to the chapel and religious activities might be retained. A variety of influences contributed to bringing about this evolution, including the growing body of literature appropriate for use in college instruction as well as the dominant role played by the leading interdenominational centers at which the increasing number of appointees to faculty positions received their training. The resultant change was so striking that by the middle of the 1960's the actual programs of study sponsored by departments of religion in explicitly Protestant schools differed less than might be expected from those made available in many nonsectarian universities and colleges.

[8] Clyde Holbrook identified and discussed this common curriculum in "Curricular Content and Evaluation" (Chap. 8), *Religion, A Humanistic Field* (Englewood Cliffs, N.J.: Prentice-Hall, 1963), 145-168.

Related developments took place during the 1950's and 1960's within Jewish and Roman Catholic circles, the latter especially undergoing an accelerated pace of change as the Second Vatican Council began to have its remarkable impact, releasing pressures which clearly had been at work for some time. Here, too, emphasis fell on expansion of the subject matter and a more straightforwardly academic approach to it. This shift required the introduction of more Christian materials into Jewish curricula and especially more Protestant materials into Catholic programs. Extra-Western religions also received increased attention, while at the same time there occurred a noticeable reduction in the strictly apologetic stance and normative tone that much of the earlier work in this area had displayed. For students in colleges representing all of the educational subcultures, this broadening of religious inquiry brought new perspectives upon common traditions, as well as interesting and important cognate materials.[9]

If, in retrospect, it may be seen that developments in the study of religion in private colleges and universities were converging toward a common type along with the changing programs in those schools under religious auspices, it must likewise be recognized that public institutions were also responding to interest in the study of religion, in a significant variety of ways. During the 1950's several state universities chose quite different approaches to the incorporation of religious materials within curricular offerings. Most of them attempted a rigorous differentiation between study of religion and allegiance to it. Here the ambiguity previously noted in the earlier practices of most religiously sponsored schools, some private colleges, and a few public ones was simply not present. But, apart this consideration, there were a variety of specific approaches adopted. A few

[9] For a brief exposition of an interesting perspective upon the Roman Catholic situation, see Gerard S. Sloyan, "Religious Studies in Roman Catholic Colleges and Universities," *The Study of Religion in College and University* (New York: National Council of Churches, 1967), 24-31. See Myron F. Wicke, *The Church-Related College* (Washington, D.C.: Center for Applied Research in Education, 1964).

institutions frankly undertook to develop "departments of religion," drawing upon the graduate programs which earlier had been so strongly influenced by Protestant neo-orthodoxy. In a small number of other universities new support and encouragement was given to "schools of religion" adjacent to the campuses, a pattern originally instituted during earlier decades of the century. In these institutions representatives of theological scholarship from various traditions fruitfully relate to each other and the cosmopolitan resources of the whole university. Academic credit is usually granted for courses taken at these "schools," although meticulous respect for the separation between church and state remains a guiding principle. Additional patterns included at least one attempt to engage prominent and wealthy denominations in continuing financial support for a department dedicated to research about religion as well as instruction in the subject.[10] Until recently the future development of religion study in public universities and colleges remained uncertain. Within the immediate past it has become apparent that, as far as general expectations are concerned, most public institutions will no longer be constrained by fear that legal principles exclude study of religion from the general curriculum or that public pressures will militate against it. Thus it seems likely that relatively modest departments or programs, thoroughly a part of the general university and college scene, will be established at most publicly supported institutions. Insofar as these developments are under way, it is evident that ties will be relatively close between such departments and the existing programs in private schools, both religious and nonsectarian.

By way of summary, it may be said that the post-war period—extending, indeed, to the present—has witnessed quite significant developments in the nature and shape of

[10] For a general overview, see *Religious Studies in Public Universities*, ed. Milton D. McLean (Carbondale, Ill.: Southern Illinois University, 1967), and Milton D. McLean and Harry H. Kimber, *The Teaching of Religion in State Universities* (Ann Arbor: University of Michigan, 1960).

the attention given to religion within colleges and universities. Study of it has become relatively widespread. Recognizably common elements now cut across the distinctions between different types of educational subcultures which were discussed in the early pages of this Introduction and which have been used up to this point. Throughout the 1950's and 1960's the major private nonsectarian institutions took the lead in nurturing the growth of religion study. But they did so by adopting programs and appointing personnel which placed them greatly in the debt of the Protestant interdenominational theological seminaries and divinity schools in which the neo-orthodoxy of the preceding decades had been so influential. Modifications in the existing programs at religiously sponsored schools moved them far closer to—and often into direct or indirect dependence upon—many of the same sources. Finally, pioneering ventures at public schools, now supplemented by what appears to be a resolve to do justice to the subject on a broad basis, have also led these institutions into dependence upon the available sources of men and ideas in their development of programs for the academic study of religion. Thus a "field"—the study of religion—has been defined, and a fraternity dedicated to its analysis has come into being. Currently the future of that field is being widely discussed, and important determinations about it are being reached.[11]

Conditions for Future Development

This historical context, which has been fixed in an extended as well as a more immediate focus, identifies the setting in which the following essay-chapters were written. They were composed by individuals who are situated at one or another location within the above landscape. Several of the authors write from the perspective of the major university-based theological training centers which have

[11] Ten case studies by Robert Michaelsen suggest both the variety of specific patterns and the elements common to them. *The Study of Religion in American Universities* (New Haven: Society for Religion in Higher Education, 1965).

contributed notably to the staffing of the developing departments and programs. Others hold, or have held, appointments in departments of religion or religious studies in a variety of private and public colleges and universities. Additionally, each author is associated with one among the recognized disciplines (some traditional, others decidedly contingent), either within existing programs or in terms of his professional study of the relevant subject matter. What unites the essays is the common experience of the context described above, as well as the shared expectation that significant evolution in the provisions for study of religion is now occurring. Without anticipating conclusions to be reached in the specific chapters, it may be useful to indicate certain general conditions which will provide the framework for further development.

One condition which will determine the future course of the study of religion in colleges and universities is scarcely unique to this particular field. It is one seemingly inevitable, affecting all of higher education. This is the increasing erosion of the distinctions which in the past have served to differentiate institutions of higher learning on the basis of patterns of sponsorship and support more than on the basis of functions. Whatever unforeseen effects may result from recent student revolts and displays of power, this trend toward "homogenization" of liberal education is unlikely to be reversed. At the very least we may anticipate the incorporation of virtually all institutions of higher education into a broadly-based national complex (even if not centrally organized), financed in large part, directly and indirectly, out of public monies. The pressures in this direction are numerous and include diverse factors: the still increasing numbers of those seeking bachelor of arts or equivalent programs; the relentlessly rising costs now pressing even hitherto invulnerable tax-supported institutions (dependent upon state legislatures which seem reluctant to underwrite expanding budgets); the mixed model of economic support likely to characterize all schools; the erosion of distinctive religious subcommunities which have nourished educational uniqueness in the past; the determined attempt of most institutions to be associated with social change through actively seeking representatives of disadvantaged groups as well as relating to that change in both curricular and extracurricular ways; the continued domination of major graduate centers in established fields which provide models and staffing for all kinds of institutions. Even the heretofore highly resistant Roman Catholic colleges will probably be drawn closer toward, and conformed more fully to, the pattern of public and nonsectarian education. Jewish and Protestant institutions have already moved far along this one-way street.[12]

On the study of religion, in particular this general condition will certainly have direct and irresistible effects. It will push even further the movement toward curricular consensus and professional identity across what, twenty years ago, might have seemed to be unbridgeable cultural chasms. Since the public sector of higher education appears to be the more dynamic and innovative at the moment, the specific developments in this sector will probably prove to influence significantly the whole pattern of religion study. The study of religious phenomena apart from chapel programs will undoubtedly become the normal pattern, and while great emphasis will be placed upon the heritages of the constituencies—basically, Judaeo-Christian sources and traditions—interest in extra-Western materials and viewpoints will no doubt grow proportionately. Thus it seems correct to anticipate the delineation with even more clarity of a field of study of those aspects of culture generally identified as "religious." This field will be common to a variety of specific kinds of institution, and the interchange between colleges and universities (involving students and

[12] An important review and analysis of "church-sponsored higher education in the United States" was authorized and supported by the Danforth Foundation under the direction of Manning M. Pattillo, Jr., and Donald W. Mackenzie. The findings were published in a volume with that title (Washington, D.C.: American Council on Education, 1966).

faculty members) which is standard in other fields will become customary in this one also.

The second condition, is, in one way, the further specification with reference to the field of religion of the one discussed immediately above. The recent and pronounced pattern of development toward the establishment of departments of religion or special programs in its study will undoubtedly be continued. In the abstract, strong arguments may be marshalled for the diffusion of responsibility for study of "religion" among relevant disciplines within the humanities and social sciences.[13] There are considerations at two levels, however, which will likely prove to be determinative on the other side of the question. One, on the practical level, involves administrative procedures and organizational structures necessary to higher educational institutions. The other, on the theoretical level, relates to the need for coresidence among humanists and social scientists engaged in the study of religion, which, after all, is a whole of related activities significantly greater than the mere availability of its constituent elements. The departments and programs which result from this pattern of development will undoubtedly be located—to use classical nomenclature—within the "arts and sciences," rather than in practical schools or traditional graduate faculties. In other words, study of religious phenomena as aspects of human culture will fundamentally be carried on in a broadly humanistic context, and not primarily within vocational schools or at the hands of a separate professional faculty. Thus the similarities to departments of politics or departments of art or music—or to programs like those in the history and philosophy of science—will be emphasized, whereas resemblances to schools of nursing or to law facul-

[13] See Huston Smith, "The Interdepartmental Approach to Religious Studies," *The Journal of Higher Education* XXXI/2 (Feb. 1960), 61-68. Also relevant to this approach are sections of a study by Alexander Miller, *Faith and Learning* (New York: Association Press, 1960).

ties, including ties to professional guilds, will be less pronounced.[14]

Increasingly there will be continuity between undergraduate study of religion and graduate work in the field. In this respect religion will undoubtedly follow the same path of development as that taken by other arts and science disciplines. Probably the curriculum will mirror this shift, becoming less dependent upon the formalities and orthodoxies of the theological traditions while placing greater emphasis upon the methodologies and disciplines shared with related arts and science subject matters. Thus religious phenomena—Eastern and Western—will more and more come to be studied in terms of rigorous philosophical and historical procedures and according to criteria held in common with other disciplines. Sociological theory, for instance, will be enlisted to aid in analyzing religious activities. Literary criticism will be brought to bear more directly upon a variety of religious texts, not simply scriptural ones. Thus different techniques already used in the study of cultural subjects generally will be systematically applied to the study of this particular class of cultural phenomena.[15]

Implied in the second condition is a third—namely, the decline in influence and significance of the theological traditions and a marked reduction of their roles in shaping the study of religion.[16] In one respect this will be a function

[14] Clyde Holbrook reviewed this basic issue in "Structures of Religion Instruction and their Evaluation" (Chap. 7) in *Religion, A Humanistic Field*, 113-144.

[15] Cf. Clyde Holbrook, "Influences of Graduate Education on Faculty and Curriculum" (Chap. 10), *ibid.*, 189-204. A series of four articles which described "graduate preparation in religion apart from the [Protestant] seminaries" during the early 1960's may be of some interest. They were published in *The Journal of Bible and Religion* xxx/2-4 (April-July-Oct. 1962), 109-114, 224-231, 291-298, and xxxi/1 (Jan. 1963), 36-39.

[16] For discussions of some ramifications of this issue, see Paul Ramsey, "Theological Studies in College and Seminary," *Theology Today* xvii/4 (Jan. 1961), 466-484, and E. Thomas Lawson, "Implications for Theological Education in Seminaries of the Study of Religion in the University," *The Study of Religion in College and University*, 76-82.

of the development of departments or programs at graduate and undergraduate levels in the arts and sciences which will become more natural centers for training faculty members. In this way existing programs fundamentally based upon the seminaries will either be metamorphosed or displaced. During the last decade the dual roles of several important seminaries have been acknowledged, and by virtue of their locations at universities they have already begun to make their graduate contribution directly in the arts and sciences (full examples would be Duke and Yale, a partial example Harvard). Other seminaries, Protestant and Catholic, are seeking out relationships to university communities and are preparing to become professional schools in that context, with this responsibility carefully delineated from the study of religion in the arts and sciences. The faculty members and library resources thereby made newly accessible to university communities will certainly render more widely available materials for graduate (as well as undergraduate) study of religion. Equally important, however, will be the greater self-consciousness about functions and working assumptions throughout the field of religion. Especially within the ranks of Roman Catholic schools, this clarification of institutional ends may prove to be revolutionary beyond the expectations of those assenting to it.

If the special influence that neo-orthodox Protestant seminaries exerted in shaping the study of religion will wane over the next several years, it will reflect, in one respect, the confused state of theology. Depending upon one's perspective, recent theological programs may be pronounced "trivial" (for example, "God is dead"—a slogan which has faded away) or "liberating" (such as Roman Catholic revision of tradition). On neither side is there a tough-minded and aggressive, widely held theological option (sociologically parallel to the Protestant neo-orthodoxy of an earlier age) so articulated and expounded as to transform (or be intended to transform) cultural attitudes and social institutions. In this sense, contemporary theological activity tends to be something of an end in itself. Accordingly, there is a fundamental skepticism about the status of religious truth. As such theology has little chance of demonstrating sufficient ideological power to give an impulse to the study of religion equivalent to that which Protestant neo-orthodoxy provided during the post-war era. Certainly, it is unlikely that an ecumenical Christian vision will replace a pan-Protestant one and even less likely that an interfaith consensus can play a constructive role in the present situation.

A final condition is the expectations widely shared regarding the field or approach frequently termed "history of religions."[17] It is commonly assumed that a unifying impulse during the coming years will be provided by systematic and comparative studies of various classes of religious phenomena across diverse traditions and cultures, Western as well as Eastern. This field—about which some ambiguity exists—already forms a significant part of the study of religion, and probably its most immediate limitation (at the moment) is in the small number of trained personnel available for academic appointments. In some respects another title, "science of religion," would suggest more exactly both the approach and subject matter central to it. For obvious reasons, this term has not been widely used in the English-speaking world. At its best, scientific study of religion would be comparative study of religious phenomena pursued in a theoretical manner. (Although up to the present the materials of the Jewish and Christian traditions have been generally excluded from analysis under *Religionswissenschaft*, there are signs that this neglect may be coming to an end.) Thus in one regard the history of religions might be expected to serve as a distinctive methodology for the

[17] Philip H. Ashby has discussed "The History of Religions" in the United States during recent decades in *Religion* (The Princeton Studies—Humanistic Scholarship in America), ed. Paul Ramsey (Englewood Cliffs, N.J.: Prentice-Hall, 1965), 3-49. A series of recent essays has been published as *The History of Religions* (Essays in Divinity, Vol. I), ed. Joseph M. Kitagawa (Chicago: University of Chicago Press, 1967).

developing study of religion, functioning in this way as a unifying impulse. If so, it will be a role in some measure analogous to that played by neo-orthodox Protestant scholarship during the past several decades. The long-run expectations for this field are great, if in the immediate future they are less so. In any event, a common feature of most reflection about future study of religion is the candid presumption that history of religions may provide an overall coherence and orientation possibly absent at present in the field of religion study. This is, in brief, a fourth condition under which current discussion goes on.

These four conditions are recognized more or less explicitly in most of the following essays. Some of the chapters are devoted, basically, to analysis of traditional subject matters and procedures, and the implicit question they address is what will happen to these "fields" as they are continued under the new circumstances and constraints outlined above. Other chapters review newer ventures whose worth may be widely acknowledged but whose specific futures are not so clear. As a whole, this volume will have served its purpose well if it provides a rigorous exploration of the activities at present constituting the study of religion as it enters upon a period of immensely significant development.

Biblical Studies in the University

KRISTER STENDAHL

THE TREND is clear. The center of gravity in the academic study of religion is moving from the seminaries to the departments of religion. This development is neither uniform nor complete. It has, however, reached a point where the question whether a religion department has a proper place within the college and graduate faculty of arts and sciences can be considered resolved in the affirmative, for state universities no less than for private schools. The major difficulties for future consolidation and growth in this area within tax-supported institutions will presumably come, not from within the academic community, but from religious groups who have enjoyed the hands-off-religion attitude of universities in the spirit of the Scopes trial. As a matter of principle, the answer of the universities to such pressures could not and should not differ from the defense of academic freedom in the study of zoology.

What has received less attention is the often almost automatic transfer of the traditional disciplines of the seminary into the structure of programs and instruction carried on in the departments of religion. To be sure, increasing attention is being given to non-Christian religions; courses and chairs in Judaica are slowly finding their rightful place in such departments; the thoughtless arrogance of American WASP culture is being overcome as Roman Catholic theology is "accepted" as part of Christianity; sociology and psychology of religion are being brought into focus, even though such areas are sometimes handled by or together with other departments where the proper skills and interests are found. But when it comes to the core of Christian studies, most departments depend on teachers who have done their doctoral work in the traditional disciplines of Old Testament, New Testament, church history, theology, or ethics. Whether they hold Th.D. or Ph.D. degrees often makes little difference, since most Ph.D. programs in religion depend heavily on the resources of adjacent theological faculties. This fact, together with the increasing necessity for specialization, has worked toward the perpetuation of the traditional seminary disciplines. The only alternative has been various attempts at interdisciplinary programs. Although these have their value, especially for very able students, they always place on the student the unfair demand of bringing together in his own mind and work what his professors have not managed to combine. Good reasons could be given for the view that such demands and challenges belong to post-doctoral research rather than to a well-conceived doctoral program.

When seen from the other side, that of the students and of the college curriculum, it becomes even more evident that, especially in smaller schools with small religion departments, we must find a new way to define the disciplines of the study of religion.

It is in such a context that we must give serious attention to biblical studies. It constitutes a venerable and obvious part of the traditional structure, although the need for specialization has led to an increasing partition between Old Testament and New Testament scholarship. Owing to the inherent tendencies and habits of historical research, these two areas have come to claim for themselves the background of their field rather than to reflect on what grew out of it. For that reason Old Testament scholars have by and large become well versed in the Assyrian, Egyptian, and Canaanite materials, while post-biblical Jewish material up to the Christian era has been handled by New Testament scholarship as far as Christians are concerned. This practical arrangement reinforces awkward terminology when we speak of the "intertestamental" period or when the German term *Spätjudentum* is perpetuated in the English designation "Late Judaism." Both terms come naturally to Christian scholars to whom the Bible is the unit of the Old and the New Testaments and to whom Judaism from the Maccabees to Bar Kokhba is the latest period of Judaism which they consider religiously or historically significant for their work. In both instances we are dealing with the early post-biblical period of Judaism or, we might say, with "Early Judaism." Terminological observations of this kind are good eye-openers for anyone who wants to assess the role of biblical studies in the university.

Such observations should also help us understand why the definition of areas of study ought not to be attempted without considering the academic structures within which they take shape and function. Prior to the recent expansion of religion departments, serious work in the theological disciplines was done in seminaries, and, as we have indicated, it was this work which set a pattern for higher studies in the field. Another of the factors of some importance here was the substantial influence exercised by the theologians of continental Europe. The names of Harnack, Barth, and Bultmann serve as symbols of that influence in this century. And it was the seminaries which saw it as their goal to emulate such heroes, although there always was a strange incompatibility in the effort—a problem to which more attention should be given. Here I can speak from some personal experience. Having studied and taught on a theological faculty in Sweden, it took me quite a few years on the American scene to discover how deep the differences were. I still find it difficult to sort them all out, since they are subtle and seem to have contradictory consequences. On the one hand, the European theologian is a man of the university, with the prestige and the ethos of "scholarship for its own sake." While he actually educates the clergy of those churches which require academic training for their pastors and ministers, his academic freedom vis-à-vis church and state is well guarded. This gives his work a university accent. On the other hand, he functions within a system where the theological faculty is related to the other parts of the university as a unit parallel to that of the arts and sciences, and not as a graduate school which builds upon a liberal arts college.

The American system makes the faculty of arts and sciences a nucleus of the university. Other graduate schools than that of arts and sciences are, by traditional definition, professional schools. If this designation has a derogatory ring in some quarters, such is neither intended nor necessary. Although good reasons could be found for arguing that much work in the graduate school of arts and sciences is at times equally professional, the anchorage of its disciplines in the college curriculum still suffices to make the traditional distinction a valid one.

This difference in the structure of the university helps to explain why European theological studies are more "academic" in ethos and at the same time more consciously theological, and even unconsciously confessional, if not denominational. The recent development in the United States toward a discipline of religious studies outside of the theological faculty has few and timid parallels in Europe, where by and large studies related to Christianity remain in the hands of theological faculties, centered in the traditional disciplines, and where the history of religion(s) tends to mean the history of religions other than Christianity. The teachers are Doctors of Theology. Even if, as we said, the difference between a Th.D. and Ph.D. in the United States is not as clear as one would expect, the fact that the majority of theological teachers in this country have Ph.D.'s has contributed to a breakdown of the concept of theology as a discipline which gives a specific faculty its academic coherence.

Impressive arguments can be mustered for defining the rationale for the traditional theological disciplines. Yet many such attempts are unconvincing because they overlook the obvious truth that such disciplines presuppose as well as express the structures delineated above. The problems are as much political as they are ideological. Take, for example, church history as distinguished from "secular history." As a discipline in a theological faculty, it can best be defined as a study of history where the selection of material is guided by what is considered important for the understanding and work of the Christian church or churches. It comprises political history, economic history, history of science, and all the rest. There is no special method peculiar to the study of church history. It is simply a study of whatever history is judged relevant for theological students. Or it is a study of history which requires understanding and sophistication on the part of those who concern themselves with religious phenomena, in the same sense as the historian of science is required to understand certain things about science, or the economic historian certain things about economics. Prima facie there is no reason why church historians should not do their work in history departments. Although some do, and more may as time goes on, they do not do so now as a rule. And the reason they do not is the traditional convention that church history is handled by the "theologians," or, more precisely, "in the theological faculty." Yet many a church historian in such faculties does not think of himself as a "theologian" or as "doing theology"—he is a historian.

The parallel to legal history is of interest. Many would argue that the study of church history is more germane to theology than legal history is to jurisprudence; only a few law schools have chairs in legal history, and their incumbents are usually historians with special competence in matters of legal process rather than lawyers with special competence in history, especially where the historical period of specialization is far removed from the present.

For these and similar reasons we could say that church history is that study of history which is deemed relevant to the needs of the seminary graduate. It is not a theological discipline, as opposed to a study of "secular history." The church historian—both in research and in teaching—covers vast areas of "secular history." He does so with the same methods as those which govern the work of his colleagues in the history departments. He becomes part of the theological enterprise by acquiring knowledge and sophistication relating to the issues of theology, ancient and present, but primarily by belonging to a faculty organized for the purposes of theological study and the education of the clergy. When such a discipline seeks its place in a department of religion, the demarcation between that discipline and the work of the history department becomes more crucial, since the pragmatic and professional *raison d'être* is dissolved.

I have used this example to make a point which I find both important and somewhat contrary to expectations. One would expect that the transfer of the theological disciplines from seminary to religion departments would lead to their increasing secularization. In a certain sense, the opposite will be the effect. How can that be?

In the seminary the different disciplines become "religious" through the aim of the total enterprise, but many of the disciplines are actually secular and the work done is identical with the philological, historical, and philosophical research carried on in various departments of the arts and sciences apart from a department of religion. Theses are written in Old Testament studies, church history, history of religions, etc., which in no way differ in method or aim from those produced in these departments.

But once a religion department begins to formulate its rationale, it will recognize that such a duplication of work and effort makes little sense within one and the same faculty. Its *raison d'être* must be more distinct. It must be defined somehow as a place where religious phenomena are examined, treated, criticized, and reflected upon *qua* religious phenomena. The study of a text, a sect, a figure, or a trend does not become study of religion merely because the object is "religious," but because it is treated as a religious phenomenon. Conversely, a religion department can treat "secular phenomena" in literature and ideas as expressions of man's religious quest and needs.

The special competence of a religion department, consequently, lies in its academic sophistication in evaluating, interpreting, and criticizing religious phenomena. It centers in the study of *homo religiosus* and the different manifestations of the *corpus religiosum*. Thus it is, by definition, not easily organized according to different religions, with or without predominance for Christianity. Its business, even in studying particular religious traditions, is to subject religious phenomena to scrutiny.

When we turn to inquire about the place of biblical studies in the university, these problems assert themselves in many ways. In the seminary biblical studies constitutes a central part of the curriculum. Its role may differ somewhat according to the theological traditions which are served, but these modifications make only for variations within the obvious. With the increasing specialization of disciplines, biblical studies has become more and more a descriptive and historical enterprise. In the biblical courses a student learns how to assess what the ancient writers of these sixty-six books—or a few more in the Roman Catholic and Orthodox traditions—meant in their own times. This is as it should be in the seminary, since the later developments of interpretation belong to historical theology and the question of possible meanings for today are central in systematic theology, ethics, and homiletics. The recent emphasis on hermeneutics has much bearing on biblical studies, but, strictly speaking, hermeneutics is an exercise in theology proper, and many outstanding biblical scholars remain innocent of the problems it deals with while they continue to be impressive contributors to their own field. This kind of innocence—some would call it historical purism—is defensible and even valuable within the team of a theological faculty and curriculum. Whereas it may be short on theological sensitivity, it is long on comparative material, earlier than and contemporary to the texts studied. If the Bible is treated as a collection of documents by which we can recapture the thought and stance of the men and communities responsible for these texts, then the canon—the lines by which these books were set apart from all other documents—has little significance. Apocryphal, pseudepigraphical, "intertestamental" writings are of equal importance and will loom large since they are less familiar and thus need more attention. New Testament studies becomes an examination of early Christian literature in the setting of Jewish and Graeco-Roman culture. Much of the progress and the excitement in biblical studies stem from this noncanonical perspective.

A discipline of this kind has its place, of course, in any study of the humanities. For all practical purposes, it is a historical discipline: it is good to know the genesis of a significant tradition. Once the historical perspective and method are clear enough, it is not difficult to handle the ambiguity of the term "Bible." Although both Jews and Christians use that term, they mean different things by it: we have a Bible with or without a New Testament. Given this approach, though, we can see not only that the Jewish Tanakh and the Christian Old Testament are identical in content but that the same standards apply for all scholars and students as they try to answer questions about the meaning of these texts at any given time in their development.

Once this point is clearly grasped, however, we must ask if this is all that is needed or expected when the Bible is studied in the context of humanistic learning. One often hears teachers in various fields of the humanities deplore the present situation when the average student lacks knowledge of the Bible which is indispensable for understanding the literature, art, and history of ideas of the West.

Where the history of ideas is dealt with in the humanities courses taking the sweep over "all the great thoughts," something is usually said about Paul—often as a background to understanding Augustine. The biblical scholar knows little about Augustine and the use to which Pauline material and elements were put in the history of Christian thought. He often wishes that survey courses were less "orthodox" in their unquestioned conviction that Paul, Augustine, and Luther were concerned with the same problems. What is needed here is more awareness of how religious texts live by reinterpretation. The very mechanics of creative interpretation in the religious realm requires that we understand the Bible, not as a philosophical text expressing certain ideas, but as Scripture, inspired and authoritative and consequently capable of assuming new meanings. This understanding leads to the puzzling insight that in the living religious traditions continuity is affirmed and achieved by discontinuity. Authority is affirmed and relevance asserted by reinterpretation. From a historical point of view, Paul did not mean what Augustine heard him say. But since Augustine and Luther read Paul as Bible, they were convinced that their problems had their answers in Paul. For better or for worse, that is how Scriptures function, and, if so, we had better take note thereof also in our treatment of the history of ideas. The biblical scholar is well equipped to torpedo the facile continuity in the history of thought.

And when it comes to "all the great books," every theologian knows how people show kindness to him and his profession by exalting the literary beauty of the Bible. These sentiments often materialize in courses labeled "The Bible as Literature." The closer such a course finds itself to the interests of the instructors of a department of English, the more imperative it is that the King James Version be used. The rationale is an obvious one, since it is in this form that the Bible has made its cultural impact on the English-speaking world. Matters of religion being a touchy subject, it also seems to help rescue such courses from any suspicion of sectarianism—although the Roman Catholics used other translations. It is worth noting, however, that we seldom conduct courses on Plato or the Greek tragedies on the basis of seventeenth-century translations.

A study of the Bible as literature can mean many things, most of which have their rightful place when clearly defined and confined. Biblical studies as we described it above—that is, as a historical discipline—devotes much attention to the literary and pre-literary forms of biblical material. Form-criticism is a refined method of sorting out these matters. The intention of the writers can be gauged only by careful attention to literary conventions, and so forth.

But the programmatic term "Bible as literature" usually points in another direction, for it tends to promote reading literature as "great literature" and aims at appreciation of the literary value of the Bible. A New Testament scholar is always somewhat apprehensive when this happens, since by and large the New Testament contains less material which qualifies as "great literature" than does the Old Testament. The relatively low cultural and educational level of primitive Christianity has had lasting consequences, although the King James Version has helped to counteract its effects by its great stylistic achievement. As Arthur Darby Nock often remarked, the Gospel according to St. John did not become beautiful until 1611.

When the Bible is approached as literature, there is one book which always receives much attention: the Book of Job. And rightly so. But it should not be forgotten that it is perhaps one of the least representative of the main line of Old Testament thought and sentiment. This does not lessen its value, but it does point up the difference between the Bible as literature and a study which aims at giving a balanced picture of biblical material as representative of the thought-world of the community in which the Bible took shape. For this latter undertaking covenant, kingship, and cult loom larger than wisdom and speculation. The student has to be aware of the tension between the study of the great and of that which is striking, as contrasted with the lives and faith of common men, who, constituting the majority, supply the continuity.

Dovetailed with the attraction to passages of literary value is the interest in those passages which are significant for associations in Western art and literature: the Creation, the patriarchs, the Exodus, the history of Israel and Judah, the life and parables of Jesus. According to these standards, the Book of Revelation should be of great significance (cf. Dante's *Divine Comedy*), but for some reasons it is often bypassed. Behind those "some reasons" lingers an apologetic tendency of the soft kind. Although the approach is supposed to be concerned purely with literary value, one often wants to show the Bible as attractive, and many teachers think that the Jesus of the parables is more attractive and more easy to present positively than the Christ speaking through the abstruse medium of apocalyptic imagery. This may well be a miscalculation in the time of LSD, science fiction, and atomic clouds. Be that as it may, such an omission leads to an anachronistic picture of the world and the emphases of the Bible and of early Christianity.

These observations point toward a significant problem. If "the Bible as literature" means that the biblical material is to be measured by the standards of great classical literature, the character of these books as a Bible, as holy writ, may well be lost. At least it will not play a significant role in the study. And yet it is precisely as holy writ that the biblical material has made its impact on Western culture. Not because of its intrinsic literary value but because of its peculiar claim to be the Word of God did it hold its grip over the minds, memories, and associations of men. It lived by recital and interpretation as sacred scriptures do.

There is no reason why literary criticism cannot become sensitive to this aspect of the biblical material. It can be done on stylistic grounds, in the way in which, for example, Erich Auerbach in his *Mimesis* discerns the contrast between Odysseus' scar and Abraham's sacrifice of Isaac and relates the latter to the implicit claim to absolute authority. The analysis can be taken even further, as Amos Wilder did in his *The Language of the Gospel: Early Christian Rhetoric*. Here the insights of the historical exegete blend well with literary criticism, and the various forms of early Christian literature are seen as expressive of distinct views of reality and distinct theological understandings of the world.

In order to reach this degree of sophistication and clarity, literary criticism presupposes an advanced knowledge in biblical studies, philology, textual criticism, source criticism, christological developments, and all the rest. The requisite competence is infrequently found in the English departments of our universities. Scholars trained in classics or in a combination of classics and comparative literature more often are better equipped for New Testament criticism. And Tanakh/Old Testament study finds a place in many Semitics departments more easily than does New Testament study in classics. There are some objective reasons for this latter difference. The Old Testament constitutes the great classic for any study of Hebrew language and literature, culturally as well as philologically. Not so the New Testament in relation to classics. According to traditional standards, it belongs to a far less glorious period of Greek language and culture. Furthermore, the time-honored division of labor in our universities has drawn the line sharp between classics and Semitics, but the New Testament scholar must have his hand in both. Although most, if not all, of the twenty-seven writings are Greek originals in their present form, they draw upon sources and traditions shaped in Semitic language and culture. There may be other reasons for the relative disregard for the earliest Christian texts in the classics, but none could be based on valid principle. Rather, it is attributable to an educational tradition where such material was deemed the proper province of the theologian.

An interesting footnote to this division of labor is that much of the progress in New Testament studies in this century is due to the decrease in knowledge of the classics. Theological students and even professors now often lack the solid grounding in the classics which was once taken for granted. They did not come to the New Testament with the sentiments and associations of the classical philosophical and cultural tradition. Thus they found it far easier to feel and discern the Jewish, Old Testament and post-biblical, even the Rabbinic flavor of much New Testament thinking. The victory of a thoroughgoing eschatological and apocalyptic understanding of Jesus, Paul, and early Christianity can be best understood as a liberation of the New Testament from its Greek pre-history and post-history. The Jewish background got a new chance, and this was felt as a refreshing development. It was often due more to less knowledge of Greek than to that better knowledge of Hebrew or Aramaic. But the two come into balance—with a rather low common denominator.

This is in no way a defense of insufficient attention to the classics. Once the balance has been attained, and that with promising results, it is high time that the study of early Christian materials, including the New Testament, be recognized as a proper province of classical studies—to mutual advantage. This becomes the more obvious as soon as we seek a viable structure for the study of religion apart from the traditional disciplines of the seminary.

When the discipline of biblical studies moves outside of the seminary, where its confines are natural and obvious, and seeks its place in the setting of the arts and sciences, we recognize that much of that discipline has a natural place in various areas of the humanities—history, philosophy, literature, and classics among them. Nevertheless, there seems to be a residue, a particular element, which requires special attention. And that element is not only one among many but the one without which all other elements are in danger of distorting the nature of these texts. I am, of course, referring to the Bible's character as holy writ. It is for that reason that we need the services of a religion department. Here we come to grips with the phenomenon of Scripture as one of the characteristics of many religions. It is not unique to Christianity. While views about the function of Scripture vary from one religion to another, there are also significant differences of opinion within the same religion. There are fundamentalists and literalists and spiritualists and allegorists and liberals in all religions of Scripture. It may well be that Jewish, Christian, and Muslim literalists or fundamentalists have more in common with each other than they have with the liberal spiritualists of their own faith.

What is important here, however, is that the primary responsibility of a religion department in relation to biblical studies is the critical understanding and evaluation of the phenomenon of Scripture and the way in which religious texts originate and function as religious documents. In that sense, also, biblical studies will become more, rather than less, conscious of the theological dimension as that discipline moves from the seminary to the religion department. Without such a focus there is no reason why such studies could not or should not be conducted in any of a number of other departments.

Biblical studies as practiced today is a historical discipline. It is a study of the formative period of two religious movements, Judaism and Christianity. Since a religion department will always need to give attention to this period, it is to be expected that biblical studies will retain its place within that department. But it could well be that the primary resources and the primary research in this area will be handled by other departments, such as Semitics, classics, history, or literature. Sometimes where the Old Testament and Judaism are concerned, and often in the case of Islam and the Far Eastern religions, this is the pattern today, and there is no reason why it could not apply also to Christian origins. What is indispensable for a religion department, however, is the attention to the phenomenon of Scripture. But the abstract study of phenomena has its grave dangers. For that reason the best work may still be done by those scholars who continue the tradition of biblical studies as it has developed in this century but who at the same time find themselves in the center of the academic inquiry into religious phenomena in a wider, global setting. In such a setting the background and the foreground are not principally Near Eastern or Hellenistic history, on the one hand, and post-biblical halakha or Christian dogmatics, on the other, but rather the glories and idiosyncrasies of *homo religiosus* past, present, and future. While such a perspective will require increased critical acumen in the historical work and vigilant avoidance of anachronisms, it will transform the climate of biblical studies. The biblical student will not be primarily the one who seeks a sound foundation for his community and his faith by his critical analyses of the Scriptures—that is the task of the seminary. Biblical studies will rather function as one of the laboratories in the analysis and critique of the phenomenon of Holy Scripture. And it will supply plenty of material for the understanding of religious phenomena over a long period of history, up to the second century of the Common Era. The historical and philological work will remain the same, but the setting will be radically different. It is too early to guess about the outcome and benefits—and the liabilities, for such there will always be. It is too early especially since we have been slow in recognizing that the creation of religion departments as integral parts of the universities' activities in the humanities does not mean a simple transfer of the seminary disciplines into the framework of the arts and sciences. The difference is not one of faith and commitment versus secularism and objectivity. Whatever can be said of contemporary biblical studies, it does not suffer from lack of critical checking of presuppositions and *Vorverständnis.* I know of few students more conscientious in these matters than the leading biblical scholars of our time. Anyone who knows the theological scene today would agree that the difference between the seminary and the humanities cannot be described in such terms or in terms of different methodologies. The difference is rather one of educational aims and academic goals. In the seminary the Bible functions as the foundation for faith, doctrine, and interpretation. In the department of religion the Bible is an object of study tending toward the understanding of religious phenomena in general. The preoccupation with the Bible opens up toward the understanding of canon and holy writ in the life of religious communities and in cultures conditioned thereby. The specific questions about Moses, Jesus, and Paul always open up toward the questions about the nature of religious men and movements as such.

Postscript

There is a second chapter to be added in this essay, and that would deal with the role of biblical studies in seminaries and divinity schools. My paper could give the impression that I envisage no changes on that side of the ledger. Such an impression would be wrong and unfortunate. Allow me to quote a statement I made in January 1968, when I was appointed Dean of the Harvard Divinity School. It may give an indication of how I would go on from this paper toward the next one called for.

> The last decades have seen a spectacular development of religion departments in colleges and universities, including state universities. The study of religion is finding its rightful place as part of the humanities. This is a promising expansion. It means, however, that divinity schools and seminaries no longer have the monopoly on such studies, or on students who want to probe into matters relating to religion.
>
> I welcome this development, partly because it is sound and long overdue, and partly because it will both force and allow the divinity schools to focus more clearly on their role as laboratories—engaged in both primary and applied research—for the work and planning of the churches.
>
> Strange as it may sound, today many theologians and students of religion are inclined to bypass the churches and take a condescending attitude toward 'organized religion.' Such an attitude can be changed only when our divinity schools recognize their direct responsibility for the renewal of the churches.
>
> Unless the insights and perspectives of contemporary theology are pumped quickly and forcefully into the life stream of the churches, theology will remain a rarefied luxury for the few, and the credibility gap between the churches and our culture will widen beyond repair.
>
> A major part of our work must be to plan for the church of the year 2000. To plan and help shape that

future is our task. We invite young men and women to prepare for leadership in the transition. In a shrinking and expanding world, they will learn how to serve a church that cannot be taken for granted, a church that will lose many of its privileges. They will accept ecumenical cooperation as a self-evident fact, not as a doubtful goal. They will find new ways to think about the relations between Christianity and other religions. They may find that the true dividing line is not between belief in God and atheism, but rather between the closed mind and spiritual sensibility and imagination. In short, they will join in one of the most drastic and promising reformations that the church has ever undergone.

Thus the division of labor between departments of religion and seminaries will lead the latter toward an agenda and a curriculum that is motivated by the needs of the churches, both theological and practical. Such an agenda and such a curriculum cannot be deduced from the traditional theological disciplines. They call for new structures in which the great gains in historical biblical studies will contribute to new and viable theological models for preaching and action. It is my guess that we shall overcome the silent presupposition in the biblical theology of the last generation—a presupposition I would describe as *Im Anfang war der Text.* The imperialism of the biblical theologians is gone, and we shall rather recognize that among its many assets the community, the church *also* has its Scriptures. The normative questions of how the church lives with its Scriptures will loom large and remain more open than heretofore. Authority is only one aspect; creativity in interpretation is another.

History and Salvation: An Essay in Distinctions[1]

WILLIAM A. CLEBSCH

It is common for most Christian theologians and for many historians who work on materials about Christianity to insist that Christianity is a "historical religion." No doubt the designation means many things, most of which can be traced to a long tradition relating Christianity and history. What the modern designations have in common is an attempt to render credible the discussion of Christian salvation during an era that is characterized by critical modes of thought. To assess the state of the arts by which historiographers deal with Christianity and Christian theologians deal with history requires drawing certain distinctions between "history" and "salvation." This essay takes up that task without presuming to complete it. I do argue to the conclusion, however, that a critical historiography of Christianity is viable so far as it is marked off from the enterprise of Christian theology.[2]

[1] The substance of this essay was delivered as the M. Dwight Johnson Memorial Lectures for 1968 at the Seabury-Western Theological Seminary in Evanston, Illinois. The arguments were summarized at a conference on "The Study of Religion in College and University" at Princeton University in 1968. Some of the hypotheses were discussed in 1967 by the Stanford–Santa Clara Ecumenical Colloquium at the University of San Francisco. A preliminary version of the essay received helpful criticism from my colleague, Professor Edwin M. Good, and a later version was read by Professor Sidney E. Mead of the University of Iowa. Adding to these acknowledgments the recollection of my debt to my students makes me wonder who should really sign the essay; mine is the blame, theirs the credit.

[2] In advancing such an argument, one should own up to its autobiographical undertones. For half an academic lifetime I have been testing means of the imagination that seemed to hold promise of bridging the intellectual gulf separating Christian theology from history. Theology, for all its interest in history, lies at a distance from critical historiography, for all its ability to deal with the materials of Christianity. The quest continues, perhaps more out of habit than hope, and has led me to this present essay—an effort, if not to bridge the gulf, at least to take its measurements.

HISTORY AND SALVATION

Two ancient ways of linking the concepts of history and Christianity are refracted in contemporary discussions of salvation and history. Since the time of Origen in the Greek-language tradition and of Augustine in the Latin tradition, human history has been seen as the stage on which agents of God played out the one meaningful drama of a cosmically significant process of salvation. Salvation-history (or "sacred history" or "theology of history") has interpreted the career of an eternal God under the appearances of time and change. Such a career could consist, to be sure, only of appearances, for on this interpretation all temporality is transcended—subjectively when salvation is tasted, objectively when salvation is fulfilled. When history and salvation are coupled in this way, it becomes possible for an investigation of temporal continuities and discontinuities to posit the divine inauguration and transmission of salvation through time and in space. Salvation-history is, then, the story—but pre-eminently the eternal reality *behind* the story—of salvation. Thus construed, the story takes place within human history, even though it does not essentially affect, and remains finally unaffected by, the stuff of history.

Since the time of Eusebius Pamphili and Lactantius Firmianus, there has been another way of linking history with Christian salvation. On this reading, an investigator of the past can learn and narrate the affairs of groups claiming to possess Christian salvation. As distinct from salvation-history (or the theology of history), the history of salvation (or the history of Christianity) becomes, not the career of God, but the progress of God's people as they dealt with the chances and changes of human existence. This view accords reality and significance to historical discontinuities, although it tends to imbue the saved with an uncommon immunity against the relativities that history inflicts on the benighted. The second way of thinking about salvation and history is akin to—but not, I think, identical with—the narrative or descriptive church histories that were devised on the assumptions and by the critical methods of modern scholars who reconstructed the history of profane groups.

In the West it was the Enlightenment thinkers, with their new perspectives on history and their new conceptions of salvation, who undercut both ancient ways of allying history and salvation. Rationalists thought that history was understandable precisely because they took man to be the decisive actor who made the human past what it was. Man was then the true creator of the episodes that historians undertook to reconstruct and narrate. The pietists were the rationalists' religious cousins. For the pietists, salvation was receivable because the recipient could locate and transact his spiritual affairs outside history and thus in disregard of historical actualities. Although the rationalists excluded what I call salvation-history, they nevertheless were able to deal with a certain human or immanent dimension of the history of salvation. Pietists were concentrating on the transcendent dimension of salvation to the neglect of the history of salvation (perhaps Jonathan Edwards is the prime example, in spite of the title of his posthumously published work).

In recent times the confidence with which the Enlightenment thinkers detached their sense of history from their conceptions of salvation has been qualified in two major ways. On the one hand, a new alliance between history and Christian theology was struck, an alliance that looked for new ways to adumbrate salvation-history in the form of theologies of history and also to develop a church history that might more fully utilize methods and procedures of critical historiography. On the other hand, a heightened self-consciousness within the the critical historical imagination has opened up the theoretical possibility that men might achieve, by their own intellectual effort, certain qualities of the spiritual freedom that Christian salvation traditionally proffered; the limits of this essay preclude my examining this interesting development.[3]

[3] If the nub of Christian salvation is construed, as certain existentialist theologians suggest, to be emancipation from constraints on

Here we pose certain questions about the recent alliance between Christian theology and history. Is the new salvation-history adequate to the modern spirit? Is the new alliance indeed the grand *entente* that some have claimed it to be, or is it only a *détente* from those conflicts between history and theology that prevailed during most of the nineteenth century? How far can the history of salvation come to terms with critical historical thinking? Is church history entering a new age in which both the stage of human action and the drama of salvation fall into clear focus? Or does the critical history of salvation yield the story of human affairs as they were engaged by people who conceived of themselves as being (or having been) saved?

As a student of the history of Christianity, I cannot avoid the converging historiographic evidence that men and women have experienced, humanly speaking, a reconciliation with God, universe, society, and self; throughout the Christian centuries their sense of reconciliation has been known as salvation.[4] This evidence remains qualified by

---

one's self-identity or decision-making by the ideology that evoked one's personhood, then the modes and stages of critical historical thinking can indeed, I believe, effect that emancipation. So I argue in a lecture on "The Liberating Function of History" delivered in 1968 at Burg Wartenstein, Austria, for The Wenner-Gren Foundation for Anthropological Research, and again in 1968 at the University of North Carolina, Chapel Hill; it is being prepared for publication. Whether such notions as deliverance from bondage to the past or openness for the future actually exhaust what Christian salvation has included (and might yet include) is, to be sure, quite another matter.

[4] One of the editors of this volume, Professor Wilson, questioned whether my argument did not assume that "salvation" and "Christianity" are self-evident categories of interpretation. I shall show below how the historian of Christianity converts testimonies about salvation and Christianity into evidences for the categories—understood, of course, not theologically but as human phenomena. I use salvation and Christianity as evidenced categories just as the military historian uses war as an evidenced category. The main point, however, is that the critical historian who seeks to identify war, salvation, or Christianity finds evidences in view of which these interpretive categories become required for the task of explanation. Needless to say, there have been varieties of salvation, varieties of Christianity,

the recognition that each age and culture lent its particularities to the meanings and expressions it gave to this salvation. As a modern critical historian, however, I cannot avoid assuming that what men and women actually experienced and have recorded in monuments or documents can be reconstructed by critical reasoning and can be represented in narratives and descriptions. This assumption is qualified by the recognition that what actually happened in one generation cannot be exhaustively reconstructed by another. The critical historian uses evidence to describe human actuality, and the historian of Christianity deals with evidence of human salvation. These facts prompt my attempt to bring history and salvation into juxtaposition, and they eventually lead me to distinguish between salvation-history and the history of salvation.

A word about the intellectual setting in which to pursue the implications of these questions may conclude this introduction. Wherever theology is regarded as beyond criticism, the legitimacy of theologizing about history (or about anything else) derives externally by privilege. Conversely, wherever the procedures of critical historical thinking are made a sacred cow, inquiry into the history of salvation is legitimated arbitrarily, as is the history of magic or witchcraft. Thus to pose the above questions is not to juxtapose history and salvation. I wish instead to ask whether salvation-history is *history* and whether the history of salvation is about *salvation.*

Salvation-History and History of Salvation

The new orthodoxy that fascinated Protestant thinkers after World War I and Catholic thinkers after World War II characteristically emphasized the historicity of salvation in two ways. First, it was asserted that salvation became normatively published and generally distributed in first-century Palestine by the death and post-mortem appear-

---

and varieties of war. I agree that the critical historian bears the burden of clarifying them as conceptual categories.

ances of Jesus of Nazareth. Second, it was maintained that the spreading and transmitting of this salvation through time and in space constituted the ultimately meaningful movement in human history. These claims of historicity arose in reaction to the threat that critical historiography might displace theology.

In 1932 Carl Becker, for example, stated quite pungently the predicament theologians had to face with respect to history. "Theology, or something that goes under that name," he wrote in *The Heavenly City of the Eighteenth-Century Philosophers*, "is still kept alive by the faithful, but only by artificial respiration. Its functions . . . have been taken over, not as is often supposed by philosophy, but by history—the study of man and his world in the time sequence."[5] Even before Becker so aptly summarized the challenge, writers concerned for the fate of Christianity were making their apologetical parries. Since about 1920 a virtual flood of books and articles has used the concept of salvation-history as the active lung for mouth-to-mouth resuscitation of the theology that Becker thought was already asphyxiated. To mention some writers whose works are already well known will recall the volume and variety of their concerns: Paul Tillich, Rudolf Bultmann, Karl Löwith, Reinhold Niebuhr, Hans Urs von Balthasar, Nicholas Berdyaev, Emil Brunner, Shirley Jackson Case, Christopher Dawson, Karl Jaspers, Karl Barth—the list is long.

Nor were all the working historians drawn up in array on Becker's side against the theologians. Two of them in particular, who disavowed being theologians, demonstrated an attractive way in which the new alliance could be hailed from the side of history. *Christianity and History* is the title given to a series of lectures by Herbert Butterfield and to a collection of essays by E. Harris Harbison. Both historians wanted to refute Becker's dictum that "In our

[5] Carl Becker, *The Heavenly City of the Eighteenth-Century Philosophers* (New Haven: Yale University Press, 1932), 17.

time, history is nothing but history, the notation of what has occurred, just as it happened."[6]

Christianity, wrote Butterfield, "presents us with religious doctrines which are at the same time historical events or historical interpretations. . . . Christianity in any of its traditional and recognisable forms has rooted its most characteristic and daring assertions in that ordinary realm of history with which the technical student is concerned."[7] Harbison did not disagree, although he was cautious enough to remark that "It has always been easier for theologians than for working historians to write convincingly of history as the work of God."[8] Yet Harbison proceeded to do just the thing he found difficult, and he applauded theologians who could do it more easily. As he saw it, the theologians were undertaking to bring about "the reconstruction of a biblical interpretation of history from the original sources"—that is, the original sources of history.[9] This reconstruction arose out of the conviction, as Butterfield described it, that "after a long period of comparative security and general progress, we in this [European] part of the world find ourselves . . . in the midst of that very kind of catastrophic history which confronted the Hebrew prophets at one period, and which the great St. Augustine, for example, had to face at another period."[10]

Wherever the new alliance between theology and history has been acclaimed, the famous Bishop of Hippo Regius has been invoked—either for comparison or for sanction or for both. It is less stylish today than it was in the 1940's to find in Rome's fall to the Goths, which Augustine contemplated, a historical parallel with (and perhaps also a spiritual solace in the face of) the fall of Paris to the Nazis, which Butterfield's and Harbison's generation contemplated. But more crucial matters than a mere parallel are at issue

[6] *Ibid.*, 18.

[7] Herbert Butterfield, *Christianity and History* (New York: Scribner's, 1950), 3.

[8] E. Harris Harbison, *Christianity and History* (Princeton: Princeton University Press, 1964), 57.

[9] *Ibid.*, 37.

[10] Butterfield, 3.

when Augustine is summoned to address our historical and theological problems. There is, for one thing, the fact that Augustine never undertook to write history in anything like the modern narrative sense. For another, although many have asserted that Augustine replaced a cyclical view of history (imputed, sometimes very recklessly, to "the Greeks") with a linear view of history, in fact Augustine taught a linear view of *time*, not history. Moreover, he made time linear in order to support his doctrine of creation, which was original by virtue of depicting creation as at once universal, unitary, and unique. He never applied this linear view of time to those problems of interpreting history with which moderns are concerned. For salvation, in Augustine's view, meant deliverance *from* history, not the transformation of this world's kingdoms into the kingdom of God or Christ. The unmixing of the two cities—rather than their historical development into a significant *civitas hominis*—was to Augustine's mind the process and the goal of Christian salvation. The church, as Augustine saw its task, was to appropriate for itself the meaningfulness normatively exhibited in the Incarnation, and it was to conserve that meaning against dissipating into the chaotic structures of the *civitas terrena.* By no means was the church, itself conceived by Augustine on the monastic-ascetic pattern, to suffuse with grace and meaning those profane institutions whose existence was historical and, on his reading, therefore transitory.

It is remarkable that only in very recent times have Christians begun to find in Augustine—or in the Hebrew prophets, or in the Bible taken as a whole—this special preoccupation with history and historicity that apologists now generally attribute to them. In fact, a fully critical study of Augustine's writings, and indeed of the Scriptures, in light of this interpretation as preoccupied with history may confidently conclude that the sharp emphasis on the dateability and locateability of crucial occurrences is the distinct mark, not of these ancients, but of the modern mentality by which we interpret them. It is because of their very modernity that moderns who are concerned for the fate of Christianity (for example) emphasize the concrete, historical, particular features of the Incarnation—or of the Exile and the Exodus as its prefigurements.

Indeed, to note this emphasis of the modern mind is also to recognize that a radically historical view of the Christian Incarnation and of Christian salvation is a radical *innovation* with respect to traditional christological and soteriological thinking. Moreover, when the modern imagination gives its account of *any* religion, there surfaces a resemblant tendency to emphasize historicity. Probably one of the most eminently retractable sentences that Paul Tillich ever wrote is this one: "The appearance of Mohammed as the prophet does not constitute an event in which history receives a meaning which is universally valid."[11] Would we not expect that every *modern* interpretation of Judaism should find in the Exodus, of Islam in the Hejira, and of Buddhism in the life of Gautama or some other Buddha, events that are dateable and locateable and that paradigmatically summarize the meaning of all subsequent or other events?

Set thus in the modern context, the recent rapprochement between Christian theology and critical historiography is seen to derive less from the rediscovery of a uniquely Christian (or even Judaeo-Christian) historico-theological motif than from our participation in a peculiarly modern—and largely *untheological*—way of thinking about the human past.

We cannot allow ourselves to forget that the linear or periodic view of time that Augustine set forth yielded over the centuries no universal historiography but only chronicles, miscellaneous with regard to human history and unified solely by the theme of providence with regard to theology. A universal understanding of history came into being in the West only when Renaissance thinkers, without

[11] Paul Tillich, *Systematic Theology*, 3 vols. (Chicago: University of Chicago Press, 1951-1963), III, 368.

discarding the idea of providence, recovered the ancient metaphor of the wheel or circle.

The Augustinian, periodic rendition of the past accounted for a continuous, sacred history by imputing providential continuity to the church. But civil history rested where Augustine had placed it, in the limbo of mere handmaidenhood to the church's career in time. The metaphoric wheel enabled Renaissance historians to counterpoise change and continuity as wrought by man in his civil institutions. By this repossessed conceptual tool the notion of novelty was restored to a humanistic place in the context of the stubborn repetitions of human experience. As Herschel Baker has noted, the English chronicles of the sixteenth century "exemplify, and often explicate, the notion that history is not a string of inconsequential episodes but an intelligible design, where repetition and recurrence provide the key to explanation."[12]

Although few Renaissance men frankly opposed their new conception of history to the old providential view, Francis Bacon spoke for his age when he alluded to the inherent conflict between these ideas by juxtaposing history and poesy. In *The Advancement of Learning* Bacon contrasted, as Baker reports, imaginative narration with the recounting of actualities. Bacon dared favor the latter. Since "true history propoundeth the successes and issues of actions not so agreeable to the merits of virtue and vice," Bacon wrote, "therefore poesy feigns them more just in retribution, and more according to revealed providence; because true history representeth actions and events more ordinary and less interchanged, therefore poesy endueth them with more rareness, and more unexpected and alternative variations." Bacon noted the realistic advantage of human actualities over divine fancies, even while conceding to poesy (and, *mutatis mutandis*, to theology) "some participation and divineness, because it doth raise and erect the

[12] Herschel Baker, *The Race of Time: Three Lectures on Renaissance Historiography* (Toronto: University of Toronto Press, 1967), 63.

mind, by submitting the shews of things to the desires of the mind; whereas reason [and, *mutatis mutandis*, history] doth buckle and bow the mind unto the nature of things."[13]

English Renaissance historians continued to elevate sacred history over profane history, even when the leading ideas of their age drove sharp distinctions between these conceptions. Bacon and Raleigh, Degory Wheare and Edmund Bolton, John Foxe and John Milton all conceded a certain truth to sacred history, especially as they found it paradigmatically set out in Scripture. Meanwhile, they applied skeptical criticism to man's own past endeavors and also to the affairs of those nations whose histories lay outside the purview of Bible and Christendom. Among those named, it was of course Raleigh who exalted sacred history to the very highest authority and subsumed profane history under it as exhibiting the will of God.[14]

But no poet after Milton, as C. A. Patrides teaches us, was engrossed in the providential interpretation of history. For prose writers who clung to the old idea we must turn to Jacques Bossuet and Jonathan Edwards. By the end of the eighteenth century the transition was so complete that, save as a conventional way of reckoning the years, the periodization of things Before Christ or *Anno Domini* had yielded, in the minds of the leading historians, to the far less continuous periodization of Western man's pilgrimage into the classical, medieval, and modern epochs.[15]

If the breach between man's historical actuality and God's overriding providence opened during the Renaissance, the gulf became fixed and final in the Enlightenment. Giovanni Battista Vico founded scientific history on

[13] *Ibid.*, 85-86, quoting Francis Bacon, *The Advancement of Learning*, in *Works*, ed. James Spedding, Robert Leslie Ellis, and Donald Denon Heath, 16 vols. (1861-1864), VI, 203.

[14] See Baker, 34-41.

[15] See C. A. Patrides, *The Phoenix and the Ladder: the Rise and Decline of the Christian View of History*, University of California Publications, English Studies, No. 29 (Berkeley and Los Angeles: University of California Press, 1964), 66-68. The idea of modernness demands updating, and so we tend to periodize our predecessors in modernity as Renaissance, Enlightenment, and Romantic men.

the principle that man can understand the human past only to the extent that he takes himself to be the creator of his own past. This principle has been employed by critical historians since the Enlightenment, and it has enabled moderns to accumulate vast data about, and to achieve profound insights into, the entire recorded human career.

Vico's principle operates only when it is accompanied by the confident doctrine that man exercised free will as he went about managing significantly large areas of his affairs. In other words, the decisively human aspect about any historical episode is, in the modern view, that the choice between alternative courses of action originates in man's decision. *Only* if that is assumed to have been the case can an episode be accurately reconstructed. This modern reformulation of the procedures by which historical thinking takes place is of course diametrically opposed to all of the three lines along which Augustine laid out his thought—providence, the bound will, and memory (not critical reconstruction) as man's entry into the past. Not insignificantly, Reinhold Niebuhr subscribed to the third Augustinian principle, as well as to some versions of the first and second. "Memory," Niebuhr apothegmatically wrote, "is . . . the fulcrum of freedom for man in history. That is why the study of history is an emancipating force in human life."[16]

All these humanistic assumptions, which were powerfully operative during the Enlightenment and have been ever since, cast long shadows of doubt across the most fundamental attitudes of salvation-history, old style or new. The doctrine of providence, which had been axiomatic to the Western mind since its pagan and Christian adumbrations, respectively, by Cicero and Augustine, became a pious opinion instead of an eternal verity. Salvation, shakily reestablished on these new assumptions, remained a tenable concept denoting a vertical relation between the soul and

[16] Reinhold Niebuhr, *Faith and History: a Comparison of Christian and Modern Views of History* (New York: Scribner's, 1951), 19.

God, but it was stripped of its potency as a description of horizontal relations between man and his fellow men—save in mutual meditation on their vertical relations to God. Precisely because they accepted these very restrictions on salvation-history, the pietists of eighteenth-century Europe and America became intellectual partners of the Enlightenment. For just the same reason, pietism appears (in retrospect) to have truncated traditional Christian theology.

The split between history and theology extended far beyond these theoretical implications. For the assumptions and methods of critical history were applied, during the nineteenth century, to explain the origin and development of Christian salvation itself. The degree to which such explanations produced a new history of salvation or church history merits attention later in this essay. But it is appropriate here to note that salvation-history suffered perhaps mortal wounds from the scientific, objective history of the nineteenth century.

On the grounds—themselves neither strictly verifiable nor strictly falsifiable—that people of the past resemble people of the present sufficiently for us to learn, understand, and narrate the thoughts and actions of our predecessors in ways that reach beyond their own self-understanding, it became possible to treat the origin and transmission of Christian salvation *objectively*. That is to say, Christian salvation became an object of investigation to whose claims its investigator was, by his own critical thinking, immunized. The dictum "Jesus Christ is Lord," whether considered as Jesus' own claim, or as the testimony of Jesus' eyewitnesses, or as the conviction of traditional salvation-historiography, lost its theological potency when it was translated into the objective, narrative statement "Jesus Christ was regarded as Lord." The history of salvation could be—and came to be—told from perspectives that perceived salvation in new, inclusive ways because these perspectives arose from outside and beyond it. Moreover, this new telling had the effect of enabling not only the narrator but also his audience to stand outside and beyond salvation-history. The so-called post-Christian—better, ex-Christian—era had dawned, perhaps originally at the University of Tübingen.

The history of salvation—viewed from the outside—exposed for the first time the multitudinous instances in which the doctrine of God's providence had shielded and sanctioned polemics, propaganda, and prejudices. The hypothesis that history created dogmas neatly unmasked the very great extent to which dogmas had in fact created salvation-history. Purportedly unique features of Christianity were traced to pagan sources. Sacred men and institutions were found to stand on feet of clay. In a word, the humanistic history of Christianity revealed that Christians had been only human.

On this objective history of salvation the commanders of a recent theological counterattack trained their mightiest weapons. Historians themselves realized that critical historiography could be raised to its conceivably most useful degree of self-criticism by going beyond nineteenth-century objectivism to an attitude in which the historian was self-critical at once of his roles as investigator, narrator, and critic. Such self-criticism confessed that historians, too, are human—and thus never wholly lacking in presuppositions. Hearing this admission made the theologians rejoice. If historians were not presuppositionless and if theologians were not presuppositionless, why not declare an *entente* between them? Few paused to ask the obvious question arising from the discovery that both parties relied on presuppositions: how defensible were the assumptions of each party? This claimed kinship of theologians and historians rested on an obviously undistributed middle term. Moreover, the heralded rapprochement between them involved a certain confusion over the meaning and effect of historical objectivity.

The terms "objectivity" and "subjectivity," of course, lose constructive meaning when they are taken as denoting simple opposites. Ranke, Strauss, and the other "objectivist" historians of Christianity were neither trying nor claiming to nullify either their own subjectivity or that of the persons about and for whom they wrote, in order to endow their narratives with sterile impartiality. Rather, in studying their data and in writing their histories, they enlisted their own subjectivity in an enterprise aimed at a high degree of intersubjective transferability. A very high degree, indeed, was achieved. By building a broad consensus on professional methods of historiography, the "objective" historians followed standards that rendered the work of each at once understandable, analyzable, and largely duplicable by another. Histories became "objective" precisely to the extent that they were genuinely critical—that is, to the extent that presuppositions were made conscious and held under control, and their effects noted.

There is, to be sure, an important feature of contemporary critical historiography which a century ago had not become a professional standard: simultaneous self-criticism by the historian in his roles of investigator, narrator, and critic. Thus the contemporary "objectivity" includes acknowledgment of presuppositions in such a manner that even the historian's own inevitable subjectivity becomes intersubjectively transferable. Such a way of possessing presuppositions, methodologically based and critically exposed as it is, can hardly be equated with the conviction that impels the theologian's work.

Of course, much contemporary theology achieves a certain "objectivity" by acknowledging its philosophical, historical, moral, and other presuppositions. It is scarcely to be questioned that a more useful historiography proceeds from this objectivity. But Karl Barth has raised a most interesting point by pleading, in effect, that true theology cannot brook an intrusion of the theologian's self-critical subjectivity and of his methodological self-consciousness, certainly not to the degree that is necessary (and, if self-critical, sufficient) to intellectual objectivity. Critical, objective, methodologically self-conscious "theology" is more accurately called philosophy of religion. The objectivity of self-consciously criticized subjectivity seems to be precisely what Barth would deny to the "theological exegete."

When the theologian speaks "from faith to faith," he concerns himself with reality which must be presumed to transcend the actualities of the human past, present, and future. Christians have always believed that this reality also was and is immanent in human experience. That belief is abundantly recorded in ways which make the *belief* an actuality of the human past, an actuality fully accessible to the critical historian. But no data available to the historian point beyond such belief to the reality of the thing believed. What is theological about a theology that stops precisely where the historian must thus stop? Notwithstanding the declamation by self-styled "biblical theologians" to the effect that God acted and spoke, acts and speaks, in "history," the critical historian can proceed no further toward knowledge of God than to conclude that men and women *believed* that God acted and spoke in their (or other) times.

Critical history as a means of understanding the past, regardless of the presuppositions its practitioner may confess, yields no knowledge of God. It does yield the important knowledge that people have believed in God. It also tells us that this belief imbued them with something we can call salvation by the God in whom they believed. On their belief and out of their salvation they thought and acted. The critical historian who studies the thought and acts of such people can describe them with respect to their salvation, a quality of life that from this perspective is no less human a phenomenon than, say, the nationalism that historians identify as having characterized the thought and acts of many different people. Christian salvation, whatever its source, exhibits itself as a human phenomenon. Therefore, the critical historian can learn much about it, albeit in a manner that prohibits his learning therefrom about God.

Here arises perhaps the most important distinction between critical history and salvation-history. Salvation-history imputes a continuous identity to peoples, movements, and institutions while it finds a high degree of change and discontinuity in the circumstances under which people have lived. Thus the true faith once delivered to the saints, the Christian ministry in its various orders, the Church, Christ, God, etc., become constant categories for salvation-history. Yet to salvation-history the ages in which (or the dispensations under which) men have lived brought in their train objectively different circumstances: B.C. and A.D., the Persecution and the Peace of the Church, pre-Reformation and post-Reformation, even Vatican I and Vatican II. "O where are kings and empires now,/" goes Arthur Cleveland Coxe's familiar hymn, "Of old, that went and came?/ But, Lord, thy Church is praying yet,/ A thousand years the same."[17] Salvation-history imbues the people who experienced salvation with a steady identity under shifting conditions.

Contrariwise, critical history tends to find that discontinuity is characteristic of the identity of peoples, movements, and institutions while the circumstances of human existence remain fundamentally the same. The French differed, according to secular historiography, before and after their Revolution and, indeed, in each of their five Republics; yet they derived continuity from their constant confrontation with Germany and England, Italy and Spain.

This important distinction between salvation-history and the history of salvation arises, at the most subtle point, out of differing emphases placed on two types of historical testimony. Salvation-historians are prone to take ascriptive testimony at face value, whereas critical historians place that testimony under suspicious scrutiny. More subtly, salvation-historians tend to identify ascriptive self-descriptions with intention-action descriptions or at least to stress the convergences of the two, whereas critical historians seek evidence by testing their divergences and by emphasizing

[17] Arthur Cleveland Coxe, *Christian Ballads* (1840), No. 382 in *The Hymnal of the Protestant Episcopal Church . . . 1940* (New York: The Church Pension Fund, 1940).

the tensions that always remain between the two types of testimony.

An example may clarify the matter we have been discussing. At Nicaea in A.D. 325 the leaders of a diverse Christian movement defined the source of salvation as a Logos consubstantial with God the Father. For the remainder of the fourth century (and even until today) Christians hotly contested the definition. If my distinctions are valid, then salvation-history will accept the self-definition of Nicaea; it will conclude that salvation in truth comes from a Logos who is HOMOOUSION TŌ PATRI; on this reading, those who rejected the Nicene teaching participated either defectively or not at all in salvation. Thus salvation-history adduces knowledge of God from the claims of men to have known God. This kind of knowledge belongs not to critical history but to theology.

Critical history learns that some men thought they were saved only if the Logos were consubstantial with the Father, and it takes equally into account the datum that other men were content with a salvation that derived from a less lofty Logos. As an actuality of the past, itself created by men, their human disagreement precludes the historian from assigning unity to the fourth-century church, and it also prevents his reaching any conclusion about the true source of salvation. From men's conflicts over their different views of God, critical history adduces only the knowledge of these men. Whatever qualities of life they may have shared as the common result of their salvation—such as a reverence for God the Father—was, critically speaking, the content of Christian salvation in their time and place. And this is not to say that salvation was whatever anybody may have thought it was.

The rapprochement between theology and history which we have noted was indeed a *détente* from the enmity between a radically subjectivist theology deriving from pietism and a radically objectivist history deriving from rationalism. Recent theologians have participated in the modern preoccupation with historicity by reinterpreting

Christian salvation according to that preoccupation. Critical historians have recognized their presuppositions for the sake of controlling them and rendering them appropriately objective. But the rapprochement is no *entente*, nor does it count for much as a *détente* today. The new salvation-history recognized defects in pietistic and liberal notions that to know a man's personal experience of God would be to know God better or to know a better God. Were God acting in history, however, it would be in a history unknowable to critical historians. The history that is knowable to critical historians is a kind of history that, by definition, yields no knowledge of God. The knowledge of God remains the business of the theologian, who will know more the less he claims about history. The historian's proper business is the knowledge of man in the past, and he will know more the less he claims about God. Where the *détente* between them is taken for a real and effective alliance, theologians may lose sight of God by looking at man's beliefs about Him, and historians may lose sight of man by looking for the God in whom he may have believed.

Church History and History of Salvation

When theological and critical-historical perspectives on the Christian past are distinguished, salvation-history is seen to be a branch of theology. Indeed, it may be suggested that salvation-history cannot be shirked by those who would carry out the full range of theological thinking. It is now appropriate to shift attention to distinctions having to do with the historiography of groups or institutions that claimed to possess and to proffer Christian salvation.

The basic question about the history of salvation (or the history of Christianity) is whether those who exhibit the phenomenon of salvation constitute as such a proper and fruitful object for investigation by the methods of critical history. I think that they do and that the critical historian can adduce answers to the question "What was the salvation they claimed and who partook of that salvation?" To elaborate on those assertions, it becomes necessary to bear in mind some distinctions between the critical historian of salvation and the church historian. To what extent, if any, does the enterprise of either subserve the enterprise of the theologian?

On this reading, of course, theology is taken to embrace more than the apologetics that try to justify it and more than the dogmatics that tend to petrify it. Theology means, in a Christian context, the knowledge and description of the God to whom salvation through Christ was or is attributed. An interesting feature of Christian theology is its attempt to identify this God as both including and transcending the deities of cultures in which Christianity flourished; thus the God to whom salvation is attributed is not only the God whom Jesus addressed as Father but also the Jahweh of the Old Testament and *the* God (HO THEOS) of Platonic thought and, later on, the *actus purus* of Aristotelian philosophy.

If theology seeks to describe this God, there remain optional methods of tracing through time such human phenomena as salvation and the ways men attributed it to God. One option is to produce in, by, and for the people who partake of salvation the story of their predecessors in the faith, for the sake of prolonging their identity. That is the task of the church historian, and I shall argue that the nature of this task establishes church history as a branch of theology. A very different option is to study the transit of the same people through time and space in order to describe the varieties of their salvation and their relations to their fellow men. The latter is the task of the historian of Christianity, engaging in the enterprise of critical history. The two tasks are further distinct in an operational (but not unimportant) way: church historiography provides data that are required for the critical historian of Christianity to do his work.

Subjects who possessed and proffered Christian salvation furnish data that meet the tests of critical historical investigation because—and only insofar as—we possess records indicating that (1) they claimed to participate in salvation, (2) these claims were affirmed and qualified by the testimonies of reliable witnesses, and (3) the identity of these subjects was established by a historiographic tradition. All three of these types of testimony can also be put to uses which are characteristically theological because and insofar as they attest to the character of God. The critical historian accepts these testimonies as data only about human subjects.

The three activities by Christian groups through the ages specifically yielding these respective kinds of testimony are (1) worship, (2) missions, and (3) church history. Liturgical writings from the Fourth Gospel to the Jazz Mass have set forth the claims of participation in Christian salvation. Insofar as their messages were seriously received and pondered, missionaries from St. Paul to Billy Graham have elicited eyewitness substantiation of their own claims to salvation. And church historians from St. Luke to Kenneth Scott Latourette have formed a historiography of and for the people of salvation.

The critical historian of salvation learns first of all to forego regarding these testimonies as evidences about God, precisely in order to be able to derive insight from them regarding the history of salvation as a human phenomenon. His work therefore differs in ways that are numerous and important from the theological enterprise that I have termed salvation-history. But these differences allow no retreat from the historiographical task of identifying and tracing this human salvation through time and in space.

The history of salvation becomes instructive if the people who bore it can be identified; thus the primary question is "What was salvation and who has partaken of it?" In our time there are two easy but quite unsatisfactory answers that may be returned. One obviously superficial solution is to say that, if a person or group only *claimed* salvation, no further critical questions may or should be asked. A more subtle but still too facile answer is the referral of questions regarding "salvation-identity" to an external, authoritative norm. By analyzing each of these ready responses to the primary question asked by the historian of salvation, we may discover that a more profound answer lies within our reach.

Our religiously plurified societies effectively dismiss as irrefragable all claims to possess or to proffer salvation. A feature of thoroughgoing freedom of religion is that claims to salvation—as *beliefs* irrelevant to society—will be allowed to be regarded as true, even if from external standpoints a claimant is seen to be deluded. Such tolerance bears the implication that the identification of those who participate in salvation is not to be taken seriously. Although the critical historian of salvation may cherish the concord and the complexity of religiously tolerant societies, his curiosity impels him to carry his inquiry further than may seem possible or proper wherever religious conviction is largely a matter of private opinion.

It is noteworthy that religious freedom arose in the interest of lifting both the restraints and the constraints on religious belief that characterized our Western societies from the Constantinian revolution down to the American and French revolutions. During this grand and long period of Christendom the status of an individual or group with reference to the *corpus christianorum*, whenever called into question, was referred to an appellate authority—parson, bishop, king, creed, pope, abbot, council, Bible, church session, holy tradition, confessor, or whatever. The duration and social significance of this practice make it appear that the determination of ecclesiastical status was tantamount to the identification of those who possessed salvation, especially in situations where the formula *extra ecclesiam nulla salus* had literal force. Actually, the external definition of status in the church usually (if not always) stopped short of a final judgment regarding the quality of the relation of the subject(s) to God; even the heretic's execution was tempered by a prayer for his imperishable soul!

Thus neither the *claim*, whether implicit or explicit, to be saved (although prominent in an era of religious pluralism) nor official *recognition* of status as a churchman (although important in the epoch of Christendom) can suffice to identify those who are saved. Accordingly, additional weight attaches to evidence that salvation has found expression in appropriate, intended *action.* (In circular fashion, such action in the modern setting tends to be seen as a mere claim on the part of the subject, whereas in Christendom it appears to have been obedience that led to official recognition.) The matter of critically identifying salvation and the saved falls into sharper focus when applied to such a concrete problem as the identification of a saint in Catholic Christianity. The holy man stakes out an implicit *claim* to be holy, but to press the claim quite explicitly is to countervail it implicitly. Official *recognition* (canonization) obviously cannot make a saint where none existed; it only publicizes a precedent phenomenon. While these two conditions are necessary to sainthood, they become sufficient only when joined to a third: *actions* manifesting sanctity, such as miracles, visions, martyrdom, etc.

By analogy the critical (or "objective") historian identifies the bearers of salvation by the convergence of three types of evidence: (1) ascriptive self-description or the *claim* to salvation, (2) crucially, the kinds of *action* which manifest the intention of salvation, and (3) *recognition* by precedent historiography. I am not suggesting that the illustrative reference to saints gives a neat model of the way critical historians establish identity, for it is characteristic of hagiography to regard the three types of evidence for sanctity as presenting neither discrepancy nor remainder; what the saint claimed to be, was, and is regarded as having been become one and the same thing—an imputation that the critical spirit could hardly accord any mortal. Yet the example is useful, first, because it places sharp emphasis on intention-action identity and, second, because many kinds of action are taken to manifest a single intention.

Thus the critical historian of salvation does not answer the question "What was salvation and who has participated in it?" simply by giving credence either to the testimony of the subject under investigation or to a judgment on the part of the religious authority operative in that subject's time and place. "Who were bearers of salvation?" is a question that remains inseparable from the question "What was salvation?" Moreover, the crucial role assigned to "intentional activity" foils any inclination to escape from relativism by resort to a theological criterion fixed for every age and place. Both St. Cyprian and the confessors during the Decian persecution against whom he strove, both St. Augustine and the Donatists or the Pelagianists whose views he disputed, both St. Bernard and the Peter Abelard he condemned, both the Renaissance popes and the Hussites they harried, both Catholics and Protestants in wars of the Reformation—all *claimed* salvation, all were by appeal to some authority *granted status* as saved people, and indeed all manifested in *action* their special salvation-intentions.

If Christian salvation, thus historically considered, shows itself in such variety, how can it be described? Only as a quality of the lives of historical persons and groups, not as a divine, ideal reality making appearances on a spatio-temporal stage. It can be described as a quality of life, understood in relation to the men and women who received, intended, and expressed it rather than in relation to the God whom they thought imparted it. As something attributed to Christ it led its recipients to resolve that their actions should be modeled after their understandings of Christ's injunctions. As a quality of life it impelled men and women in various measures to achieve and to articulate their reconciliation with God, the universe, the polis, and the self. All this (and of course much more) can be said historically to have been Christian salvation, and all of it is adduced from human data about those who possessed and proffered salvation.

The history of salvation, so identified, is not, however, church history, insofar as church history posits a continuous institution existing under changing circumstances. To identify subjects bearing Christian salvation is not simply to know what the Christian church has always been. Church history is at once an enterprise more certain of itself and an intellectual discipline more given to theology than is the history of salvation.

In 1952 Gordon Rupp, a church historian then at Cambridge and later at Manchester, voiced this lament: "It is one of the disabilities of our time that the two disciplines of history and theology remain in separated compartments, and the wayfaring Christian who tries to make sense of his Bible and his newspaper must be concerned to know what the historian and the theologian mean when they speak about a historical religion."[18] It becomes increasingly clear that they mean different things. A simultaneous lament by another church historian, James Hastings Nichols, then at Chicago and later at Princeton Theological Seminary, noted that the theologians of history "do not locate the community which is the bearer of this fragmentary emergent meaning, which is a challenge the Marxists do not fail to meet. . . . [O]ne cannot discern direction and meaning in history in general without a concrete perception of particular redemption and new life in the church. This is the task which both the theologians of history and the church historians have generally burked, and which would be the common ground on which they might most effectively stimulate each other."[19]

Both laments serve to remind us that only in modern times have theologians and church historians—and by no means all of either class—burked that task. From the Acts of the Apostles down to denominational chronicles still in print, church history has been set forth as the centrally meaningful strand of history, borne by an identifiable institution or movement. I suggest that the frustrations church historians articulate over this issue derive from a profes-

[18] Gordon Rupp, *Principalities and Powers: Studies in the Christian Conflict in History* (New York: Abingdon-Cokesbury Press, 1952), 7.

[19] James Hastings Nichols, "The Art of Church History," *Church History* xx (March 1951), 8.

sional double-mindedness that refuses to distinguish between church history as a branch of theology and the history of salvation as a branch of critical history. Or, more simply, the kind of historical study of Christianity that is appropriate to a theological seminary or divinity school must—if we are rigorous—be delineated from, and in important respects be set at odds with, the kind of historical study of Christianity that is appropriate to the arts and sciences faculty within the university. The two should not and cannot be identical, because it is precisely this church historiography that provides the third level of data without which, on the above terms, the critical historian of salvation is unable to do his work.

Church history, confidently identifying the church as the locus of salvation and God as its author, is a legitimate aspect of theological studies, but it cannot at the same time separate itself from salvation and salvation-history in the manner necessary for it to be the history of salvation. It is this distinction that lends cogency to an otherwise apparently arbitrary principle of church history that, as Sidney E. Mead puts it, "every historian of 'the church' ought ideally to be a practicing, responsible member of a denomination. It is this existing 'church' *as is* that he ought to be trying to understand, and to help to a self-understanding of itself by reminding it how it came to be what it is." Continuing to explain church history, Mead wrote: "Hence the study of the history-that-happens [by church historians] is always somehow the study of the works of God in history—and by his works we shall know Him, though now we see only through a glass darkly."[20]

There are, to be sure, important distinctions to be drawn between church history on one side and salvation-history or the theology of history on the other, but these distinctions do not remove church history from the circle of theological studies. Referring to salvation-history as "sacred

[20] Sidney E. Mead, "Church History Explained," *Church History* XXXII (March 1963), 27, 29.

history," Paul Tillich has traced the line of demarcation in a pithy passage:

> . . . [O]ne cannot call church history "sacred history" . . . . Sacred history is in church history but is not limited to it, and sacred history is not only manifest in but also hidden by church history. Nevertheless, church history has one quality which no other history has: since it relates itself in all its periods and appearances to the central manifestation of the Kingdom of God in history, it has in itself the ultimate criterion against itself—the New Being in Jesus as the Christ. The presence of this criterion elevates the churches above any other religious group, not because they are "better" than the others, but because they have a better criterion against themselves and, implicitly, also against other groups.[21]

Whatever one may think of Tillich's terminology—and I, for one, object to his equating "history of salvation" with "sacred history"—the distinction is clear. Although church history may flirt with critical history by day, by night she goes to bed with theology, her true husband.

From the standpoint of critical history, the problematical features of church history are not only the very high degree of continuity imparted to an institution related "to the central manifestation of the Kingdom of God in history" but also the tendency to leap over the difficulty of identifying the groups which comprise this institution. A twentieth-century trend toward writing church history from an ecumenical point of view has gone far toward overcoming the polemical and sectarian spirit with which church historians for many centuries had anathematized one another's churches. There is a possibility that, beyond a historiographical harmonizing of Protestant and Catholic Christianity since the Reformation, the schism between Eastern and Western churches may be sufficiently healed to afford the mutual recognition of both parties as belonging to one, historiographically-reunited church.

[21] Tillich, III, 381.

But however one may play down the divisiveness of Christian churches in the present millennium, the story of the first millennium exhibits divisions and contentions which no historiographical erasers can expunge. Ebionites and Docetists, Marcionites and Montanists, Arians and Apollinarians, Nestorians and Donatists, Monophysites and Monothelites, Origenists and Iconoclasts are only a few of the anathematized heretics or schismatics who people the era. The church historian is counseled to lay aside their claims to Christian salvation not simply on the testimony of their enemies but by applying theological criteria that, being retroactive in their force, cannot be adduced or defended historically. The historical fact is that the Christian churches in all their appearances have been contentious, fissiparous, divisive institutions—the more and not the less so when they held themselves under the concept of *una sancta*. That fact can be deemphasized, properly enough, by church historians who work within the theological circle. Historians of salvation must, however, face the evidence and interpret it in terms of different criteria.

The trouble arises when the theological principles of church history are confused, especially by theologians of history, with the critical principles of the historiography of salvation. There has been, to be sure, an attempt to join church history with critical history, and in America it was the theologians who foiled the attempt. Harbison has aptly noted that "Theology yielded her queenly throne in American seminaries to 'scientific' church history sometime during the early 1900's, but recently she has reclaimed her rights and put the usurpers to rout. The result is . . . that the writers in question [Barth, the brothers Niebuhr, Brunner, Temple, Berdyaev, Bouyer] are like Isaiah and Augustine: most of them are prophetic commentators *on* the historical process rather than chroniclers *of* the process itself—closely interested in history but suspicious of any who see salvation in the historical process."[22] In these same seminaries the church historians by and large are giving

[22] Harbison, 39.

renewed and appropriate allegiance to the reenthroned queen.

During the early 1960's there arose in the pages of *Church History* a brief but in retrospect fascinating argument, which I will trace briefly. The argument not only revolved around the question of the continuity of the Christian church but also involved a more fundamental question about the very survival of the church through its early history. On the basis of his study of patristic writings, Hugh Nibley scored all church historians since Eusebius for describing rather than questioning the survival of the church through the early centuries. That Nibley took a Mormon's viewpoint on the nascent Christian movement does not make any easier the defense of its identity and continuity against his attack. "By its very definition," he wrote, "church history requires unquestioning acceptance of the basic proposition that the Church did survive. . . . Church history seems to be resolved never to raise the fundamental question of survival as the only way of avoiding a disastrous answer, and the normal reaction to the question—did the Church remain on earth?—has not been serious inquiry in a richly documented field, but shocking recoil from the edge of an abyss into which few can look without a shudder."[23]

An incensed retort from Hans J. Hillerbrand, who confessed that it was to him a "bread and butter" issue, pleaded the Reformers' distinction between the church visible and invisible as the knife Nibley should have used to cut his knot. Further, Hillerbrand proposed the viability of considering church history "as the *history of the interpretation of the Sacred Scriptures*" (Gerhard Ebeling) or as "the *history of the Gospel and its consequences in the world*" (Heinrich Bornkamm). "Or, more simply but quite adequately," according to Hillerbrand, "one can define church history as the *history of Christianity* or the *Christian reli-*

[23] Hugh Nibley, "The Passing of the Church: Forty Variations on an Unpopular Theme," *Church History* xxx (June 1961), 131.

gion and avoid thereby the theologically dangerous term 'church'. . . ."[24]

At the request of the journal's editors, Robert M. Grant arose to referee the debate. Without accepting Nibley's conclusions, he dismissed Hillerbrand's first proposal by saying he did "not believe that the Protestant Reformers can be regarded as guides to the study of early church history, of which they knew practically nothing. . . . A Catholic understanding of the church is the only one which makes any sense in church history, especially in early church history, essentially the history of Catholics by Catholics for Catholics." A further paragraph by Grant merits quotation in full:

> To treat the object of church history as history of interpretation or the history of the Gospel is to make church history the history simply of ideas. Those who do this are, in Mr. Hillerbrand's phrase, "ecclesiastic docetists." The fact that "history of Christianity" or "history of the Christian religion" avoids "the theologically dangerous term 'church' " does not necessarily suggest that such terms are adequate. Since "a history of the movings of the Holy Spirit" is beyond the church historian, why shouldn't he write church history?"[25]

Not long afterward Philip Hefner showed that church history was central to the theological work of Albrecht Ritschl and that in Ritschl's view only the establishment of the continuity of church history—the delineation of "a continuous tradition . . . that . . . moves from Christ to Saint Paul to Luther to Ritschl . . ."—could bring church history fully into the service of theology.[26] Every generation and

[24] Hans J. Hillerbrand, "The Passing of the Church: Two Comments on a Strange Theme," *ibid.* (Dec. 1961), 481.

[25] Robert M. Grant, "The Passing of the Church: Comments on Two Comments on a Strange Theme," *ibid.*, 481-482.

[26] See Philip Hefner, "The Role of Church History in the Theology of Albrecht Ritschl," *Church History* XXXIII (Sept. 1964), 338-355, esp. 352.

school of theologians needs such a continuity to be established, and it is the church historians to whom they rightly assign that sometimes very onerous task.

In the following year the same journal published the 1964 presidential address to its sponsoring society, and the issue was settled—by assertion—according to Nibley's prediction. "Can the church in history be delineated, warts and all," Albert C. Outler asked rhetorically, "with a modesty born of uncertainty and a confidence born of a glimpse of God at work not only in the Scriptures but in all succeeding ages?" The possibility flowed, according to appropriately theological but quite dubiously historical logic, from the imperative: "If this is impossible, then more than the enterprise of church history is at stake, for the Christian faith itself will not long outlive its major premise: God's real presence in human history—past, present, and future."[27]

Indeed, the church historian must assume the survival of his object of investigation, at least down to his own present, and, since hard data indicate as much discontinuity as continuity in the church, the precarious balance has to be tipped by a presupposition that neither arises from nor is verified by the data. The possibility of church history does not turn on the absence of such presuppositions, and as such they are basically neither less nor more verifiable than the critical historian's assumption that man survived the discontinuities of all his institutional endeavors, or the belief that man in any place in the past can be understood by man here and now.

The important clarification to make is that the assumption of every critical historical thinker about man's endurance and solidarity are historical assumptions that may be tested by reference to the rest of *humanistic* knowledge, whereas the assumptions of the church historian are, as

[27] Albert C. Outler, "Theodosius' Horse: Reflections on the Predicament of the Church Historian," *Church History* XXXIV (Sept. 1965), 261. Cf. Georges Florovsky, "The Predicament of the Church Historian," in *Religion and Culture: Essays in Honor of Paul Tillich*, ed. Walter Leibrecht (London: SCM Press, 1958), 140-166.

Outler made plain, *theological* assumptions buttressed in the last resort by their congruence with Christian doctrine. On the particular issue of an idea of the church that allows church history to proceed, once we are clear that all such ideas are theological, perhaps we should concede that Grant was accurate with reference to the early church but too narrow with reference to the rest of it. Church history is certainly the history *of* institutional Christians *by* institutional Christians *for* institutional Christians.

To reduce church history to the history of Christianity, which I have also been calling the history of salvation, might indeed be to merge church history unfairly into the history of ideas. But if the activities of man in the past are, as humanistic and critical historians must insist, explainable in the final analysis by reference, not to God, but to human decisions—themselves properly understood as ideas—there remains another sense in which the history of salvation (or of Christianity) is the proper nontheological mode of the study of this religion in time and space. For the history of Christianity can be studied and narratively reconstructed without resorting to theological presuppositions and, just as important, without eschewing what lies at the heart of Christianity as a historical religion—its possession and proffering of salvation. The same assertions apply, *mutatis mutandis*, to the historical study of any religion that is in a similar sense historical with respect to its concept of salvation.

Christianity belongs in a sense to the church and in a different sense to Western culture. What it has been and what is is to become—of, by, and for the church—is the proper concern of church historians and is properly the task of historical studies in seminaries, in allegiance to Christian theology. What Christianity has been and what it is to become—of, by, and for Western culture—is the proper concern of historians of Christianity and is properly the task of historical studies in universities, in allegiance to the humanities.

Neither the church historian nor the historian of salvation can escape the particular fate of modern man's ability, now a necessity, to think historically about every feature of his past, present, and future. "We must have the courage to profess our own historical total fate because we cannot get out of our historical skins," wrote Ernst Troeltsch. Troeltsch's application of that imperative to the European can be truly read as applying to Western man, who "strives to win a consciously guided future by [means of] a consciously preserved past. But his historical philosophy therefore must restrict itself to a penetration and unification of his own total becoming from the point of view of present experience[,] and to an outline of the future[,] building by critical continuation and creative transformation of that which has become."[28] In a word, the identity and the story of Christian salvation are built by the church historian out of theological principles by means of his allegiance thereto. The historian of Christianity builds them, to be sure less confidently, out of equivocal historical data by means of his "own total becoming."

Currently church history is being restored to its traditional and rightful place in the theological curriculum, in subservience to the search for the knowledge of God. The critical historiography of salvation is thus free to take its place in the curriculum of the humanities, in subservience to the goal of understanding the finished past and of shaping the unfinished future of man.

[28] Ernst Troeltsch, *Der Historismus und seine Probleme* (Tübingen, 1922), undated English translation by Gerda Hartmann, unpublished typescript, Union Theological Seminary Library, New York, 530.

Student Concerns and Philosophical Analysis: Unscrambling Theological Uses of "Contingent"

MALCOLM L. DIAMOND

In his *Tales of the Hasidim* Martin Buber tells the story of a tortured young disciple of a Hasidic master who wanted to tell the master about his inner torment but lacked the nerve. One day he could not restrain himself, and he ran weeping to his master, who asked him what was wrong. The young disciple answered: "I am after all alive in this world, a being created with all the senses and all the limbs, but I do not know what it is that I was created for and what I am good for in this world." His master admonished him, saying: "Little fool! That's the same question I have carried around with me all my life. You will come and eat the evening meal with me today."[1]

Told in the context of a discussion of the study of religion in a modern university, this story is pregnant with disastrous possibilities. The directness of the master's response makes an important point. In effect, he acknowledges to his disciple that there are no clear-cut answers to some of our most vitally significant questions. He explains to him that working on these questions of ultimate purpose is a lifelong enterprise. It is part of the effort to become a man, and that "man" is what the philosopher Gilbert Ryle calls a "process word," like running in football, rather than an "achievement word," like scoring. Moreover, the story makes the point that genuine religion is a matter of personal relation even more than a matter of the transmission of information. Thus the master's response, "You will eat the evening meal with me today," suggests the sacramental character of this meal as a shared act of communion in the

[1] Martin Buber, *Tales of the Hasidim, The Later Masters* (New York: Schocken Books, 1948), "Master and Disciple," 261.

face of ultimate mystery. It is only a short step from reflection on this sort of authenticity to the notion that the job of the professor of religion on the university campus is to convey meaning to students by being with them in an authentic way and sharing what Paul Tillich called "ultimate concern."

In the continuing effort to dissociate religion as an academic discipline from the traditional occupational pattern of the chaplain-teacher, it is essential to distinguish human problems from academic ones. In one sense, the increasing emphasis on the professionalism of graduate schools has precipitated a crisis for liberal arts education as a whole. The emphasis on specialization and on research for the learned associations and journals undercuts the emphasis on the human touch and encourages the development of a bloodless type of scholar who regards undergraduate teaching as a chore. This is, of course, a problem that permeates all fields. Yet it will not be helped by cheapening the academic respectability of the study of religion in an attempt to have professors in departments of religion compensate for the deficiencies—on the human level—of their colleagues in other departments.

The confusion between the roles of chaplain and of the professor of religion is an institutional one, but there is also an important intellectual source of the notion that the professor of religion ought to assume a special responsibility for the spiritual well-being of students. The emergence of departments of religion after the Second World War coincided with the vogue of religious existentialism in the Protestant seminaries of the United States. One of the central themes of religious existentialism has been the primacy accorded participation as a precondition for understanding the ultimate questions concerning human beings in their historical relations and in their relation to God. Whereas the rationalist and the empiricist traditions in philosophy have mistrusted emotional involvement and personal commitment and regarded them as the most common source of bias in human affairs, religious existentialists have extolled them. They have all followed Kierkegaard's lead in claiming that detachment is only possible and effective with regard to relatively trivial matters. They do not deny that a patriot may be partial to the cause of his country or that a believer may be prejudiced in favor of his own religion; instead, they stress that a detached approach to these problems might involve greater distortions. Unless one participates in the phenomenon with one's whole being—body, will, and intellect—one cannot even realize what is at issue. It would seem, for example, that a detached Frenchman or Norwegian could make an objective, and therefore valid, judgment about the American Civil War. A religious existentialist, however, would view the matter differently. He would claim that this very detachment would preclude the Frenchman or the Norwegian from resonating to the American ideals that were at stake, so that he could not come to any meaningful conclusion concerning the authentic interpretation of these ideals by one side or the other. Thus, with regard to the most crucial issues that human beings confront, religious existentialists have insisted that the objective attitude of the detached spectator will not only be inadequate but will not even set one in the position of being able to make a judgment.

The result of this "two story" theory of knowledge has been to imbue men who have been trained in religious existentialism with a sense of the great urgency of transcending mere objective communication. They want to enter into what Martin Buber called "dialogue" with other persons, and certainly they would not exclude their students. They stress the importance of teaching the "whole man," and although they are not at all anti-intellectual, they are apt to demand that education be more than merely intellectual.

The influence of this point of view upon education has resulted in the same unfortunate misunderstandings that characterize its application to political discourse. It has led to a confusion between that which can be accomplished by conscious volition and that which is a by-product of the best that we can do by means of conscious volition. The confusion is implicit in the ambiguity of Buber's term "dialogue." This term refers both to things we can consciously intend, such as attendance at an ecumenical conference, and certain desired benefits that may result from such a conference, as for example, an apprehension of the faith of the other party from the "inside." The sort of thing I have in mind is the way that a Protestant might come to empathize with the Catholic attitude toward the Blessed Virgin Mary. This is a mode of illumination that goes beyond the merely intellectual level, say, the acknowledgment in purely logical terms that, if one grants certain premises, a few propositions do hang together. Yet that greater degree of sympathetic internalization is not something that can be consciously willed, any more than one may consciously plan to fall in love. The deeper involvement cannot be forced; an element of spontaneity must be present.

What has just been said of efforts at "dialogue" holds for liberal arts education as well. Students can be coerced into memorizing facts and subsuming them under prefabricated schemes of greater or lesser generality, but no teacher can compel them to incorporate into their own lives the facts, the generalizations, or the values implicit in the study. Yet the existentialistic emphasis upon participation as a source of privileged access is one that tempts teachers to try to achieve this result. It intensifies the penchant for religious advocacy that is apt, in any case, to infect faithful men when they become professors in a department of religion. The apologetic tendency of religion, against which H. Richard Niebuhr warned us so eloquently, is likely to be reinforced by an existentialistic approach to knowledge.

The universities and, of course, the faculties that have such a dominant role in giving direction to them, can institute procedures that upgrade or downgrade the importance of teaching. They can also make decisions that will raise the professional competence of their faculties. They cannot, however, legislate guidelines that will insure the communication of basic perspectives in the field of religion or anywhere else. Professors at a university simply cannot undertake responsibility for the faith of their students.

There is an emerging consensus on this point with regard to the philosophy of religion. Frederick Ferré, Ninian Smart, and others who teach the philosophy of religion in the English-speaking world have stressed the necessity of dissociating the philosophy of religion from its traditional involvement with Christian apologetics. No one has put it more succinctly than John Hick:

> What is the philosophy of religion? Until recently it was generally understood to mean religious philosophizing in the sense of the philosophical defense of religious convictions. It was seen as continuing the work of "natural," [as] distinguished from "revealed," theology. Its program was to demonstrate rationally the existence of God, thus preparing the way for the claims of revelation. But it seems better to call this endeavor "natural theology," and to term the wider philosophical defense of religious beliefs "apologetics." Then we may reserve the name "philosophy of religion" for what (by analogy with philosophy of science, philosophy of art, etc.) is its proper meaning, namely, *philosophical thinking about religion.*[2]

It would, however, be naive to suppose that philosophical thinking about religion is what students are looking for when they enroll in religion department offerings in the philosophy of religion. Very often they are seeking answers to questions of meaning and value, and they want them to be taken seriously. This demand is fair enough. Yet it is just at this point that the individual teaching the philosophy of religion should be aware of the crucial distinction between what he can control by conscious intention and those matters of great moment which are not subject to that sort of control. A student may be emotionally concerned with basic questions of life's meaning. The teacher, how-

[2] John Hick, *Philosophy of Religion* (Englewood Cliffs, N.J.: Prentice-Hall, 1963), 1.

ever, cannot determine the way the material will interact with these concerns. What the teacher can do is to channel the student's interest into disciplined paths. Part of his job is to provide the student with a technical vocabulary for expressing the questions and beliefs that he already entertains. It is also his responsibility to introduce the student to the history of reflection on these issues and to confront him with the hard options that philosophical reasoning ferrets out of the consideration of these matters. By way of illustration, I should like to relate some of the concerns that students are apt to bring to a course in the philosophy of religion to the theological concept of "contingency" and to see some of the options that he may be confronted with when philosophers work it over.

Let us begin by acknowledging that not all students are alike. Some may be troubled by ultimate concerns regarding their origin and goals, whereas others may be seeking only to discover the quickest route to their first million. For those who are troubled by ultimate questions, the arbitrary character of existence may become a special focus of concern. Members of the white race in contemporary America begin life with a tremendous advantage, at least with regard to the material blessings that most men have sought throughout history. It does not take very much reflection on the part of a student to realize that this advantage of birth is accidental. It is not difficult to imagine the circumstances of one's birth as being other than they were; or, again, any child on learning of the peculiar set of circumstances that led to the mating of his parents may wonder that he was born at all. In other words, it is easy to conceive of the possibility of one's nonexistence. And this is one of the basic meanings of the term "contingent": that which might be otherwise without contradiction. Once a person is infected with the sense of the notion, he cannot readily dismiss it from his mind.

This sense of the contingent and arbitrary character of existence is an example of the sort of concern students may bring to the study of the philosophy of religion. Reflection on these matters is what they seek. This reflection may be carried on in different ways. One way would be to analyze the various responses to these questions found in the great religious traditions. Each of them must, in some fashion, cope with the arbitrary inequalities that exist at birth and that persist through life. One manner of coping with them is provided by the doctrine of Karma as it appears in Hinduism; here it is claimed that the inequalities of birth are explicable by reference to past lives which were, in effect, qualifying examinations that determined one's status in this life. By contrast, traditionally, both Judaism and Christianity have had recourse to the afterlife as the place of compensation for the arbitrary inequalities of this life.

The sense of contingency not only may lead a student to wonder at his own existence in the form and time and place that it is actually manifest but may also affect his values. The Book of Ecclesiastes is a sustained expression of surfeit with the contingent character of existence. All is vanity because all things exist at the same level of mere happenstance. Perhaps Macbeth's "tomorrow and tomorrow" soliloquy has given us the most eloquent expression of the way that the experiencing of life as one little thing after another is able to devalue all things and all events. And Paul Tillich maintained that this kind of meaninglessness is a greater threat to human well-being than death itself.

A student overcome by the meaninglessness that can be elicited by this awareness of contingency may be drawn to a consideration of the cosmological argument from contingent to necessary being. In this tour de force of Western religion the contingent character of the things and events of our everyday experience is not denied, it is underscored. And yet the argument seeks to move, in a compelling form that resembles that of logical demonstration, to the conclusion that beyond the experienced nexus of contingent beings and events there is a reality of an utterly different character—necessary being. Within the context of Western religious thought the argument is used not simply to establish the mere existence of necessary being but to relate it to contingent beings as the North Star is related to the compass. Necessary being gives purpose and direction to life by providing assurance that contingent beings do not exhaust reality but that above and beyond them lies an utterly different order of being that endures after they perish and that assures contingent human beings that their being is ultimately grounded in an order where "must be" prevails, rather than mere "might or might not be."

The stake in the argument is a great one. Although Pascal's dichotomy between the God of the philosophers and the God of the Patriarchs has been very much in vogue of late, it is misguided. What is at issue is a matter of different levels of discourse. We may accept or reject the claim that the character of God is disclosed to us in the Bible. Those who accept it, however, must face the fact that the God whose character is purportedly disclosed in the Bible is strikingly anthropomorphic. This applies as much to the exalted God of the prophets who manifests his sovereignty in moral terms as it does to the God who walks through the Garden of Eden in the cool of the day looking for Adam and Eve. We can cavalierly dismiss the God of the proofs as irrelevant to faith only as long as we refuse to confront the task of distinguishing God from human agents who are also just, loving, and possessed of creative power. The Bible does this after its own fashion, giving us poetic grounds for the distinction, as when we read: "The grass withers, the flower fades when the breath of the Lord blows upon it; surely the people is grass. The grass withers, the flower fades; but the word of our God will stand forever." A formal theological way of getting at this distinction is the contrast between contingent and necessary being.

The argument from contingent to necessary being not only helps us to say what we mean by "God" but, if it is successful, gives all rational men a compelling reason for thinking that God exists. The statement of the argument which follows will rely on statements of the so-called vertical version of the argument that has been advanced by contemporary Thomists.

The argument from contingent to necessary being may be momentous in its conclusion, but its point of departure is prosaic. It does not appeal to special experiences, say, the experience of the numinous. (I shall challenge the argument on this point later in the essay.) Rather, it asks us to look around ourselves and to reflect on cabbages and kings and all the other things we come across. Reflection convinces us that all these things are changing and that sooner or later all these things which have come into being will cease to be.

This generalization applies not merely to such obvious instances of generation and degeneration as living entities but to inorganic things as well. Heinrich Zimmer, in *Myth and Symbol in Indian Art and Civilization*, notes that a day in the life of the high god Brahma is 3,004,000,000 of our calendar years. In time spans of that magnitude, the mountains—which the Hebrews regarded as the pillars of the world—undulate like waves! They undergo a continuous process of erosion back to sea level and then of violent upheaval that thrusts them up once again toward the sky. All things that we can point to, whatever their level of being, come into existence and pass on out of it again.

This combination of observation and reflection yields the data of the argument: things come into existence, keep changing while they exist, and then cease to be. Next comes the assertion that we know the existence of these particular things is not something to which the verb "must" is appropriate, but rather something to which we ought to apply the verb "might." In other words, the myriads of beings that we encounter in our everyday life do in fact exist, but there is nothing necessary about their existence. They might have existed with different properties, or at a different time or place, or they might not have existed at all; they are contingent.

An important assumption of the argument must be noted at this point, namely, that what is true of each and every individual is true of the aggregate. Just as a great number of zeroes added together yield only zero, so it is maintained that a limitless number of contingent beings, taken together, would still be radically contingent. It follows, then, that, if the world is composed of nothing but the sorts of things we can point to, the world is radically contingent.

The next step is crucial. Our reflection on the nature of the contingent things all around us shows that their existence depends upon something external to themselves. A child depends upon its parents for the act whereby it is conceived, a statue depends upon the sculptor for the act whereby it is formed, and a lake depends upon a complex set of factors both to bring it into existence and to keep it filled. Therefore, since it has been demonstrated that the world itself is contingent, it likewise must depend on something to bring it into existence. And the obvious question that follows is: "On what can a contingent world depend?" If the world is held to depend on anything else that is also contingent, we have not accounted for its existence in an ultimate way. We would then have to ask the same question of this contingent being on which the world is said to depend, namely, "On what does it depend?" We are, therefore, driven to conclude that the world, as an aggregate of the contingent beings that we experience all around us, must depend for its existence on a being of an altogether different sort—necessary being.

The argument involves a number of philosophical issues, among which are the infinite regress, the meaningfulness of talking about the world as a whole, and the metaphysical contrast between contingency and necessity. In this discussion I shall concentrate upon the last issue. But, before proceeding, I should like to make an observation regarding the perspective from which it will be carried on.

It has been noted that ancient and medieval philosophers were "substance-oriented"; they sought to unravel our experience of the kinds of things there are in the world by classifying them. Post-Cartesian philosophers, on the other hand, were more oriented toward epistemology and focused on those factors in our experience which justify our claims to knowledge, especially on the problems of perception. Contemporary philosophers are most urgently concerned with problems of language and devote their efforts to probing the justifications that underlie the use of the terms we employ in communicating experience. An examination of the term "contingent" will help to underscore this distinctive emphasis of contemporary philosophy. In theological discourse the term "contingent" is linked to the term "necessary." In the past eras philosophers have often stressed the problematic character of "necessity." It is, after all, hard to identify a "necessary substance" or to regard a precept as rooted in necessity (a point made so tellingly by Hume). At the same time, these philosophers have not regarded the term "contingent" as equally problematical. By focusing on linguistic considerations, I intend to show that the theological use of the term "contingent" is a loaded one. This point has been obscured by the practice of theologians who borrow nuances from legitimate philosophical usage in an effort to provide theological doctrines, such as creation out of nothing, with philosophical support.

Let me, then, begin this evaluation of the cosmological argument by considering a statement of St. Thomas that suggests that the term is a fairly straightforward description of things we encounter. It should be noted that, although St. Thomas does not actually use the term "contingent" in this context, this statement has had an important effect on its subsequent theological employment. "We find in nature things that are possible to be and not to be . . . ."[3] This seems as straightforward as the statement that "We find in nature things that are possible to fly and not to fly," and we might expect that both statements could be verified in the same way. When it comes to checking out the second statement, we look and discover that birds

[3] *Summa Theologiae* I, 2, 3.

fit the description very nicely. When we seek confirmation of the first statement, by examining things in our environment, we confront an embarrassment of riches. Everything we come across falls within the scope of its meaning. In short order we find that the term "contingent" is a relative of the term "exists" and that, just as "exists" plays havoc with the ontological argument, so "contingent" plays havoc with this version of the cosmological argument. It seems to be descriptive, and yet it does not serve to distinguish any things in nature from any other—a most peculiar way for a descriptive term to function. Furthermore, it differs from "exists" in that no one has claimed for "contingent" the status of a transcendental, that is, a term whose significance is so basic that we must affirm it of all things in order to make significant predication of any kind possible.

The term "contingent" as used in the cosmological argument is, then, not a straightforward descriptive predicate like "yellow" or "can fly." That it is not will become even clearer later in the paper when I deal with formulations of the term proffered by contemporary Thomists. There is, though, a nonproblematic use of "contingent." It occurs in logic, a discipline that has no tolerance for ambiguity or vagueness. In contemporary logic the term "contingent" is linked to the terms "impossible" and "necessary" in a trichotomy. As they function in logic, the term "necessary" refers to statements that can never be false, the term "impossible" refers to statements that can never be true, and the term "contingent" refers to statements that can sometimes be true and sometimes false, depending on circumstances. To illustrate: (1) The statement "This figure is conical, or it is not conical" can never be false, and it is therefore necessary. (2) The statement "This figure is conical, and it is not conical" can never be true, and it is therefore impossible. (3) The statement "This figure is conical" will be true if the figure designated *is* conical, and it will be false if the figure in question is *not* conical; this statement, then, is contingent.

The use of "contingent" in this context is clear, and its application follows formal rules. When confronted with complex statements, logicians break them down into their component elements, check their truth values by means of truth tables, and determine which label—"necessary," "impossible," or "contingent"—applies. The results have the intuitive clarity and coerciveness of mathematics, and the procedure is unexceptionable. The reason that the procedure is unexceptionable, however, is that no existential claim is involved. In the context of logic the terms "contingent," "necessary," and "impossible" do not legislate concerning what there is in the world; they merely help us to determine the consistency of statements by means of a rule-governed symbolism. The point at issue has to do with what W. V. O. Quine has called the "referential opacity" of the term "necessary." The statement "Nine is necessarily greater than seven" is true, but if we substitute for the number nine "the number of planets," we get the false statement that "The number of planets is necessarily greater than seven."[4]

All that my discussion has accomplished so far is to advance rapidly to the rear, in fact to "advance" all the way back to the positivistic dichotomy of the analytic and the synthetic as it was popularized by A. J. Ayer in 1936.[5] In effect, I have contended that the term "contingent" as it functions in the cosmological argument is not used synthetically to provide information about things that we find in nature. I have then added that it is used effectively in analytic contexts, that is, in contexts that deal with the meanings of words but that tell us nothing about the way things are.

Raising the issue in these terms is obviously inadequate

[4] Willard Van Orman Quine, "Reference and Modality," *From A Logical Point of View* (Cambridge: Harvard University Press, 1953), esp. 143f. See also "Three Grades of Modal Involvement," *The Ways of Paradox* (New York: Random House, 1966).

[5] *Language, Truth and Logic* (London: Victor Gollancz, 1936).

from the point of view of the contemporary scene. In 1951 Quine published his essay "Two Dogmas of Empiricism" which repudiated the analytic-synthetic dichotomy.[6] Since then philosophers have become increasingly wary about making glib references to the analytic-synthetic distinction. In this post-positivistic era it is no longer fashionable to dismiss metaphysical statements as nonsense by means of quick demonstrations of their deviation from standard instances of analytic and synthetic usage. It may therefore seem promising for the theologians to argue that the effective functioning of the terms "contingent," "necessary," and "impossible" in logic ought not to preclude their use in metaphysical contexts and, indeed, that the logical use might serve as a model for the metaphysical one. Thus a "contingent being" might be defined as one that might possibly exist or possibly not exist, a "necessary being" as one that cannot possibly not exist, and an "impossible being" as one that cannot possibly exist.[7]

To bolster this point regarding post-positivistic analysis, we may direct attention to A. N. Prior's comment that even positivistic philosophers make liberal use of the categories "necessary," "contingent," and "impossible" in dealing with *nonexistence.* Within the domain of things that do not exist, they distinguish between those whose nonexistence is contingent and those whose nonexistence is necessary. No existing animals exemplify the concept of "unicornhood," but there is nothing about this concept which precludes its exemplification. It merely happens to be the case that there are no unicorns. On the other hand, it is necessarily the case that the concept of "noncubical cubehood" cannot be exemplified, because it has the property of "self-contradictoriness" which absolutely precludes its exemplification. "Why," Prior asks, "could there not be a similar distinction among *exemplified* concepts? . . . why should there not be

6 "Two Dogmas of Empiricism," *From a Logical Point of View.*

7 Jacques Maritain, "Reflections on Necessity and Contingency," in *Essays in Thomism,* ed. Robert E. Brennan, O.P. (New York: Sheed & Ward, 1942), 27f.

properties of concepts which necessitate their exemplification?"[8] In effect, Prior wants to know why the same philosophers who freely permit purely conceptual considerations to legislate what cannot possibly exist obdurately refuse to permit purely conceptual considerations to legislate what must necessarily exist.

The criticism is impressive, but not persuasive. At issue is the question whether philosophers who claim that the concepts of "noncubical cubehood" or "square-circle" cannot be exemplified really are legislating what cannot possibly exist on the basis of purely conceptual considerations. As I see it, when one classifies a statement as self-contradictory, one is engaged in a more modest activity, namely, stating that this concept cannot be formed within the framework of a given logical system. And even if one does form such a concept and use it in a *reductio ad absurdum* argument, one is still not legislating what can and cannot occur in the world, but rather exposing the fallacious conclusions that follow within the system when a self-contradiction is introduced. In the same way, if one maintains that the concept of "square-circle" cannot be exemplified, one is not sitting in an armchair and telling surveyors what they can and cannot construct out there in the field. What one is saying is that within the rule-governed framework of Euclidian geometry the concept of "square-circle" is incoherent or, in other words, is not a well-formed concept. In this connection it is worth recalling Einstein's remark: "As far as the laws of mathematics refer to reality, they are not certain; and as far as they are certain, they do not refer to reality."[9] Thus I reject the claim that the gap between

[8] A. N. Prior, "Is Necessary Existence Possible?" *Philosophy and Phenomenological Research* xv (1955), 545-547. See also Richard Taylor, "Introduction," in *The Ontological Argument*, ed. Alvin Plantinga, xviff., and Anthony Kenny, "God and Necessity," in *British Analytical Philosophy*, ed. B. Williams and A. Montefiore (London: Routledge and Kegan Paul, 1966), 138ff.

[9] Albert Einstein, "Geometry and Experience," in *Readings in the Philosophy of Science*, ed. H. Feigl and M. Brodbeck (New York: Appleton-Century-Crofts, 1953), 189.

logic and ontology has been bridged on the negative side, that is, on the side of the necessary nonexemplification of concepts. And I therefore find little justification for appealing to it as a precedent that validates the construction of a bridge parallel to it on the side of the necessary exemplification of concepts.

The question whether there is or is not a bridge between logic and ontology is a live one. I am not proposing to make a contribution to this discussion. I am merely reporting that the use of "contingent" and "necessary" in the domain of formal logic remains noncontroversial only when those who employ these terms do not seek to extend their use to the making of existential claims.

It will be useful to recapitulate the argument by way of showing why theological proponents of the cosmological argument—the very theologians I am attacking—would nevertheless be reasonably happy with the course of it. What I have done is to show that (1) "contingent" is not a straightforward empirical predicate which sets off some objects of our ordinary experience from others, (2) "contingent" does have a clear-cut use in logic which sets one class of statements apart from others ("impossible" statements and "necessary" statements), and (3) the use of "contingent" and "necessary" with regard to beings, as opposed to statements, is controversial.

In one sense, the appeal to a controversial sense of "contingent beings" and "necessary being" is all that theologians require. They can invoke the greater permissiveness of the post-positivistic era in urging a use of "contingent" that makes a difference, because they claim that this usage discriminates among the different things that are. The term "contingent" as applied to beings sets contingent beings apart from "necessary being." It is not a contrast between physical objects, for this contrast does not hold between two classes of observable phenomena. It places the class of contingent beings, that is, the class of all entities that are observable in principle, in contrast to "necessary being," which cannot, even in principle, be observed. This clarification is helpful, but the point is not acceptable. Although the post-positivistic philosophers who engage in analysis may be permissive, they are not antinomian. They are suspicious of a contrast of this kind because it seems to be drawn between two birds in hand when, upon examination, one of them turns out to be as systematically elusive as any bird in the bush. Therefore, this reference to necessary being smacks of obscurantism and needs a great deal of justification.

In looking for arguments to back up traditional metaphysical positions, such as the meaningfulness of the contingent-necessary contrast, many metaphysicians have found support in the later work of Ludwig Wittgenstein. In the *Philosophical Investigations* he reacted against the positivistic tendency to set up restrictive models of meaning, such as the "analytic" and the "synthetic."[10] He thought the positivists had succumbed to armchair speculation and dogmatism with regard to meaning, just as earlier generations of philosophers had been speculative and dogmatic with regard to being. By means of such admonitions as "Don't think, but look!" he urged philosophers to look at the way we actually learn to use words and at the many applications that different sets of words, intimately related to one another, actually have. He called a network of interlocking terms "a family" and the context in which they function together a "language game." The job of the philosopher is not to tell the participants what their game should be; his is a more modest function than this. He should tune in on a game and see how its rules actually work. If he does that, he might be able to contribute to the game by showing the players that they are using some words inconsistently and that they are abusing rules by transferring them from one game where they work very well to another game where they do not belong.

If consistency of usage within a framework of discourse is a criterion for legitimacy of meaning, then theologians

[10] Ludwig Wittgenstein, *Philosophical Investigations* (New York: Macmillan, 1953), *passim.*

can justly claim that the contingent-necessary contrast is legitimate, since their use has been both long-established and reasonably consistent. Anselm formulated the concept of "necessary being" as a "being that cannot be conceived not to exist." In the third of his five ways Aquinas refers to "something the existence of which is necessary," and in the *Contra Gentiles* he defines a substance as necessary "if it cannot not exist." Charles Hartshorne has recently reformulated the contingent-necessary contrast by listing a number of limitations that apply to contingent beings but do not apply to necessary being. The main contrast is that, whereas contingent beings are, obviously, conceivable as not existing, necessary being is *not* conceivable as not existing. Contingent beings are also compatible with some sets of genuine possibilities but not with others (for example, a person with a given genetic structure is compatible with one sperm having fertilized a given egg but not with others), and a contingent being is limited by being dependent upon other beings to bring it about (as a child is dependent on its parents). Furthermore, unlike necessary being, contingent beings are limited to a given segment of time and space. Finally, contingent beings are limited in value, necessary being is not.[11]

Despite the impressive consistency of the use of the contingent-necessary contrast over the centuries, many philosophers have reservations about its validity. As it operates in the theological context, the distinction seems contrived rather than discovered. This is not to say that only discoveries are genuinely helpful and that contrivances never are; on the contrary, some contrivances are among the most useful things we have. Nevertheless, they are only useful if they can get some job done. The invention of the term "dormitive faculty" as an explanation for sleep does not get a job done; it merely restates the job description. Many philosophers are convinced that the appeal to the

[11] Charles Hartshorne, "Ten Ontological or Modal Proofs for God's Existence," *Logic of Perfection* (La Salle, Ill.: Open Court, 1962), 74ff.

contingent-necessary contrast does not do the job of demonstrating the existence of God but is, rather, an elaborate way of restating the theistic claim. Indeed, in a philosophical era that is dominated by a concern for language, it ought to be clear that Ockham's razor applies to terms as well as to entities. If the theological use of the term "contingent" is found to be either parasitic on the legitimate logical use of the term or else merely contrived for the purpose of advancing a theological doctrine, then it ought to be abandoned.

Having said this much, we should note that philosophers who would deny the legitimacy of the theological use of the contingent-necessary contrast must take account of its prima facie plausibility. Consistent and enduring use of a distinction does constitute an argument for its legitimacy. This point was urged by H. P. Grice and P. F. Strawson against Quine's effort to blur the analytic-synthetic distinction. However, they added a qualification that undermines the parallel to the theological use of the contingent-necessary contrast. As they put it, "in general, if a pair of contrasting expressions are habitually and generally used in application to the same cases, *where these cases do not form a closed list*, this is a sufficient condition for saying that there are *kinds* of cases to which the expressions apply; and nothing more is needed for them to mark a distinction."[12] The underscored qualification introduced by Grice and Strawson is crucial to the case in hand, for on the contingent side the class is so open that any being we can encounter belongs to it, whereas on the other side the list not only is closed but is limited to a single member, God. The class of necessary beings must be limited to one member if it is to have theological significance. If there were a number of necessary beings, theologians, *qua* theologians, would not be interested in them. These necessary beings would merely constitute a set of extra items in the world and would, for monotheists, perforce lack saving power.

[12] H. P. Grice and P. F. Strawson, "In Defense of a Dogma," *The Philosophical Review* LXV (1956), 143.

This consideration leads one to suspect that the contingent-necessary distinction may be contrived, and this suspicion is reinforced when we reflect on the language used by contemporary Thomists in defining the term "contingent being." Maritain uses the term to describe a thing that "is by reason of something else," Copleston uses it to refer to a being that does not "contain within itself the reason for its existence," and Gilson uses it to denote a being that "has not its existence from itself."[13] The most revealing illustration of this type of theological use of "contingent being" we find in Mascall, who uses contingency as the fundamental mark of finitude: "the fundamental characteristic [of finite being] is a radical inability to account for its own existence. . . . in which, therefore, existence is not self-maintained but is received from without and, in the last resort, is received from a being whose existence is not received but is self-inherent."[14]

These definitions are like St. Thomas' statement that "we find in nature things that are possible to be and not to be." They seem to be empirical and appear to be telling us something about what we observe. Reflection on the use of these definitions, however, will show the extent to which they are contrived for doctrinal purposes. What we find in nature are things in continual transformations. A mineral ore is transformed into metal, which is transformed into an automobile, which then degenerates until it becomes part of a pile of scrap metal that is melted down and transformed into typewriters. At no point in these processes do we encounter things which are dependent upon something else for their very existence; rather, they are dependent upon other things for their specific configura-

[13] Jacques Maritain, *Approaches to God* (New York: Harper, 1954), 48; F. C. Copleston, S.J. "A Debate on the Existence of God" (with Bertrand Russell), in *The Existence of God*, ed. John Hick (New York: Macmillan, 1964), 168; E. Gilson, *The Christian Philosophy of St. Thomas Aquinas* (New York: Random House, 1956), 68.

[14] E. L. Mascall, *Existence and Analogy* (London: Longmans, Green, 1949), 71.

tions. They neither undergo annihilation, nor are they produced from nothing. Yet observable processes of transformation will not serve the purposes of contemporary Thomists, because this view of the process would allow for the Spinozistic thesis that the universe itself is necessary being. The stuff would be eternally present, and we could observe the processes which result in continual changes of existing configurations. In this connection it is illuminating to note the difference between St. Thomas himself and those Neo-Thomists who are his most prominent commentators in the English-speaking world. St. Thomas maintained that there is no rational way of demonstrating that the world is not eternal. He regarded the creation of the world as an article of faith and realized that a great deal of argument was needed to link the necessary being of the third way to the God of the Bible. Contemporary Thomists, in order to derive God, *who creates the world out of nothing*, as the one necessary being, have to stipulate a more radical definition of "contingent" than St. Thomas himself gave. They have to define contingent beings as those which depend upon something else for their total existence—atoms, molecules, and all—and not merely for their specific configurations. Yet there is no empirical evidence for this radical use of "contingent being." It seems especially tailored for the purpose of getting a sense of "contingent" that can be fed into the cosmological argument and made to yield the God who creates the world out of nothing as its conclusion. The radical sense of "contingent" that appears in the work of contemporary Thomists is not the result of empirical observation, but rather of stipulative definition.

Once we have clarified this point, we need not regard these definitions as intrinsically pernicious. All sorts of inquiries—scientific, legal, and historical—are advanced by stipulative definitions which begin with the formula "By 'x' I shall mean. . . ." The problem now before us is whether anyone who is not already convinced of the truth of theism would find any reason for adopting these definitions of "contingent."

To raise this question is to recall our point of departure. The radical sense of "contingency" that we find in some contemporary statements of the cosmological argument provides a link between a sophisticated philosophical category and the visceral responses that lead the philosophically uninitiated to a preoccupation with these issues. If we break this sense of "contingent" down into two components, we can see the connection. We remarked earlier about the preoccupation of students with the arbitrary character of the way things are. This concern is spoken to by the use of "contingent" in the sense of "dependent upon something else for its actual configuration." At the outer limits of speculation, however, we confront the ultimate metaphysical question "Why should anything exist at all?" This question is spoken to by the use of "contingent" to mean "dependent upon something else for its total existence, for its substance as well as its configuration."

These definitions are persuasive, and powerfully so, because they are bound up with emotional reactions to universal elements of human experience. The interesting philosophical question is whether they have any use beyond that of articulating these reactions—whether, for instance, they are useful in uncovering some things, like "necessary being," that can be legitimately added to a list of what there is in the world.

Thomists, as a specific example, begin the cosmological argument with an empirical premise from which they move on to argue for the existence of God. Many contemporary philosophers are convinced, however, that in such a use "contingent" has undergone so many refinements for purposes of its theological deployment that it has been rendered incapable of serving any other function. Alasdair MacIntyre puts the matter this way: "to accept that there are contingent beings, to accept the use of 'contingent' as a word applicable to everyday objects of experience, is to accept already the thesis that these objects can only be explained by reference to God."[15] MacIntyre is charging the Thomistic theologians with "begging the question," that is, with giving the impression that they are arguing to a conclusion when what they are doing is assuming the controversial points at issue. On this reading, what the Thomists really do, then, is to advance a stipulative definition of "contingent" which is drawn up in such a way that, if it is accepted, there is no need for argument. The existence of God has already been tacitly conceded in adopting the terms in which the discussion is to be carried on.

These stipulative definitions of "contingent" undermine the cosmological argument at the point where it is intended to be strongest. The argument was designed as a corrective to the procedure of the ontological argument, where the effort is made to derive the existence of God from reflection on the definition of God. By contrast, theologians who advance the cosmological argument claim that it begins with empirical observations. They propose to derive the existence of God as an inference from that which is seen to exist. My contention is that the point of departure for the cosmological argument is not empirical at all but consists rather in a stipulative definition. Ironically, the starting point for the cosmological argument then turns out to be the same as that of the ontological argument, the very argument it was intended to correct. Both begin with a metaphysical contrast between the contingent and the necessary. But where the ontological argument focuses on the necessary side of the contrast, the cosmological argument emphasizes the contingent. This analysis points to an intimate relation between the arguments, which has been noted by Charles Hartshorne, who treats them as variations on a single theme.[16]

In connection with the relation between the ontological and the cosmological arguments, we come upon another

[15] Alasdair MacIntyre, *Difficulties in Christian Belief* (London: SCM Press, 1959), 82.

[16] Charles Hartshorne, *Man's Vision of God* (Chicago: Willet, Clark, 1941), 251f.

important issue generated by the necessary-contingent contrast as it applies to being. It was for all intents and purposes launched by an essay of J. N. Findlay, "Can God's Existence be Disproved?"[17] The essay was important because it combined religious sensitivity with philosophical acuity. On the level of religion, Findlay analyzes the most distinctively religious action, the act of worship. Bending the knee in adoration, he asserts, is an action that would be utterly inappropriate in an encounter with a being who merely differed from us quantitatively. The act of worship implies (when we think about it, it does not follow that everyone who worships actually entertains the notion) that the object of our absolute adoration should be a being who does not merely happen to exist but rather must exist necessarily. Thus the idea of "necessary being" is seen to be demanded by the religious consciousness of philosophically reflective believers.

Findlay continues by invoking one of the basic tenets of the positivists, the analytic-synthetic dichotomy, in order to show that this inescapable demand of the religious consciousness involves a philosophical absurdity. According to the positivists, "necessity" is a property of propositions or statements, and it cannot be used in dealing with situations that actually obtain in the world. On the other hand, "existential" assertions—that is, assertions of the form "There is a such and such"—are never necessary. Thus Findlay confronted religious thinkers with a dilemma. If they assert that God exists, then the term "exists" must function as it always functions when it functions properly, namely, in making a claim that may or may not be true. But this sort of claim is clearly inappropriate when it is directed to the object of worship. To accept the logical status of mere possibility for "God claims" is to reduce God to the status of an idol. On the other horn of the dilemma, the religious believer must, in order to do justice to his

[17] J. N. Findlay, "Can God's Existence be Disproved," in *New Essays in Philosophical Theology*, ed. A. Flew and A. MacIntyre (New York: Macmillan, 1955).

religious sensibilities, affirm the existence of God as "logically necessary." But the notion of a *logically* necessary existence involves a meaningless concatenation of concepts; it involves what Gilbert Ryle calls a "category mistake." Since Findlay saw no way out of this dilemma for believers (at the time he made this point), he clearly regarded it as a disproof of the existence of the transcendent God.

Findlay had no sooner set forth this dilemma than A.C.A. Rainer replied on behalf of the theological tradition.[18] He noted that the necessity theologians attribute to God had never been understood as logical necessity in the contemporary sense. Rather, it involved the claim that God is not dependent on any other being for His existence. Since Rainer first made this point, it has been repeated many times over by such prominent philosophers as G.E.M. Anscombe, P. T. Geach, John Hick, and C. B. Martin.[19] Perhaps the most succinct statement of it is found in the remark by Anthony Kenny that "something [that is 'being'] is necessary if and only if it is, always will be and always was; and cannot nor could not, nor will not be able not to be."[20] In Kenny's terms, God did not depend upon anything else to bring Him into existence and is not dependent upon anything else for His continued existence because, by His very nature, God cannot come into or pass out of existence. This proposition follows from the assertion that he cannot, nor could not, nor will not be able to, not be. In various formulations of the point, the thinkers mentioned above agree. They maintain that they thereby avoid the category mistake of attributing *logical* necessity to something which exists and that they have cut the ground out from under Findlay's clever dilemma.

18 *Ibid.*, 68f.

19 G. E. M. Anscombe and P. T. Geach, *Three Philosophers* (Oxford: Blackwell, 1961); John Hick, "A Critique of the 'Second Argument,'" in *The Many-Faced Argument*, ed. J. Hick and A. C. McGill (New York: Macmillan, 1967), 343ff; C. B. Martin, *Religious Belief* (Ithaca, N.Y.: Cornell University Press, 1959), 156ff.

20 Anthony Kenny, "Necessary Being," *Sophia* I (1962), 8.

This discussion is an interesting illustration of a not uncommon phenomenon. A difficulty in a traditional position is met by a new departure, which is adopted with enthusiasm as the "way out." Then the departure itself comes under rigorous attack. Ironically, the response to the new difficulty takes the form of a reversion to the traditional position. In this step the difficulty which had elicited the new departure is overlooked. Such has been the course of discussion concerning theological use of the concept of "necessary being." The problem of reference has been a perennial one for believers in a transcendent God. They have always been challenged to produce hard evidence for His existence, and by "hard" the skeptics have generally meant sensible evidence or the sort of correlations with sensible data that scientists have recourse to in talking about subatomic particles. Religious thinkers have used the idea of necessary being to turn the tables on the skeptics by insisting that a God who could be referred to by means of hard data would not be the true God known in faith, but an idol known by processes akin to magic. Theologians have come to cope with this difficulty by arguing that, since God is not a contingent being but necessary being, then the type of verification appropriate to establishing the existence of all other entities whatever are strikingly inappropriate to establishing the existence of God.

The difficulty with that position was sharply stated by A. J. Ayer in *Language, Truth and Logic*, and it has been urged many times over.[21] The problem is that, if necessary being is so utterly transcendent as to be beyond correlation with any sensible phenomena whatever, then what difference does its existence or nonexistence make? The resolutely empirical cast that analytic philosophy has assumed is a reaction against the populating of philosophical discourse with myriads of metaphysical entities that have no discernable effects in our physical domain of existence. Therefore, the unblushing espousal by modern thinkers of the

[21] Ayer, *Language, Truth and Logic*, 115.

traditional theological notion of necessary being as a response to Findlay's dilemma strikes me as a retrogressive move, because it makes their position extremely vulnerable to attacks like Ayer's.

The retrogressive character of this move may be further underscored by considering a passage from C. B. Martin's *Religious Belief.*[22] "Let us suppose a being of the following sort: (1) A being for whose existence nothing else need exist. (2) A being that has always existed. (3) A being upon whom everything else depends for its existence." Martin is a philosopher who has responded to the anti-metaphysical thrust of positivism that issued in the challenge of verifiability; therefore, he is not prepared to let matters rest there. He adds the following: "One can even have a kind of verification procedure for such qualities. For (1) take away all other things and the being would remain in existence [although unimaginable, this condition of Martin's does not seem to be inconceivable]. For (3) take away the being and everything else would pass out of existence. [This condition of Martin's is also conceivable because, although unimaginable, it does not involve a contradiction.] For (2) at *any* time in the past this being could be observed to exist."

The final point reveals the foolishness of Martin's verification procedure. The nub of the philosophical difficulty raised by talk of the transcendent God is that necessary being cannot be observed to exist at any time whatever. As we have noted, if such observation were possible, we would not be talking about the transcendent God of the Judaeo-Christian tradition. To press the point further, all thinkers who have responded to Findlay's challenge stress the point that necessary being, as traditionally understood by theologians, is considered to be without beginning or end. Thus if we were, for the sake of argument, to concede Martin's point that at *any* time whatever necessary being could be observed, how could one ever establish that neces-

[22] C. B. Martin, *Religious Belief*, 156.

80555

sary being had no beginning and will have no end? One might show that necessary being existed before the beginning of even the oldest galaxies, but how could one ever prove that it had no beginning and how, short of mere stipulation, could one demonstrate that it will have no end? By stipulating such a definition, one may have bypassed Findlay's dilemma, but only at the price of doing traditional metaphysics with a vengeance. Furthermore, there seems to be a reasonable doubt whether the negative method of removing limitations from observable entities by way of specifying the character of necessary being as eternal, unconditioned, and the rest is meaningful. As Kant put it, "The transcendental idea of a necessary and all-sufficient original being is so overwhelmingly great, so high above everything empirical, the latter being always conditioned, that it leaves us at a loss, partly because we can never find in experience material sufficient to satisfy such a concept, and partly because it is always in the sphere of the conditioned that we carry our search, seeking there ever vainly for the unconditioned—no law of any empirical synthesis giving us an example of any such unconditioned or providing the least guidance in its pursuit."[23]

What does this add up to as far as our point of departure —namely, the student seeking the meaning of life—is concerned? Clearly, the student seeking the meaning of life has not been given a redemptive word. Rather, he has been introduced to disciplined philosophical analysis of the term "contingent" and has been shown that a nest of complex problems lies just beneath the surface of this superficially simple word. One might also be tempted to maintain that he has been handed a conclusively negative verdict on the validity of the theological deployment of the term "contingent." This, however, would be a misguided claim, for it would be based on what I regard as a misconception of the character of philosophical discourse. Students approach philosophy with the ambition of obtaining clear-cut answers

[23] Immanuel Kant, *Critique of Pure Reason*, B 649.

to major problems because their expectations are molded by the two types of material they encounter in secondary school, namely, mathematics and history (which they tend to regard as the accumulation of hard facts).

The first thing to be said in correcting this misconception was noted by Aristotle more than two thousand years ago: "It is the mark of an educated man to look for precision in each class of things, just so far as the nature of the subject admits."[24] I would argue that what Aristotle says about precision applies to conclusiveness as well. Even in our time, when so many philosophers have consciously coupled their cars to the scientific engine, there seems to be little sign that philosophy has been able to emulate science with regard to either the conclusiveness with which hypotheses are resolved or the cumulative nature of the enterprise. After all, no issue in philosophy seemed deader than the ontological argument; almost all philosophers and even all theologians agreed that Kant had buried it more than one hundred and fifty years ago. Yet Norman Malcolm, a respected philosopher, wrote one essay in the idiom that is *au courant*, and this issue once again moved into the forefront of controversy.[25] The present consensus clearly runs against Malcolm's defense of the argument, but to refer to a consensus is already to acknowledge that at least some philosophers do not adhere to it.[26] In any case, the astonishing thing is that the argument is discussed with respect by a generation and school of philosophers whose outlook is emphatically secular.

Thus a concerned student seeking answers to the gut issues would, regardless of the outcome of the discussion, have received a serious response to a serious question. He would have been exposed to the range of meanings, in-

[24] Aristotle, *Nicomachean Ethics*, Bk. I, Chap. 3.

[25] Norman Malcolm, "Anselm's Ontological Arguments," *The Philosophical Review* LXIX (1960), 41-62. See esp. *The Philosophical Review* LXX/1 (Jan. 1961), which was devoted to essays critical of Malcolm's position.

[26] Norbert Samuelson, "On Proving God's Existence," *Judaism* XVI (1967), 21-36.

cluding emotive meanings, of the term "contingent," as when Maritain says, "If we grant to a speck of moss or to the tiniest ant the value of its ontological reality, we can no longer escape from the terrifying hand which made us."[27] He might, as a result, join with J. J. C. Smart in feeling a sense of momentousness in a category that he finds intellectually inadequate. Smart, in dealing with what is widely regarded as the basic metaphysical question, has linked its significance to the sense of numinous awe that reflection on the cosmological argument engenders:

> . . . now let us ask, "Why should anything exist at all?" Logic seems to tell us that the only answer which is not absurd is to say, "Why shouldn't it?" Nevertheless, though I know how any answer on the lines of the cosmological argument can be pulled to pieces by a correct logic, I still feel that I want to go on asking the question. . . . That anything should exist at all does seem to me a matter for the deepest awe. But whether other people feel this sort of awe, and whether they or I ought to is another question. I think we ought to. If so, the question arises: If 'Why should anything exist at all?' cannot be interpreted after the manner of the cosmological argument, that is, as an absurd request for the nonsensical postulation of a logically necessary being, what sort of question is it? . . . . All I can say is, that I do not yet know.[28]

In response to the many criticisms that have been directed against the arguments for the existence of God, many theologians have reworked them or reassessed their significance. No one has gone so far in this direction as Paul Tillich.[29] He accepts Kant's strictures against their rational cogency. He insists, as rigorously and consistently as anyone has ever insisted, that necessary being cannot be re-

[27] Jacques Maritain, *Distinguer pour unir*, as quoted by E. L. Mascall, *Existence and Analogy*, xiii.

[28] J. J. C. Smart, "The Existence of God," in *New Essays in Philosophical Theology*, 46.

[29] Paul Tillich, *Theology of Culture* (New York: Oxford University Press, 1959), Chap. II.

garded as a super-being divested of the limitations of contingent beings. Tillich claims that the entire conceptual scheme that is equipped to handle contingent beings breaks down when we try to apply it to necessary being. Another way of putting the point is to declare that, when we deal with necessary being by means of categories drawn from conceptual systems that are oriented to contingent beings, we convert necessary being into an idol. Tillich asserts that using our ordinary concepts in speaking of necessary being inevitably leads us to talk as though the correspondence theory of truth could be effectively deployed in dealing with necessary being. To think that it could, however, is to radically misunderstand what necessary being involves. Necessary being is not something that can be observed, not in this life nor in any other. To use Tillich's favorite formulation, God is not a being alongside other beings, and neither, quite obviously, is necessary being.

According to Tillich, the traditional arguments for the existence of God do not demonstrate the existence of a super-being who exists beyond the range of our instruments of observation. Rather, they focus on urgent problems of the human situation to which God, as revealed in the Judaeo-Christian tradition, provides answers, albeit answers saturated with mystery. God is the "yes" that corresponds to the "no" that is manifested in so many situations. God is the ground of being that withstands the many threats of nonbeing that assail us. And these threats are formalized by the traditional arguments.

> Finite being includes courage, but it cannot maintain courage against the ultimate threat of non-being. It needs a basis for ultimate courage. Finite being is a question mark. It asks the question of the "eternal now" in which the temporal and spatial are simultaneously accepted and overcome. It asks the question of the "ground of being" in which the causal and the substantial are simultaneously confirmed and negated. The Cosmological

> approach cannot answer these questions, but it can and must analyze their roots in the structure of finitude.[30]

And Tillich claims that the questions formulated by means of the cosmological approach are answered by the revelation in Jesus as the Christ.

Thus a student who becomes engaged with the issue of contingency out of deep personal involvement can, by virtue of philosophical analysis of its spectrum of meanings, attain clarification of the intellectual cogency of his personal concerns. He may come up with a positive evaluation of the force of the traditional theological use of the term, or he might reject it outright by deciding that it is a deceptive term that hypostasizes certain intense emotional states. He might equally well arrive at less emphatic conclusions. He may, for instance, find himself agreeing with Tillich that the term is meaningful and carries ontological weight, even though the theological tradition has misrepresented the meaning and misread the weight. Or he might adopt the view of J. J. C. Smart that the term "contingent" points to a genuine mystery whose cognitive significance has not yet been clearly discerned. Yet, whatever the student's final attitude toward contingency might be, if the philosophical approach affected him at all, his interest in contingency would have taken an academic turn—which in a university setting is a most appropriate turn to take.

[30] Paul Tillich, *Systematic Theology,* I (Chicago: University of Chicago Press, 1951), 209f.

The Ambiguous Position of Christian Theology

ARTHUR C. MC GILL

TO SPEAK OF the discipline and teaching of Christian theology within the faculty of arts and sciences in a modern "secular" university is to broach a very complicated problem.

On the one hand, Christian theology seems to be fundamentally at odds with the kind of intellectual discipline to which the faculty of arts and sciences is committed. It proceeds from a posture of belief, not from the critical, open posture of neutral reason. In a way quite consistent with this perspective, certain principles or orientations are simply taken by it as given and thus considered to be beyond judgment by the free play of man's native intelligence. Furthermore, in proceeding from this posture of belief, Christian theology belongs within the sphere of a religious community. In theologizing the theologian serves the special interests of the church; otherwise, he would not be doing Christian theology. In this way he obstructs one of the aims of the faculty of arts and sciences, for this faculty seeks to free human reason from the control of special interests, practical institutions, and ideological communities. Within the total life of a university, such theology may find an appropriate place in one of the professional schools, which are designed precisely to help disciplined rationality serve the needs of practical communities. But within the arts and sciences, theology appears incongruous.

This is one side of the situation, but there is another. Some faculties of arts and sciences, within their departments of religion, actually provide instruction in Christian theology. And by that I do not mean instruction simply in the philosophy of religion, or in the history of Christian ideas, or in the "religious factor" in Western thought, but instruction in the analytic and constructive work of specifically Christian theology. Certainly without any intention of identifying themselves with the interests of the Christian Church, and without any thought of compromising or even modifying their ideal of critical rationality, these faculties nevertheless employ Christian theologians, grant them tenure, and compete against professional divinity schools for their services by making them unconscionably lucrative offers.

Such, in brief, is the confused state of affairs at present affecting the place of theology among the arts and sciences. In the following remarks I shall attempt to sort out some of the elements in this complex picture.

Religious Truth

Perhaps the most important point to note is that, in some respects at least, the problem of Christian theology is but an aspect of the problem of the study of *religion itself* within the faculty of arts and sciences. For it is in their preoccupation with *truth* that all religions pose such difficulties within the academy. We must therefore consider the peculiar features of truth within the sphere of religion.

Let me characterize religion as the human response to those superior powers from which man sees himself and his communities deriving life and death. In this sense, religion does not primarily pertain to a certain set of objects defined in terms of their own natures, but rather to a mode of relationship between man and that which has his fulfillment or destruction at its disposal. This characterization of religion is certainly not final or completely comprehensive, but it does identify a feature conspicuous in all religions and one that is fundamental for the problem at hand.

1. A religious attitude on the part of an individual or a community entails the judgment that such and such a thing or power or presence does in fact have some kind of control over human life. The word "life" may have too narrowly biological a connotation; we might better say

"control over the fulfillment or impoverishment of human existence." Obviously, such a judgment can never be a matter of indifference. What is at stake is the attainment or the loss of life itself. For a community to orient itself toward realities that have no authentic power while ignoring those that bring life and death would be folly and perhaps fatal folly. For instance, if full life comes through the clarity of understanding, so that the power of intelligibility is the authentic life-giver, then submission to the forces experienced in sensuality would be debilitating and ultimately destructive. On the other hand, if expanded sexuality is man's way of participating in true life, then monogamous marriage may simply be the way of living death.

Concern for truth is therefore absolutely central in religions—concern, not for any truth, but for truth regarding the sources of life and death. In other words, in religions truth is not a matter of satisfying the intelligence but of fulfilling existence. To be sure, this religious way of construing the human situation may be wrong. Perhaps the powers over life and death do not lie beyond man, to be received from certain supernal realities. Perhaps these powers lie wholly at his disposal and under his control. Perhaps the fullness of life is simply a matter of improving his moral character, or turning aside his hostilities, or releasing his suppressions, or improving his machines, or purifying his drugs, or merely manipulating the right bits of genetic information. But insofar as the human situation appears to be religious in character, in the particular fashion just described, then the truth-question is central and decisive. The quality of a person's existence is seen to depend on that which is not himself, that which is beyond him, that about which he must learn by being attentive to what is *extra se*. Such attentiveness is identical with a preoccupation with truth. In religions, therefore, the question of life and death is seen as a truth-question, as a matter of judging truly about reality.

In religions the truth-question itself becomes part of the religious venture and is not something preliminary or detached. An element in being nourished by the gods of one's personal and communal existence is knowing them and thus being able to live "properly" in relation to them. Therefore, pursuit of this kind of truth is urgent, since a beneficial relation to the gods depends upon its success. In moments when knowledge of religious matters becomes confused, this sense of urgency produces a deep uneasiness, even anguish. In moments of insight and assured knowledge, it comes to expression as advocacy. Because his own and his community's life and death may be hanging in the balance, no man can deal with religious truth without feeling the impulsion toward either uneasiness or advocacy. The one impossible attitude is what medieval writers called *curiositas.* To consider the gods as if they were not gods, to approach the powers which are thought to have control over life and death with an attitude of curiosity, that is, in abstraction from urgency, apart from any religious relationship, as if the fulfillment or destruction of one's own life were not at stake in this consideration, is nothing but self-deception. For departments of religion the posture of advocacy has always been a matter of distress. These departments sometimes act as though their reason for being could be fully justified once they disinfected themselves of this posture. Advocacy, however, has its roots, not in the peculiarities of individual temperament, but in the urgency of the subject matter which these departments study.

Christian theology, at least the kind of theology that poses a problem in the faculty of arts and sciences, pursues the truth-question precisely within this kind of religious framework. It responds to what it takes to be disclosures of the authentic source of all power over life and death. It understands its own pursuit of truth as in some way constitutive of a fruitful, rather than a destructive, relation to that source. It shares the urgency which is inseparable from the religious attitude, and whether it has the form of apologetic theology or confessional theology or kerygmatic theology or dogmatic theology, it is always informed by either uneasiness or advocacy.

Whether the Christian God might be considered in a nonreligious way—that is, not at all as a god who holds sway over human life and death, but as a necessary explanatory hypothesis, say, or as a factor in cosmic history—remains open. Nonreligious theology is often pursued. But for our purposes it is religious theology which poses the difficult problem.

2. The matter of life and death refers to the self in its actual existence. This actual existence is not primarily biological. It is constituted of hopes and memories, of daydreams and nightmares, of intelligent insights and covert symbolizations. In these various dimensions every actual self experiences an endless sequence of fulfillments and deprivations, and does so in ever new and unexpected situations. Some disastrous circumstance, some unforeseen enormity, some suppressed hunger or unappeased wish grips the self, and all the careful strategies it has developed for handling the sources of life and death now become useless and discredited. The religious orientation of previous moments has been complicated and challenged by the impact of reality, either from outside the self or from within and behind the self.

Take a native New Yorker and set him in the African jungle. He will not know how to identify the source of his nourishment or where to perceive the signs of danger. He will not even be able to tell what life and death will be within himself in this new world. This kind of upheaval is experienced by a work-oriented man who is suddenly dismissed from his job and by every person emerging out of young adulthood into the unfamiliar contours of middle age.

But dramatic change of this sort does not occur simply in the lives of individuals. It is a significant feature of community experience as well. A sustained drought makes a mockery of a people's long loyalty and deep identification with the land. A nation that has never lost a war becomes demoralized when its military power is successfully challenged. The American democratic way of life proves incapable of handling the complexities and ambiguities and long-term horizons of international leadership. In such situations it appears that the beliefs and rituals which previously aligned concrete existence with the powers of life and death in a successful manner become confused or inadequate when confronted with new circumstances.

This fact of existence should lead us to recognize that at the religious level *the truth-question is never closed.* The gods who seemed so clearly to have control over a people's life and death yesterday now become impotent and irrelevant. No reality has so clearly, so universally, and so unavoidably manifested its lordship over all life and death that every new experience at the level of actual existence immediately confirms that lordship. To be sure, people may use the term "God" to refer to something so abstract, so devoid of any manifestation in contemporary existence that it is unaffected by the shifts and surprises of concrete experience. But by the same token all that then remains to them is a god void of all religious significance, who stands in no relation to the concrete actualities of life and death. So far as anything has been experienced in some sense or at some level as having real control over some dimension of life in an individual or community—that is to say, so far as anything is taken as religiously important—people will discover that its status is questioned, complicated, or challenged by later experience.

The life of every community is deeply affected by the uncertain character of its religious truth. Some societies accept this uncertainty as one of the essential features of divinity. Polytheism, for instance, assumes the existence of innumerable unknown gods that the people have not yet encountered but that may suddenly appear tomorrow. Dynamistic religions expect the extraordinary to erupt in new modes and at new places, and Hinduism emphasizes the inexhaustible capacity of divinity for assuming new forms. These might be called "open" religions. But even "closed" religions, which believe in a final and decisive disclosure of the realities of life and death, recognize that this disclosure is not yet fully appropriated, that the truth-question keeps becoming confused even for believers, that some kind of darkness—the darkness of *maya* in Buddhism, say, or of sin in Christianity—allows people to be distracted by unreal gods and to refer authentic life and death to powers that do not in fact hold sway.

The consequence of this unsettled character of religious truth is obvious: it means that *change* is inherent in all the forms and expressions of the religious attitude. It is not the case that, at the level of the actual religion of actual people, there is some fixed entity called Islam, for example, and that the history of this religion is a record of the maintenance, the compromising, perhaps the corruption, but also the repeated recovery of this fixed entity. There is no such thing as a fixed religion. No person anywhere has discovered a source of life and death that is immediately and unavoidably decisive in every situation. All religious judgments, therefore, are constantly being shaken and transformed by new frames of reference. And because these new frames of reference bring with them new dimensions and new experiences of life and death, every reaffirmation of a god followed yesterday really entails a change in the understanding of that god.

Transformation in religions, then, is not a matter of external compromise and infection; it is an inherent and essential property. Not only does religion have the posture of truth as its central preoccupation, but it also has the *problematic* of truth as its fundamental dynamic. In the extreme case this transformation may entail the conscious and deliberate abandonment of an entire fabric of religious forms and the turning to new gods and new rituals. Usually, however, it involves an ever-shifting sense of the actual identifiable content of authentic life and, therefore, a changing expectation of how the god will concretely reaffirm his lordship over the forces of life and death. Thus a single religious orientation, which at one time follows a world-renouncing, sacramental way toward a trinitarian God, can at another time, while committed to the same Lord and guided by the same Scriptures, seek the perfection of worldly possibilities for suffering men.

The uncertainty of truth at the religious level has been very central in the history of Christianity. The Jews had expected the Messiah to be God's agent in closing the truth-question in religion once and for all.

> For in the last days it shall come to pass that I will pour out my Spirit upon all flesh, and your sons and your daughters shall prophesy, and your young men shall see visions and your old men shall dream dreams . . . and I shall show wonders in the heavens and on the earth. (Joel 2:28-30).

The Lord of all life and all death shall become unavoidably manifest. The earliest Christian community saw Jesus as the bearer of this decisive event, for the blind see, the lame walk, lepers are cleansed, the deaf hear, the dead are raised, the low are exalted, and the hungry are filled with good things. Yet the momentum of disclosure begun in Jesus was not completed. The *parousia*—the decisive, unambiguous, and universal "presencing" of this God as the authentic Lord of life and death—did not occur.

The Christian community has always been caught up in the same problematic of truthfulness as other religions. It is always being perplexed internally by shifting experiences of apparent life and apparent death. It was shaken at first by the prospect of antinomianism, then by the prospect of persecution, and after Constantine by the prospect of acculturation. In fact, the theological doctrines of the Christian Church have been established precisely because the truth keeps becoming unsettled in the concrete life of Christian people. According to one Protestant tradition, for instance, the Christian community is one that is constantly falling into arrogant forgetfulness. It cannot, therefore, let itself be measured by any agent or any order or any historical moment from within its own life. It must allow itself to be recurrently reformed by that which stands beyond it—in short, by the claims of the Scriptures. On the other hand, according to one Roman Catholic tradition, moments of uncertainty and confusion are too concrete, too contemporary, too immediate to be dispelled by statements made in the past and preserved in writing. Over and above the Scriptures, the Christian community must have an infallible living voice to remove uncertainties, and this God provides through the office of the Pope.

This problem of uncertainty is not just a feature of community life, however. Every individual Christian must wrestle repeatedly with the question of religious truth. That is why he develops faith to hold on to that which he does not yet see. That is also why each Sunday he seeks a revindication of God's life-giving power, a re-presenting (*anamnesis*) of God's victory in Christ in the liturgy of Word and Sacrament.

However far Christians may want to advance beyond the "old" dispensation of the Jews, and however rhetorically they want to stress the fullness of the revelation given in Jesus Christ, they still cannot break out of the condition of recurrent uncertainty and tension and change in which all religious truth stands. A hiddenness remains. It is not without reason, therefore, that in the New Testament the word "revelation" is reserved for that final unavoidable disclosure which has not yet occurred. And it is not without reason that in the Schweitzer school of theology the delay of this final disclosure is seen as the decisive fact that has shaped Christianity through every period of its history.

In the Christian tradition the pursuit of the question of truth takes the form of theology. This not only means that theology is grounded on and shaped by the religious attitude. It also means that the activity of theology is enveloped by the religious problematic. The religious truth with which Christians seek to be identified keeps becoming obscured. Christian theology thus can never proceed from and can never attain a final form for its truth, a form that is persuasively valid for all peoples everywhere. No insight, no assertion, and no belief is immune from uncertainty at the religious level.

For this reason it cannot be assumed that past theologians have completely taken care of certain doctrines, that in these areas it is simply a matter of repeating their work, and that, if the contemporary theologian wants something to do, he must find a doctrine not already "covered." The theologian can never adopt the posture of Alexander the Great looking for new worlds to conquer. Not a single fragment of Christian truth has been conquered so securely that the theologian can take it for granted and need not constantly listen for obscurities and confusions in people's understanding of it, at least at the religious level. Every act of theological reflection begins with a *questio.*

What the theologian finds true in others' work must also be true in his own. Nothing he can say will at any point carry Christian awareness out of the circle of recurrent confusion. He works with seriousness, because he expects his efforts to be successful. He expects actually to penetrate through a particular religious confusion and to attain a clarifying insight regarding Christ's lordship over life and death in some specific area of existence. But he knows that such success will be provisional and that his insights, far from forestalling further obscurities in the future, may themselves become the source of new confusions in the face of changing situations.

Not for one moment, therefore, can the Christian theologian detach himself from the *problem* of religious truth and pursue other tasks. He cannot turn away to some other order of problem, for example, to the problem of building an intellectual system out of a number of individual truths that may be taken as settled. He cannot turn from the Church and ask himself about the views of non-Christians toward Christianity—as if the difficulties regarding Christ which plague non-Christians were not simply pale reflections of the truth-question that constantly breaks open at the very center of the Christian religion itself. In Christianity what is uncertain is the very center, the viability of Christ as Lord and Savior. That viability becomes obscured at ever new points as changes occur in an individual's or a community's awareness of life and death. That Christian theology cannot detach itself from this religious problem poses a severe difficulty for the faculty of arts and sciences.

3. If religious truth—the truth about the sources of life and death—becomes confused, how can this confusion be removed?

Normally confusions are dispelled intellectually by the mind taking initiative and bringing into view from its vast storehouse of knowledge some datum or some principle or some analogy which dissolves the obscurity. Where uncertainties of a religious sort are concerned, however, this is exactly what cannot be done. Such uncertainties arise because the actual sources of fulfillment and deprivation in experience have become blurred. People have difficulty in making out which god really counts. Therefore, to remove this difficulty is not a matter of thinking better. It is a matter of the authentic source of life and death being revindicated as such in their lives. Its action upon them must be perceived anew so that they may again have a taste of the actual life or death which they believe to be at its disposal. Without this *concrete vindication* the confusion will remain, at least religiously.

The religious attitude finds control over the powers of life and death not finally at man's disposal and, therefore, also not at the disposal of his desire to resolve religious confusions. Gods cannot be made to come out and show themselves as gods whenever devotees so wish. If men could dispose of their religious confusions by such efforts, that would simply mean that the problem had ceased to be of a religious kind and had been transferred to another frame of reference.

Religions do resolve their religious uncertainties in a religious way. That is, when the sources of life and death become obscured in some area of existence, the authentic gods are *invoked* to show themselves. The difficulty is not solved by men. It is referred to the gods themselves, and men wait for them to deliver such impulsions of life or death as will exhibit the truth.

This act of referral and waiting is rarely as dramatic as the contest between Elijah and the priests of Baal. But this basic structure has always been present. Over time rituals of invocation and referral are developed within every religious tradition as it is embroiled in religious uncertainties; it is expected that the authentic god will again affirm himself to the people as the true source of life and death for them and will thus revindicate his power and dispel their confusion.

No exception is presented within Christian theology. For all their conceptual precision and concern for rational proof, theologians do not themselves have the means of disposing of the confusions which they face. Such matters are not academic. They depend for their clarification upon the actual re-presencing of the lordship of Christ. Theologians must therefore align themselves with the means of grace and be responsive to the illuminations of the Spirit. The complete dependence of the entire Christian life on Jesus Christ pertains just as much to the process of theological clarification as to deeds of charity. And if the theologian does succeed in his work, if he exhibits religious (not intellectual) truth with a restored clarity, this achievement will be manifest in the attitudes of the people actually oriented toward Jesus Christ. In short, the Christian theologian belongs to his religious community both in the processes and in the fruit of his work.

Such, then, are three important features of religions. First, they consist in a particular attitude about truth in the matter of life and death, namely, that life and death are received by man from beyond himself. Thus all religions convey what they hold to be authentic and fruitful knowledge about the sources of life and death. Second, the flux of actual experience results in confusion about this knowledge; therefore, it must be constantly recovered in fresh forms. Third, this restoration is believed to be carried out, not by man, but by the revindicating action of the sources of life and death themselves. If Christian theology stands at odds with the faculty of arts and sciences, it does so because it is a religious activity and thus necessarily embodies these three features of religions.

The Antagonism to Christian Theology

By tradition the faculty of arts and sciences has been identified by its subject matter—the arts and the sciences. This has come to embrace, first, the study of the languages, writings, arts, and other self-conscious modes of human expression; second, the investigation of natural phenomena; and, finally, the study of man himself and his sense of the world by means of philosophy, history, psychology, and so forth. As to methods and goals, however, the faculty of arts and sciences has no fixed direction. There is no ideal paradigm by which its activities in various universities can be judged. The intellectual aims and procedures of faculties change according to what use is made of their work and according to what methods prove most fruitful for the purposes at hand. In one age the study of the arts and sciences may be pursued in order to serve the Christian Church and its theological inquiries. Then the liberal arts become the handmaid of theology. In another age an arts and sciences education may offer the best preparation for political leadership. In still other circumstances this education and knowledge are thought to provide the fullest development of human power, the most effective way for mankind to gain mastery over itself and its environment and for the individual to realize his latent capacities.

Recently, however, there has flourished a somewhat different view of what the faculty of arts and sciences should be, a view that has been—and still remains—decisive for the status of Christian theology. As its model for responsible inquiry, this view looks to the kind of detached and critical reasoning which was first developed by the new physical sciences in the seventeenth century. It maintains, therefore, that one condition is absolutely necessary for genuine understanding, and it insists that only an intellectual enterprise which fulfills this condition can be legitimately included within the faculty of arts and sciences.

This primary condition is that true knowledge must arise from *autonomous inquiry*. Reasoning must serve only its own demand for clear understanding. Accordingly, it must keep itself free from entangling alliances with ecclesiastical communities or nationalistic ventures or commercial interests. On this view, the search for truth begins when reason poses *its own questions* about the object of inquiry. These are not questions which have their roots in the practical life of social groups, but rather questions which the mind finds pertinent to its own endeavor to comprehend. Further, the search for truth is advanced, not when the mind has recourse to long-accepted principles or to religious beliefs or to wish-fulfilling values, but when it formulates answers that are entirely at the service of its own rational requirements. And, finally, the search for truth is completed when reason, in order to justify its answers, can provide probative evidence that will be intelligible to any rational person. All reliance on esoteric knowledge or external authority to support the truth is excluded.

In recent times this condition of autonomy has been widely adopted by faculties of arts and sciences as the proper norm for their activities. They exist, it is maintained, to seek understanding of the arts and the sciences in complete independence from all external claims, which is to say, from all the claims that may arise from nonrational impulses within the scholar and from all those that may be imposed on his thinking by his social environment. We find the presence of this norm of independence everywhere in the modern university. There is, for instance, the practice of tenure and other such procedural stratagems by which these faculties attempt to resist control by the church money or the corporation money or the government money that supports them. For the individual scholar there has developed the now universal demand that he secure the

Ph.D. degree and in that way give evidence of his ability to pursue a lengthy technical inquiry without once being subverted by any nonrational, nontechnical interest.

The true autonomy of reason, however, requires more than this independence from extrinsic forces. Beyond social institutions and personal emotions, the mind may also become falsely imprisoned by one of its own momentary insights or by the impact which some object happens to make upon it at one particular time. Reason, therefore, must also keep watch over its freedom even in the course of its own work. That is to say, it must learn to review its own attainments continually and to submit them to the criticism of others. It must refuse any hint of dogmatism. It must insist on seeing its subject matter from various sides, letting the knowledge gained from one approach be qualified by and integrated with the knowledge gained from others. In short, reason must maintain what is called "critical distance" with respect to its own achievements.

Today we have a shorthand term to convey this elaborate notion of the faculty of arts and sciences as the citadel of rational autonomy. The term is *scholarship.* When a faculty measures its attainments, promotes its members, and assesses the work of its students in terms of their scholarly competence—that is, their competence in pursuing an objective, methodologically self-conscious and self-critical inquiry, their competence for formulating rationally urgent questions, for finding rationally satisfying answers, and for providing rationally probative evidence—then this faculty has defined its essential function as the exercise of autonomous reason.

The adoption of this ideal of rational autonomy by the faculty of arts and sciences is the chief reason why, over the past two centuries, the entire domain of religion has become alien to this faculty. For the religious attitude, in one of its essential features, involves man's seeing himself in relation to powers that prohibit any trace of autonomy. When men come to realize that their lives and deaths depend on the movement of enormities that lie beyond their control—that is to say, on the movement of gods—then the posture of scholarship, with its detachment, its leisurely and many-sided inquiry, and its critical distance, is neither possible nor desirable. Above everything else, man in the religious situation must be attentive to what stands beyond himself. He must be ready to respond immediately to any signs that the impulses which nourish his life are about to wax or wane, that his own existence may be moving out of fruitful alignment with these decisive powers and into a position where they cease to nourish him and become destructive. The whole of a man's existence is thought to be at stake here. He has no vantage point, therefore, to which he can withdraw in order to rationally examine and observe the gods. There is no safe center from which he can direct questions at them. As gods, they are related to him only in ways that exclude objectivity and distanced consideration. He does not judge them; they judge him. His life and death depend on movements that are utterly beyond his competence, for they issue out of the depths of these inscrutable powers.

Religion thus requires a very demanding attitude of attentive responsiveness, an utmost willingness to follow the movement of God or the gods. In religion—and in any intellectual discipline that partakes of the religious attitude—truth does not mean a knowledge that satisfies the demands of reason, but a knowledge that is fruitfully responsive to the movement of the gods.

Turning now to the other side of this issue, we can see clearly that religion represents a fundamental enemy of truth as conceived from the standpoint of autonomous reason. For the religious attitude is not simply a purveyor of erroneous assumptions or false information or faulty inferences. From the perspective of rational autonomy, it is wrong through and through to its very essence; it is an intrinsic perversion of the human capacity for truth. Instead of opening man to the real world and liberating his awareness with authentic knowledge, it closes him off from the world. By its very concern with the question of man's own life and death, it fosters in him a narrow, egocentric preoccupation with himself and encourages him to judge everything from that perspective. The exhortation that men should be willing to lose the world in order to gain their own souls perfectly expresses the self-absorption which the champions of rational autonomy find inherent in the religious attitude and which they decisively reject.

In order to exhibit the essentially closed and untruthful posture of religion, the rationalists of the eighteenth century emphasized the role of fear in the religious attitude. Religions arise, they said, because men feel themselves in the grasp of unknown powers, powers utterly beyond the control of their paltry strength and the ken of their crude perception. They find themselves helpless and ignorant. Naturally, therefore, they are filled with fear. The gods with whom religions people this world are expressions of this fear. Because men can pray to these gods, however, and perhaps appease them, religion also provides men with a way to cope with this fear. According to this analysis, then, religion exists first to foster a fearful attitude toward the world and then to allay it.

The force of this rationalistic account lies in the recognition that fear is the most claustral and defensive of all human emotions. In maintaining that religion was grounded on fear, the eighteenth-century rationalists were simply trying to exhibit how thoroughly closed this attitude is. How, they asked, can religion be based on an openness to the real, how can it be capable of any rational truth whatsoever, when it insists on seeing man's basic situation as one of ignorance and helplessness—that is to say, as one of dependence on uncontrollable powers—and therefore demands an attitude of fear? The catchword for describing religion in these terms was "superstition."

Today this negative judgment upon religion has become more subdued. There is less talk about ignorance and more about mystery. The term "awe" has replaced the word "fear." Myths have been rehabilitated, and no one now speaks of superstitions. Yet nothing we have learned about religions in the last hundred years challenges the fundamental accuracy of this description. In the religious attitude men do conceive their existence, at least in its final dimensions, to be at the disposal of superior and undomesticated powers and see it, therefore, as something of which men will always be somewhat ignorant and always somewhat fearful. Such a vision of human existence cannot be neatly integrated with efforts to attain truth through the discipline, the autonomy, and the detachment of scholarly reason.

In the course of the nineteenth century this ideal of rational openness became widely influential in the faculties of arts and sciences. Their methods and their criteria for legitimate investigation and competent personnel fell increasingly under the dominion of this ideal. Consequently, religion, both as a viewpoint from which to teach and as a way of life for which to teach, was more and more excluded from these faculties.

This process of excluding religion constituted a long and bitter struggle, a struggle not only against religion in general but, above all, against the religion at hand, against Christianity. This new autonomous rationality did not, after all, have virgin territory to conquer. The Christian religion had a controlling hold on every single area of learning, and the new perspective had to fight every step of its way against these entrenched interests.

The theology advanced in defense of the Christian religion in this struggle was not a neutral, detached, purely rational kind of theology, but a thoroughly religious theology, that is, a theology shaped by and dedicated to a belief in Jesus Christ as the sole Lord of life and death. Through the work of its theologians, the Christian religion sought to limit the autonomy of reason and subordinate intellection to the requirements of a religious posture. Theology directly challenged the commitment of autonomous reason to truth.

The course of this struggle has long been over, but the memory remains. The condemnation of Galileo and the opposition to Darwin which Christian theologians sponsored continue to be recalled. Thus each new generation has exhibited to it the lack of truth, the fear-ridden closedness, and the essential enmity against autonomous reason that allegedly characterize the Christian religion. Yet it is not simply the echo of these great public events that continues. For, in fact, every faculty of arts and sciences that is over a hundred years old still carries the marks of that struggle within itself, and long after local incidents and personalities have been forgotten, there remain deeply implanted the quite justified *feelings* of hostility toward the theological aspect of the Christian religion.

To suggest that religious theology be pursued and that religious theologians be trained under the auspices of the faculty of arts and sciences is therefore to reawaken this conflict between two incompatible modes of truthfulness. Irenic claims that such conflict is unnecessary, that Christian theology and a faculty devoted to scholarship really share a common ground or pursue a common belief in reason, are simply false. Scholarship does not measure truth according to the degree of its participation in the life-giving power of Christ. And the Christian theologian does not submit the religious issues of life and death to the judgments of his own autonomous, self-critical, and publicly verifiable reasoning. There can be no question of appealing to fair-minded tolerance in the interests of "giving the Christian faith a chance in the intellectual world." Nor is there any point to the contention that Christian theology, in its subservience to the beliefs of its religious community, merely exemplifies the way in which all rational inquiry depends on fundamental assumptions. The religious sense of dependence on lordly powers means that in theological reflection the moment of responsive submissiveness has a positive and fulfilling significance that is quite unknown in good scholarship. No amount of clever intellectuality in theology should be allowed to conceal this difference.

The proposal to bring Christian theology under the aegis of the faculty of arts and sciences, then, makes visible once again the tension between religion and the posture of autonomous rationality.

The Establishment of Departments of Religion

The recent establishment of departments of religion must be viewed in the light of this tension between religion and autonomous rationality. For these departments did not arise out of a purely neutral curiosity about a new field of learning within the faculties of arts and sciences. The question of their establishment was never wholly separated from the conviction that religion as such is not the way of truth and that the Christian religion in particular has been the most formidable enemy to the development of rational truth.

Departments of religion represent the positive attitude of objective, scholarly reason toward religion. Without once forgetting its fundamental opposition to the claims made by the religious attitude, the advocates of autonomous reason have never imagined that their only responsibility was to repudiate and discredit religion. On the contrary, they were bound to take religion with utmost seriousness for two reasons.

In the first place, religious truth involves not simply a posture of attentive responsiveness, for it also has a content. It consists of ideas about the divine and the world, about human origins and human destiny. If autonomous rationality is to vindicate itself as the way of truth, it cannot ignore all this content. If it claims to provide the mind with an open and luminous relationship with what is real, a relationship not dependent on the action of superior forces but available simply through the subjective action of the rational power that lies within man himself, then it must demonstrate its capacity to discover and validate the truth of "religious" matters. It must undertake a positive program to bring the content of man's religious awareness under its own judgment and to show its effectiveness in this decisive area.

Second, the way of reason would be false to its own nature if it were to adopt a purely negative and repudiating attitude toward the sphere of religion, for such an attitude of closed hostility has always been one of the major faults of the religious posture. What would be gained if reasoning were simply to substitute for the closed intransigence of Christian dogmatism an intransigence of its own toward everything religious? Autonomous rationality has not claimed that it possesses a certain content of truth which is infallibly correct and that any conflicting content ought therefore to be suppressed. It simply maintains that its method of arriving at the truth yields such clear, reliable, and objective knowledge that no defensive repudiations are necessary anymore. It is in this same spirit that it ventures upon the study of religion, for the advocates of rational autonomy have always wanted to penetrate and understand this whole region of life and, in fact, to understand it so profoundly that even religious men will be compelled to admit that autonomous reason provides the best access to the truth of religious matters.

But how can this inquiry best be carried out?

We may take René Descartes's approach as typical of one procedure. It is fascinating to observe in his work how subtly and yet how thoroughly autonomous reason establishes itself in the area of religion.

He makes it clear that he thinks of truth only as that which can be accepted by autonomous reason. The only things which he will consider to be true, he says, are those ideas which are completely clear and perfectly defined to the rational intellect, or which can be inferred with absolute certainty from such clear ideas. Anything confused or obscure, anything on which the least doubt can be cast—in short, anything which does not satisfy the mind's own inherent demand for satisfying knowledge—will be rejected as if it were absolutely false. This criterion eliminates the entire domain of religion, which by his own account (*Discourse on Method*, Part I) concerns those matters that are wholly beyond the capacity of human knowledge.

Proceeding in this way, and beginning with a clear idea of himself as a thinking being who lacks perfection, Descartes immediately establishes therefrom a secure and unshakable knowledge of God as the being with all perfection and as the source of all the reality and truth in the world.

It is at this point that the full significance of Descartes's purpose becomes evident. For it now appears that he is not interested simply in satisfying his mind. He uses the truth secured by his mind to inspire the whole concrete existence of living man with an attitude of confident openness toward the world. As he explains it (*Discourse on Method*, Part IV), because reasoning has shown that everything real and true in human experience proceeds from a perfect and infinite being, men may be assured about their judgments, so far as they are based upon clear and distinct ideas, and about the world which their judgments assess. In short, by the use of autonomous reason, men not only may satisfy the demands of their minds but may also escape the oppressive feelings of dread and uncertainty about the human situation and may release their energies for a confident engagement with the world. It is no wonder, then, that Descartes can exclaim: "I have every reason to render thanks to God, who owes me nothing yet who has given me all the perfections I possess" (*Meditations* IV).

This familiar Christian theme of God's unmerited goodness must not conceal from us what Descartes is here doing. Having set aside the truths of religion as wholly beyond the grasp of thinking, he then shows how autonomous reason can establish some of those very truths entirely out of its own resources. He first authenticates the foundation on which religion rests—the awesome idea of an utterly perfect and utterly infinite being. And then, on the basis of that idea, he lets his reasoning show how proper it is that men take an affirmative attitude toward the world and toward their own subjective judgments. Finally, in this setting, he exhibits the free graciousness of God to men and thus validates the claim which God makes upon their thanksgiving. In short, reason in the writings of Descartes does not criticize the religious posture. Rather, by its own light it establishes the content long associated with religion and purports to do so with a subjective persuasiveness far greater than anything provided by religion itself. Precisely for that reason it will presumably be more effective than religion in generating the basic religious emotions of awe at God's infinite perfection and thanksgiving at God's unmerited goodness.

In this aspect of his work Descartes may be seen as representative of one positive approach which autonomous reason may take to religion. In seeking to understand religion, that is, in seeking to bring the religious aspect of human experience into the orbit of intelligence, this approach examines the fundamental tenets of religion—for example, the existence and goodness of God—and tries to reconstitute these in its own terms, judging them according to how well they satisfy the mind's demand for rational clarity.

This procedure has flourished for three centuries after Descartes, usually under the name *philosophy of religion.* In it man is viewed primarily as mind, and religion, therefore, is regarded as one of his ways of groping for a full cognitive knowledge of reality. But religion is an inadequate way, it is maintained, and man can fulfill the aim of his religious life only by applying the disciplines of autonomous rationality to religious questions.

This thesis has been formulated in various ways. According to the deists, for instance, religion fails because the natural reasoning by which every human being knows the one same universal truth about God and human destiny becomes mixed with the products of irrational fear—with magical practices, with an authoritarian priesthood, and with deified heroes. Autonomous reason brings out the true content of religion by removing all this excrescence and exhibiting religious truth, not as true in a religious way—that is, not in terms of the life- or death-bringing action of divinity—but as true rationally, in terms of its power to grasp and satisfy the demands of autonomous reason.

According to someone like Hegel, on the other hand, nothing in religion is to be eliminated as false or superstitious. It is inadequate, not because it represents a mixture of fragments of falsehood and bits of truth, but because in religion men express the truth about the Absolute through the imperfect medium of concrete sensuous things. In all their rituals and myths, their holy objects and holy places, people manifest their true awareness of the Absolute. But, for Hegel, this mode of expression is not an adequate medium for conveying the truth of ultimate reality. Men therefore can fulfill the inner intention of their religious consciousness only if they transform their religion into philosophy and grasp the truth about the Absolute in purely rational terms, devoid of concrete events and physical images. Hegel assigns to autonomous reason the task of teaching men to carry their most fundamental questions beyond the areas of the concrete life, where the life-giving powers wax and wane. It must help them to *think* the non-concrete content of their religious pictures and to replace the certainty of religious faith—faith in certain concrete events or actions as manifestations of divinity—with the certainty of self-conscious knowing.

Within the study of the arts and sciences, the approach of the philosophy of religion came most fully into its own in the nineteenth century. While the religious theologians seemed entrammeled in the quagmire of dogmatism, scripturalism, and denominational self-justification, the religious questions of God and man were being successfully clarified by autonomous reason. Why shouldn't any practitioner of such reason, any scholar in the arts and sciences, whether his speciality be Hellenic archeology or vertebrate zoology, be able to speak out on the true—that is, on the rational—meaning of religion? And so in the nineteenth century many chose to do so.

By the turn of the present century, however, there came into being a new awareness of primitive religions and of the religions of the ancient Mediterranean. It was then that the whole enterprise of the philosophy of religion itself began to be seriously questioned. For in its preoccupation with the views held by religions concerning God and the world, this approach failed to grasp the peculiar way in which religious men see themselves *related to* these beliefs. The new study of less advanced and less rationalized religions showed clearly that religion is not primarily a cognitive effort to understand the world, that myths are not erroneous explanations of natural phenomena, and that the effort to prove the existence of God to the satisfaction of reason—the nerve center of the philosophy of religion, for if this point is not settled, the reasoning mind has no grounds for even considering divinity—is either entirely absent or quite peripheral in actual religions. Accordingly, it became obvious that the philosophy of religion did not understand the human side of religion, the motives and the attitude toward reality that operate here. And hence it did not succeed in gathering religion into the domain of autonomous reason. Instead, it made the religious posture a mirror of its own rationality and only overcame the problem of religious truthfulness by ignoring it.

In response to this crisis there has arisen a much more rigorously descriptive and inductive approach to religions. There has been no change, however, in the fundamental project: rational autonomy is still held to be the only guarantor of true openness and, therefore, the only reliable means of securing the truth. In dealing with religion, the scholarly mind is expected to ask its own questions, to seek answers satisfying to it, and to establish those answers on the basis of publicly available evidence.

But this new descriptive approach is more modest and indirect than the philosophy of religion. It does not simply look at a religion's views of God and man in order to judge of their truth or falsity. It tries to suspend the modern Western rationalistic preconceptions about what constitutes reality and how men should think and act. It tries to let every element in a people's religious behavior stand forth in its own right—their legends, their rituals, their sacred officials, and their holy days. It wants these to disclose what meaning they have, not for the philosophic quest of Western man, but for the people who believe in them. It moves to grand generalizations only very slowly, almost with reluctance.

The success—or, better, the promise—of this descriptive approach in recent years has led to the establishment of departments of religion within faculties of arts and sciences. To put this in another way, in view of the failure of the philosophy of religion to handle the immense range of data about religion that is now being accumulated, that is to say, in view of its failure to comprehend the whole truth-posture of religion within the more radiant truth of scholarly reason, some faculties of arts and sciences have looked to the new descriptive approach to achieve this goal. Accordingly, they have set up departments of religion.

Obviously, many interest groups, including an important segment of the Christian community, have out of their own motives sought the formation of these departments. The very real influence of these groups may be seen whenever departments offer courses on Catholicism, say, or Judaism, covertly oriented to the needs of believing Catholics or Jews. The philosophy of religion is also usually represented in courses within the departments of religion. As faculties of arts and sciences have made the decision to form these departments, however, they have not been interested in providing young people with instruction in the faith of their choice, and they have expressed no strong demand that philosophic clarity be achieved on religious matters. What they have expected is that these new departments will study something of the variety and history of human religions and will do justice, in whatever way reasoning may find best, to the almost unmanageable range of phenomena in religious behavior.

If we survey the actual work of departments of religion and look below the sometimes rather confusing surface of their course offerings, we find that the descriptive approach does indeed dominate the scene. An unremitting effort is made to avoid any one-sided preoccupation with the local religions of the West. Even when competent personnel cannot be found, departments still try to give some instruction about Eastern or primitive religions. There is a general willingness to get along without a particular methodology and certainly without a definition of religion. Philosophical analyses jostle happily along in the company of sociological and phenomenological studies. The subject matter is felt to be too complex, too pluriform and many-sided, to permit any broad theoretical generalizations. As to vigorous scholarship, departments of religion today almost universally stress the value of historical sophistication. This emphasis simply follows from the recognition that every religious phenomenon belongs within the matrix of life of some particular place and time. By requiring historical skills, departments are able to demand of their descriptive work the highest standard of accuracy.

The faculties of arts and sciences have made it quite clear that their departments of religion are to be agents of rationality and not of religion. These departments are expected to exclude all confessionalism, all advocacy and indoctrination. They are not to represent any particular religion or even religion in general. They are not to let reason become the instrument of some faith, nor allow the religious posture to hold sway. They are to show how the power of descriptive reasoning can penetrate and understand the phenomena of religion. In short, they are to proceed by the same canons of competent scholarship as every other department in the faculty of arts and sciences.

In this climate it is obvious that Christian theology in the religious sense still has no place in a department of religion. Its posture of faith and its preoccupation with life and death as mediated concretely through an incarnate God and a religious community remain at odds with the commitment to reason that is still voiced in faculties of arts and sciences.

Nevertheless, because of their descriptive approach, present-day departments of religion frequently do set aside a place for what is often called "Christian theology." This situation corresponds very closely to what happened to theology during the nineteenth century when the philosophy of religion flourished in the arts and sciences. At that time many Christian theologians accommodated themselves to the prevailing approach. They investigated how well various Christian beliefs could be reconstructed on the basis of natural knowledge, without making any reference to special revelation or to life-giving events at the concrete level. Although they themselves were believers, their work, which came to be known as philosophical theology, was very eagerly accepted in the world of rational autonomy. For it completely ignored the religious problematic of life and death and examined the truth of Christian teachings from the quite nonreligious perspective of rational cogency.

In a similar fashion, departments of religion as they exist today also have need for a certain kind of Christian theology. If they wish to describe so theological a religion as Christianity, they must present the theological aims and insights of the important theologians who have shaped the Christian awareness. They must have "historical theologians." But these theologians are no more called upon to wrestle with the problems of religious truth than were the philosophical theologians of the last century. They are asked by their departments, fundamentally, to be intellectual historians, to explain what Tertullian or Jonathan Edwards may have thought, but not themselves to take up these theological questions in all their religious urgency.

The Attraction of Theology

The fact remains that Christian theology in the strict sense has been included in certain departments of religion. Some theologians have been appointed, not as philosophers of religion or as intellectual historians, but as believers who conduct rational inquiries under the control and for the sake of their beliefs. Notwithstanding the traditions of scholarly research and autonomous rationality, some faculties of arts and sciences prove not to be averse to the presence in their midst of minds that work within the religious problematic, that let their thinking be wholly responsive to the life- and death-giving power of the divine, and that therefore serve the interests of the religious and not the rational posture. To be sure, the outer forms of scholarship are insisted on. Any theologian appointed to a faculty of arts and sciences is expected to attain the technical competence entailed in the Ph.D. degree and to have a certain command of historical knowledge and historical methods. But there seems to be a certain relaxing of the rationalistic demands which would have been made upon him previously. The legitimacy of his activity does not depend on his avoiding the religious pursuit of theological questions or on limiting himself strictly to those matters that seem evident to natural reason.

On this basis it would appear that the tradition of rational autonomy is being questioned today within faculties of arts and sciences. The rejection of the religious posture is less assured than it used to be, and this hesitancy indicates that the basic purpose of these faculties is again under question. When described in this way, however, the situation is made to appear far more clear-cut and self-conscious than it actually is. Behind the tentative steps now being taken here and there to include Christian theology in departments of religion, there lies a variety of concerns, none of which is decisive in itself and all of which together do not constitute anything like an explicit challenge to the tradition of rational autonomy. Yet their presence clearly points to a certain blurring in the sense of purpose that controls the arts and sciences. The problem of fundamental goals has thus begun to be raised at the heart of the university.

Let me indicate briefly the three concerns which are most frequently voiced by those who support the inclusion of Christian theology within departments of religion. It should be remembered that I am not considering the views of religious groups or of seminary graduates or of anxious parents. I am interested exclusively in the ways in which the presence of Christian theology is justified in terms of the overall responsibilities of the faculty of arts and sciences.

1. The most important factor is simply the character of theological writing actually being done today. No member of a faculty of arts and sciences can escape some engagement with the work of contemporary theologians. Their ideas are discussed everywhere, and some acquaintance with Buber or Niebuhr or Tillich has become the normal mark of a literate person.

When a faculty member reads this theology, however, what he encounters has none of the obvious irrationalisms which he has been taught to distrust. There is nothing closed or defensive or compulsively doctrinaire in this enterprise. Instead of a mechanical repetition of dogmas and authoritarian proof-texts, he meets intellectual insights that ring true far beyond the precincts of the church-going religion which he may have known. Instead of subservience to narrow ecclesiastical interests, he finds all kinds of questions—even skeptical ones—explored openly and at times with a seriousness that seems almost unfair. There can be no doubt that these writers are religious: rational clarity is not their overriding criterion for the truth. But from within their religious perspective, they are able to shed light on a whole variety of problems in a way that autonomous reason finds strangely satisfying. The religious factor is decisive but nevertheless not altogether obstructive.

The impact of this kind of theological literature on faculty members in the arts and sciences should not be underestimated, for it has raised a doubt about the simple and straightforward manner in which theology had been judged. This faculty has its primary allegiance, not to certain views about what reason can or cannot do, but to every intellectual enterprise that does in fact yield clear and compelling understanding, however unlikely its credentials or fragmentary its achievements. From this point of view, it has not been difficult for some faculty members to suggest that the unsectarian and anthropologically self-conscious theology now in fashion might well have a place among the arts and sciences.

2. Among the highly educated class there is present today a new feeling of urgency about religious questions. This has nothing to do with the revival of any particular religion. It seems to be connected rather with a loss of confidence in the competence of rationality to provide answers in this area. After several centuries of liberated rationality, there are many who feel oppressed by the weight of religious uncertainty, that is, uncertainty about the real source of life and what might be judged its authentic character.

This mood is not a matter directly pertinent to faculties of arts and sciences, though it does reflect on certain claims made for the autonomy of reason. But it is the sign of a new sense among intellectuals of the importance and the irreducibly religious nature of religious matters, and this in turn has deeply influenced the technical work in various departments in the arts and sciences. It has become apparent that religious beliefs and the religious posture may be far more deeply present throughout the whole scope of human life than was previously suspected. Far from being a crudely primitive way of groping for the truth or a set of special actions that are universally recognized as religious, religion now appears as a vital perspective that gives shape to man's political life at one extreme and his works of art at the other. Once the full urgency of the religious question was perceived, it was easy for literary critics and political scientists to discover its influence in great novels or political revolutions.

For numerous faculty members in various departments, this discovery has drastically changed the bearing of religion on their technical work of scholarship. No longer can it be dismissed as merely the consciousness of religious institutions or reduced to purely rational terms. The demands of their subject matter have required them to consider the religion pertinent to their data—usually Christianity—in terms of its own urgency and according to its own sense of truth. For this purpose the presence of Christian theologians in the faculty of arts and sciences has seemed both useful and appropriate. After all, if religion has such a profound bearing on the most creative and the most communal aspects of human life, and if theology breaks beyond ecclesiastical forms and is willing to think into the mysteries of life-giving power at this deep level, it can be excluded only at the price of intellectual impoverishment.

3. Finally, serious questions may be raised about the descriptive approach which now prevails in departments of religion.

In contrast to the professional schools, it is said, the faculty of arts and sciences considers knowledge only with regard to its truth and falsity, not with regard to its practical effectiveness or its public acceptability. The descriptive program in departments of religion is criticized on this ground. For religion is not a "thing." It is a tissue of attitudes and judgments about reality. A faculty of arts and sciences cannot fulfill its responsibility here simply by *describing* what religious people believe and how they act. After performing this necessary first step, it must then go on and raise the truth-question. It must itself enter into the problems which activate religion and must judge those religious judgments. In adopting the descriptive approach, departments of religion have proved far more successful than the older philosophy of religion in coping with the immense volume of data. But they have paid a price. The approach lacks the seriousness which gave the philosophy of religion its commanding stature. It avoids coming to grips with the question of truth. Or, rather, with the limited aim of securing a true account of a particular religion, it ignores the more obvious fact that each religion is itself an account of reality which must be considered on the merits of its own truthfulness. Specialists in these departments sometimes offer the ludicrous spectacle of being more interested in what other specialists think about a religion than in what that religion itself actually thinks.

The call for Christian theology to be established as a corrective in this situation does not represent any conviction about the truthfulness of Christianity. It is simply suggested that Christian theology would be the most effective enterprise for getting the truth-question off the ground again, for reminding everyone that all religions are preoccupied at their very centers with the question of truth and falsity and that no faculty of arts and sciences can afford to forget this fact for one moment.

What are we to say about these three reasons for including Christian theology within a department of religion? They certainly involve no religious conversion to Christianity on the part of faculty members. Of more significance, they do not grow out of any self-conscious ideology about the meaning of scholarship in relation to life. The only fully stated ideology one ever hears in the faculty of arts and sciences is the familiar theme of critical reason, rational autonomy, and "sound scholarship." The interest in Christian theology, however, betrays a new and not well-articulated reservation about that ideology. When it comes to the religious dimension of human life, is the old ideal of autonomous reason a proper model for successful inquiry? Or does this involve a pose of such detached objectivity and a commitment to such narrowly rational satisfactions that it proves unrealistic and fruitless in this area?

On the matter of the place of theology, the overwhelming impression in the faculty of arts and sciences, then, is one of confusion—not the confusion of two perspectives in conflict, but the confusion of a habitual self-understanding in the process of erosion. The place where that confusion is manifested most fully is the department of religion. Is religion to be drawn into the domain of rational clarity and transmuted into terms that are satisfying to reason? Departments continue to maintain programs in the philosophy of religion. Is religion to be described in all its phenomenal complexity, without pressure for hasty judgments about truth or generalizations? Departments provide a large battery of descriptive courses. Or is the religious posture to be allowed to maintain its kind of truth-seeking, subordinating the rational demands of reason to the life-giving claims of some divine power? There are departments which offer work in Christian theology. Given this incredible troika, it is a wise departmental chairman who avoids policy discussions.

That religious theologians are being given professorships indicates how deeply this confusion extends beyond the department of religion to the whole faculty of arts and sciences. It almost seems as if, in its commitment to deal with religion, this faculty finds that it has a tiger by the tail—a tiger which has broken free from the cage of rational philosophy and has overcome the tranquilizing of phenomenal description. Some faculties, of course, are kindly appointing Christian theologians to hold on to that tail!

Catholic Studies in the University

VICTOR PRELLER

THE EXPRESSION "Catholic studies" is highly ambiguous and misleading. In fact, I should argue, it has already misled more than one academic institution. Part of the academic backwash of the ecumenical movement has been a wave of enthusiasm for what we might call a cross-denominational approach to the study and teaching of religion. Jews are appointed to Protestant theological faculties; Catholic colleges bid frantically for recent graduates of Ivy League seminaries and departments of religion, often to discover with some disgust that the man of their choice is himself a Catholic. Administrations of traditionally Protestant universities suddenly find enough money for a second man in religion and poetry when, of course, it happens that the candidate is either a Catholic or a Jew. In one sense, this flurry of ecumenical hiring is both understandable and justifiable. More than one sort of criterion ought to be brought into play in determining the make-up of any college or university faculty. Generally speaking, it has turned out to be the case that the most liberating and humanizing sort of education is produced in the context of maximal social diversity. Just as universities tend nowadays to substitute a well-rounded class for the well-rounded student, so also ought they to have some concern for the well-rounded faculty. I cannot help but think, for example, that Princeton University is somehow derelict in its hiring policies when it allows whatever criteria it may use to select an entirely white faculty. There are legitimate sociological criteria that ought to play a role in determining the specific nature of faculty appointments (in which I include diversity of social, cultural, and intellectual background), as well as purely academic criteria. There are times, I believe, when sociological criteria may even be permitted to outweigh the abstract considerations of academic criteria.

The notion that abstract academic criteria should be the only ones to figure in a faculty appointment policy has application, not to any historically contingent, that is, actual university, but only to the Platonic idea of the university, where pure methodologies inform the Student Mind. What I have called sociological criteria for faculty hiring have in practice real educational value, and on that basis alone the attempt to provide denominational diversity within faculties and departments of religion can be justified in abstraction from the exigencies of curriculum and methodology. This view, of course, does not at all imply that methodological considerations are simply to be abandoned to the sociological value of maximum diversity. I am not suggesting, for example, that maximum diversity in methodologies is necessarily of any educational value—the notion that the university hires a man and lets him "do his thing" with no thought of how his method and discipline fit into the total pattern of university education. The two sorts of criteria, sociological and academic, should be kept distinct and each granted its own integrity.

Often, however, they are in practice confused. Thus Catholics and Jews are hired by Protestant institutions, or Protestants and Jews by Catholic institutions, on grounds that purport to be wholly academic in nature, and as a result curricular and methodological categories are hopelessly compromised. I can think of only one circumstance in which purely academic considerations might in theory demand the appointment to the faculty of a Catholic or a Protestant or a Jew *as such.* If proper curricular desiderata should require the appointment of a *practitioner* of Protestant, Catholic, or Jewish theology, as opposed to an expert *on* such theology, denominational allegiance would seem to be crucially involved. One cannot practice Catholic theology—make the truth claims of Catholic theology—without being a Catholic. For reasons I shall mention later, I do not think such curricular demands could *legitimately* arise in a secular college or university (and, for that matter, I am not certain they would arise in a theological college or faculty). The most, at any rate, that the legitimate curriculum of a liberal arts college or a secular university might require is the appointment of an expert *on*, say, Catholic theology, and such an expert need not in theory be a confessing Catholic or even a confessing Christian. This point brings us to a third sort of criterion that is relevant to faculty appointments. It is a contingent *historical* fact—and, I should argue, a regrettable fact—that nearly all academically qualified experts *on* Catholic theology happen to be confessing Catholics; thus, on contingent grounds, to appoint an expert on Catholic theology is usually in practice to appoint a Catholic. There could never be, however, a valid *academic* reason why that should be so.

There are, then, three sorts of criteria that may be operative in the appointment or designation of a faculty in the field of "Catholic studies," and all three must be kept separate in our minds, lest we misconstrue the very nature of Catholic studies as an academically possible and desirable activity in the university.

In order to clarify the interrelationships between these three sorts of criteria, I shall discuss briefly the role of historically contingent factors in producing the current demand for Catholic studies in the secular university. If I were asked in a general way whether or not I thought that Catholic studies ought to be a recognizable field or program in a department of religion in a secular university, I should be tempted to answer "No!" Certainly, Catholic studies ought never to be an independently definable program or field within a religion curriculum. The only possible role for Catholic studies which I could in the abstract conceive would be as a subdivision of the history or phenomenology of religion, parallel, for example, to Buddhist or Hindu studies. Indeed, as a subdivision of Christian studies, it would probably be a subsubdivision, parallel rather to something like Hinayana Buddhism than to Buddhism itself. Personally I look forward to the day when Christianity, and hence Catholicism, is generally taught at the university in precisely the same terms and categories as non-Western religions. We are, however, dealing here—at least *immediately*—with departments of religion in their present state of development, and that is the primary historically contingent factor. Most departments of religion at secular colleges and universities either have developed out of intentional or unintentional transplantations of miniaturized Protestant seminary faculties to secular campuses or have been so largely staffed by graduates of such institutions that they have been conceived along the lines of the disciplines traditional and proper to the Protestant theological seminary. One of the results of the ecumenical thaw, and the consequent spread of nonpolemical information across church boundaries, has been the recognition by the faculties of departments of religion that their curricular offerings are (as a result of Protestant inbreeding) intolerably one-sided. The history of the Catholic Church since the Reformation is largely ignored, Christian ethics is almost entirely identified with such thinkers as Reinhold Niebuhr, and few students learn anything whatever about modern Catholic interpretations of the meaning of Christian revelation. A contingent factor in the historical development of American secular universities has produced what is generally recognized as an immediate curricular need for Catholic studies. Academic considerations alone require that attention be paid to ways in which Catholic studies might be introduced into the curriculum as the most obvious and immediate means of restoring balance to existing departments of religion. The academic necessity of appointing experts on Catholicism happens historically to involve the practical necessity of appointing Roman Catholics, since few non-Catholics qualify as experts in the field. That historical necessity, however, is rightly taken as a welcome occasion for satisfying the sociological criterion of maximal denominational diversity among the faculty. Departments of religion particularly and rightly desire to have Catholics represented on their faculties, and what better and more fitting way is there to achieve that end than to appoint Catholics in order to satisfy the legitimate academic demands of the curriculum, which, because of historical happenstance, cannot in any case be met without the appointment of those same Catholics.

Everything seems to have worked out very nicely indeed, as all three of the criteria point happily in the same direction. But it is precisely here that caution is required. The agreement between the three sorts of criteria has led in practice to their confusion. For example, there has been in the past few years a growing tendency to establish in secular universities a so-called chair of Catholic studies. Such a chair may conceivably be of permanent value in a denominational seminary, but it represents a distinct danger in the department of religion of a college or university. It is, of course, an obvious way of taking care of the immediate problem at this stage of historical development: through the establishment of a chair of Catholic studies the curricular imbalance in favor of Protestant subject matter may to a great extent be corrected. And, because of contingent historical factors, one ends up in practice with a real live confessing Catholic. One would not think, indeed, of appointing anyone but a Catholic to such a chair, since that is what is, in any case, desired on independent grounds. The evident danger, of course, is that being a Catholic is implicitly or explicitly written into the job description itself and is thereby confused with purely academic criteria. As a result, Catholic studies comes to be interpreted, almost without reflection, as something which *in theory* only Catholics can or ought to teach, although, oddly enough, Protestant students are presumably able to study and learn it. An unfortunate historical contingency—that only Catholics are trained to teach Catholic studies—and a happy sociological desire to have a Catholic "on the job" are allowed illogically to imply that being a confessing Catholic is somehow an academic requirement for remedial teaching of a basic subject within a department which purports to have a legitimate place in the liberal arts faculty of a secular university. The ambiguous phrase "Catholic studies" is so interpreted that the word "Catholic" functions as an adjective and the studies themselves become Roman Catholic in nature. The occupant of the chair of Catholic studies is viewed as a spokesman for Catholicism, a purveyor of Catholic interpretations, or a supporter of Catholic truth claims. In order to see really how intolerable such an interpretation is, we need only substitute "Near Eastern" for "Catholic"—an expert on Near Eastern studies is not taken to be a supporter of Near Eastern truth claims. The reason, I think, that some departments of religion so readily define a chair in Catholic studies as a Catholic chair is that those departments have not become clear methodologically on what they themselves ought to be on purely academic grounds. Departments of religion are construed as departments of religious studies, where "religious" again functions as an adjective. Such departments have, as a matter of historical fact, represented religious values and truth claims on and to the campus, and that regrettable carry-over from the seminary archetype has been considered part of the legitimate academic function of the field, even when a crudely apologetic approach to the material is consciously avoided.

If, owing to a confusion of sets of criteria which in fact help determine specific academic appointments, it is understood to be *academically* desirable that Protestants teach *about* Protestantism, Jews *about* Judaism, and Catholics *about* Catholicism, it is almost inevitable that the mistaken notion will be incorporated into the academic job description that Protestants teach Protestantism, Jews teach Judaism, and Catholics teach Catholicism.

Even when such a serious confusion does not arise, the "chair for Catholic studies" will probably prove to be dysfunctional in terms of the ongoing historical development of any department of religion. Chairs once established are hard to get rid of, particularly if they are endowed by name. To take refuge in such an obvious solution to the immediate academic needs of the typical contemporary department of religion is to interpret the historically contingent present need for Catholic studies (the need, that is, for a counterbalance to Protestant one-sidedness) as a theoretical academic need for the whole future of the study of religions. It is to commit oneself to the proposition that Catholicism ought to be studied under its own rubric as a self-contained specialty. Catholic studies is elevated to the level of an academic discipline per se and is simply placed alongside the traditional disciplines, taken over from Protestant seminaries, which presumably continue to dictate the shape of the department. Needless to say, the commendable but mistaken desire to have an official academic reason for guaranteeing the presence of a Catholic on the faculty simply feeds the misconception.

My thesis is that Catholic studies as such can be academically justified only as a temporary solution to a problem contingently inherent in the present and, I hope, transitional stage in the historical development of departments of religion. Catholic studies, I shall argue, has no inherent justification as a separate discipline within the academic study of religion but derives its rationale solely from its temporary status as an antithesis to the traditional constitution of departments of religion. To continue the horrible Hegelian imagery, Catholic studies, as an antithesis to the Protestant seminary image of the department of religion, has for its inherent historical end the simultaneous fulfillment and destruction of both the thesis and the antithesis, as the present fragmented department of religion is *aufgehoben* into the academically and methodologically more unified department of the future. On the contrary, however, the confusion of historical and sociological criteria with properly academic criteria has often led to a definition of Catholic studies, and to subsequent faculty appointments, which tend to perpetuate that which ought to have been an unfortunate temporary expedient.

One cannot, then, answer the question of what role Catholic studies should play here and now in the university without raising the broader question of the kind of academic and methodological unity that might be appropriate in the future for a department of religion. However important sociological and contingent historical criteria might be in determining the concrete way in which a program in Catholic studies is *instituted*, they must remain subordinate to abstract academic considerations when one sets out to *define* that program. What, then, would Catholic studies look like when *aufgehoben* into some future and more methodologically unified program in the study of religions?

We may begin by asking another question: what sorts of truth claims could legitimately be advanced precisely *as true* within such an academic program? And what sorts of arguments could legitimately be used in support of those claims? I should argue that, since a department of religion is an integral part of the liberal arts faculty of a secular university, no truth claims ought to be put forward within it, precisely as true, unless they can be made intelligible to the natural light of the human intellect—unless they can be stated in terms of a language which is in theory public—which can be understood without the introduction of special and gratuitous forms of perception, intuition, or illumination. Such truth claims could be legitimately supported, only by appeal to criteria of evidence, standards of interpretation, or canons of explanation which themselves derive from the syntactical conventions or exigencies of a normative human language system which is also in theory public. So far as I can see, this requirement of theoretical publicity within the natural universe of human discourse excludes only one sort of truth claim that one might be tempted to put forward in a department of religion, and that is a *theological* truth claim. Theology as such, I would maintain, should play no methodological role in an academically defined program or course in the study of religions.

The reasons are not hard to see. The fundamental propositions, for example, of Catholic theology fail to meet the criteria for permissible truth claims that may actually be advanced in a teaching situation through application of properly academic methodologies as understood within a liberal arts faculty. The fundamental truth claims of theology are not intelligible and cannot be made intelligible to the natural light of human reason. That, at least, is itself a dogma of Catholicism, which maintains that revelation veils or conceals its subject in the very act of revealing. The sort of intelligibility that theology does reserve for its basic truth claims results from a problematic and absolutely gratuitous illumination, the nature of which is reflected in Augustine's disclaimer: I see the Son of Man; I believe the Son of God. Yet it is not I, but the Holy Spirit who believes in me. In the second place, the kinds of arguments put forward in support of theological truth claims are themselves not appropriate as modes of *academic* disputation. They do not derive their authority from the conceptual patterns of public human language, but rather from the *sui generis* authority of faith. In no case, then, should a theological method which involves the setting forth of the claims of faith precisely as true be allowed to determine the proper structure of an academic program in the study of religions.

That stipulation does not entail, however, that theology—Catholic and Protestant—would not be *studied* in such a program. It would simply not be *done*. It is important to note that not everything that comes today under the general rubric of "theology" is methodologically committed to the truth of essentially theological propositions. The historical task of determining, for example, what has in fact been claimed in the name of Christian truth—that discipline sometimes known as "positive theology"—is clearly independent of the validity of religious belief. In addition, it should be noted that systematic theology itself makes use of methodologies and advances certain kinds of truth claims that do not fall under my characterization of what it is to *do* theology. Indeed, the average systematic theologian may well spend the major portion of his time and energy, both in research and in teaching, in establishing and supporting the kinds of truth claims that are by any standard appropriate to a liberal arts faculty. An essential moment, for example, in any vital systematic theology is creating out of the richness of human language and experience new ways of expressing or illuminating what it is that one takes theological truth claims to be about. The imaginative development of new analogies for the nonintelligible truth claims of faith offers no more methodological difficulties than parallel moments in the history or phenomenology of religions when an attempt must be made, in spite of hermeneutical obstacles not only to repeat the language of non-Western religions but to find some way of reexpressing for oneself the sort of thing the language seems to intend. That may be done without understanding in any intelligible fashion the meaning of either the original or the analogy. Such moves and methods *from* theology might well be represented in a unified academic program in the study of religions. We shall have later to ask the question where and how. At any rate, we may now say that such moves always involve the making of truth claims *about* theology, and never *within* theology. Thus the systematic theologian performs in the practice of his essential methodology a number of second-order analyses which terminate in truth claims about theology. He does this, however, in the context of, and in methodological subordination to, the first-order business of theology, which is to present the fundamental truth claims of faith, and to present them *as true.* In that enterprise the methodologies proper to a unified academic program in the study of religions cannot participate.

Having made a basically negative judgment about the academic criteria for defining a proper *aufgehoben* version of Catholic studies, and a judgment involving the elimination of essentially theological methodologies, is there anything positive that can be said? Whatever succeeds Catholic studies, it seems to me, will have to be controlled by the following kinds of general methodological patterns which ought to be found in any future program in the study of religion.

1. No methodologies will be permitted in that program that could not in theory be represented in some other department or departments in the university. The only meth-

odology strictly proper to the subject matter of religion is theology, and that methodology would have no place in the program.

2. All religious traditions and phenomena across the board, will be fair game for the application of any methodology or discipline constitutive of the study of religions. Thus the artificial division between Western and non-Western religions could be overcome, both with regard to such methods as phenomenology and also with regard to such disciplines as religious ethics. The Judaeo-Christian tradition, and thus Catholicism itself, would be subject to the same sorts of historical, phenomenological, typological, sociological, and anthropological investigations that now characterize rather broadly the complex field known—here at Princeton, at least—as the history of religions, a field too generally restricted to the neutral territory of Hinduism and Buddhism. By the same token, the philosophy of religion would in theory range over all forms of religious language, and thus the languages of Buddhism and Catholicism would be equally fit objects for the analyses of contemporary philosophy. Those interested in the nature of religious ethics might just as readily research and teach about what is ethically the case in Catholicism or in Hinduism as restrict their attention to contemporary Protestant ethics or the ethical teachings of the New Testament. Catholicism, along with and to the same extent as any other religious tradition, will be open to the inquiries of the psychologist or the sociologist of religion, or of any other practitioner of a method suitable to the academic study of religions. In short, disciplines will be defined in terms of the application of appropriate methods across the board, and only as a matter of specialization within those disciplines will such distinctions as Christian, Protestant, Catholic, Jew, or Hindu be pertinent.

Obviously, such a projection into an unknown future is questionable in more than one sense. To start with, its presuppositions might be false. Not all theologians, for example, would agree that what I have said about the epistemological status of the essential claims of faith in fact describes anything with which they find themselves dealing as theologians. It may be that I am simply blind to the public meaning of statements about the Trinity, say. With regard to Catholic studies, however, the vast majority —if not all Catholic theologians—would accept my contention that such language is *not* intelligible in any naturally public sense. I, at any rate, am committed on more than one ground to such a view, and I therefore have no choice but to construe the future of Catholic studies in terms of that view. Luckily for the university, no individual has the power to legislate his own opinions into operative policy.

Another sense in which my projection is questionable is that it seems to imply that every proper and unified program in the study of religions must be so extensive that every religious tradition would be treated in it from the standpoints of an unrealistically large set of interrelated and complementary disciplines and methodologies. Thus the *aufgehoben* Catholic studies of the future would *consist* in the investigation and interpretation of the whole array of Catholic facts, movements, and phenomena under the various rubrics of sociology, psychology, philosophy, religious ethics, history, phenomenology, and perhaps any number of other methodologies and disciplines, which would in theory be applied to all religious traditions, Eastern and Western, in the same department. The key expression here is "in theory." What I have defined in outline is not a department, but a field. It is clear, however, that every department of religion would have to select for itself a unified and meaningful cluster of disciplines and specialties drawn from that larger field, which it could responsibly and coherently handle. That choice would, of course, be made with the entire situation of the university in view. Opportunities for interdepartmental cooperation and regard for the needs of other departments would play a role in determining how the broad categories of the field as a whole would be specified at any particular institution. The notion that every department of religion ought ideally to cover exhaustively the whole field of the study of religions is a mistake carried over from the seminary model of religious education. It is a mistake for which most departments of religion have been paying dearly in terms of superficiality and chaotic breadth. It might be desirable, for instance, that Catholic studies at some universities be represented *only* as a subsubdivision of the history or phenomenology of religions. In another department philosophical and ethical interests might form a basic grouping of methodologies in terms of which the study of Catholicism would *also* be carried on, along with the investigation of other religious traditions. Any number of clusters and specializations might be developed, always subject, of course, to the broad methodological rules and restrictions that would define the field.

My major point with regard to Catholic studies is that it would not, if approached in this manner, appear as a discipline or self-contained body of methodologies and subject matter but would in theory fall under all of the disciplines and methodologies properly constitutive of an academic program in the study of religions. The function of Catholic studies here and now, in what I hope will be a transitional stage in the development of such a program, is fundamentally to contribute toward the creation of conditions that will make a program of this kind possible. How can Catholic studies serve that function, however, if it is also conceived as a necessary counterbalance to the *present* structure of the typical department of religion, with its generally seminary-oriented curriculum? Is there not a danger of fulfilling a proximate and pressing curricular need only at the expense of losing a future and academically crucial opportunity? Is there not, that is, a danger of reinforcing the present unsatisfactory structure of a department by simply duplicating it insofar as possible with Catholic counterparts? Is there not a tension between abstract academic definitions of the ideal role of Catholic studies and the role forced on it by contingent historical demands?

Thus if a member of the department teaches Christian ethics and makes use of a traditional Protestant seminary methodology in so doing, ought we not to compensate for his bias by importing a Catholic moral theologian who can teach the *proper* Christian viewpoint on birth control? Or if we now have a theologian who puts forward the truth claims of faith (precisely as true) from the standpoint of traditional or contemporary Protestant theological categories, ought we not to get hold of a sharp Jesuit who can advance the same truth claims of faith (precisely as false, on a Protestant reading) but in terms of traditional or contemporary Catholic categories? Does not the historically contingent counterbalancing function that we have assigned here and now to Catholic studies tend to reinforce the very categories that might be most inappropriate to the future of the field?

Some alternatives might suggest themselves if we go back to the example of Christian ethics and ask two questions: what was meant by saying that our hypothetical incumbent makes use of a traditional Protestant seminary methodology in teaching Christian ethics, and what other kinds of things might he in fact be doing? Without suggesting that there is, strictly speaking, a single method of teaching Christian ethics used in all Protestant seminaries, I would nonetheless claim that the following generalizations characterize a mode of doing Christian ethics most appropriate, and finally *only* appropriate, to a seminary curriculum. First, the fundamental concern is the doing of ethics and not of meta-ethics. The dynamics of the methodology itself tend to terminate in ethical judgments or directives. The truth claims advanced pertain to what is permitted, forbidden, or commanded on the basis of first-order ethical analysis. Second, the authority for putting those truth claims forward (precisely as true) is essentially theological. It is revelation or the Gospel or the Word of God or faith itself that ultimately authorizes or does not authorize those truth claims that are made or rejected. The incumbent who actually followed such a method would indeed be, in the root sense of the word, a "professor" of Christian ethics on and to the campus, just as our true theologian would be a "professor" of Christian truth on and to the campus. Such a profession, I would argue, has no place within a liberal arts faculty.

I should like to make it clear that I do not disapprove of such a mode of doing Christian ethics merely because it involves in its primary intention the doing of ethics rather than meta-ethics, but rather because the ultimate authority in the doing of Christian ethics *so conceived* is taken to be essentially theological—a matter of faith and not of publicly persuasive argument. It is only in the realm of religious ethics, I want to contend, that the doing of ethics is methodologically antithetical to a liberal arts faculty. Outside of religious ethics the first-order analysis is methodologically possible but involves so many practical and theoretical problems at the present time that I, for one, should not like to attempt it.

Let us suppose, nonetheless, that our Protestant incumbent so conceives and so does Christian ethics in the department. It is extremely important to point out that, just like our theologian, our Christian ethicist of necessity will also be doing many other things preparatory and in addition to the undertaking of first-order Christian ethical analyses. Just because the controlling intention of his methodology so conceived will inevitably *terminate* in the making of truth claims with regard to what is permitted, forbidden, or commanded, it does not follow that the major part of his effort in research *or* in teaching will consist in the making of such truth claims. Indeed, he will undoubtedly spend most of his time, like the theologian himself, doing second-order analysis and making truth claims of a kind quite acceptable to the secular university. In the first instance, and most obviously, our Christian ethicist will of necessity be doing the meta-ethics of Christian ethics: he will be clarifying to himself and to his students how and why Christians in fact think they can and should make first-order truth claims about the moral nature of actions based on what they take to be the implications of revelation. Like the theologian, he too will be concerned with the kinds of things Christians do take to be implied by revelation and the queer sorts of reasons they give for so construing revelation. In all of this work he will be doing second-order analysis—a kind of meta-ethics. He will be presenting Christian truth claims, *not as true*, but in order to talk about them in a public, analytical, and critical way —with the intention, that is, *not* of arguing for or against their truth value, but of showing that and how Christians take them to be true. In those moments, and they should be many, he will be talking *about* Christian ethics, not *doing* Christian ethics.

There are, of course, other activities that such a Christian ethicist might pursue in addition to making first-order ethical analyses on the basis of appeals to Christian faith. He might, for example, find it illuminating to take the conclusions of Christian ethics proper and test them in the course of nonreligious first-order ethical analysis. He might attempt to show that the prohibitions and commands of Christian ethics can also be argued for in publicly persuasive terms—in terms, that is, of some conventional or proposed mode of making ethical judgments without appealing ultimately to revealed or nonpublic authorities. And he might make that attempt whether or not he accepted that mode of doing ethics. Or he might systematically contrast the sorts of grounds Christians normatively cite in order to justify their moral decisions with the sorts of grounds suggested in philosophical meta-ethics as appropriate to moral decisions in general.

Our Christian ethicist, even if he conforms to what I would call the "seminary pattern" in ultimately defining the proper and controlling intention of his discipline, might nonetheless engage in an almost unlimited number of kinds and levels of analysis that do not per se involve the naturally opaque references of the language of faith and that are in theory separable from the first-order analyses of Christian ethics.

I have gone through this lengthy and somewhat imperious account of another man's methodology in order to make two points. First, the ground and the germ of a possible future reconstruction of the field is already present in the most conservative version of what I regard as the ultimately undesirable seminary model. Second, it would be possible to introduce a Catholic counterbalance to our mythical Protestant ethicist without reinforcing those aspects of the current show that may not be wanted when the curtain goes up on tomorrow.

With regard to the first point, there is not a single *material* aspect of what goes on in present departments of religion that could not in theory reappear in a nonseminary version. In many places it already has, if not always with methodological clarity. The difference, the change to which I, for one, look forward, is a *formal* change, but an important one nevertheless. It makes all the difference in the world whether one conceives of oneself as setting forth the first-order truth claims of Christian ethics *as true* or as setting them forth simply in order to discuss and clarify them according to a method which itself is not the method of Christian ethics and which could just as well be used to discuss and clarify the claims of non-Christian or even anti-Christian ethics. As soon as that latter step has not only been taken but methodologically clarified, then certain traditional labels, such as "Christian," lose their power to dictate the categories in terms of which a department of religion must or ought to be set up—categories already suffering from dangerous arteriosclerosis. Once a person concedes on methodological grounds that he is not or ought not to be engaged in first-order religious analyses or procedures, he comes to see that the method to which he is in fact committed has in theory a much wider application than he himself has given it or, indeed, necessarily ought to have given it. The man who realizes that he is not, strictly speaking, doing Christian ethics or Christian theology may come to see that what he is doing might better be defined in terms of broader disciplinary categories that have equal relevance to Buddhist ethics or Hindu theology.

With regard to the second point, if appointments are to be made in Catholic studies in order to offset such Protestant bias as there might be in a particular department of religion, one should be careful in drawing up the job description. Not only, in order to safeguard the integrity of academic criteria, ought sociological and historical criteria to be excluded (hence allowing for the possibility of having Catholic studies taught by a Protestant or a Jew, a Hindu or an atheist, or even a peculiarly well-educated minister of the Los Angeles Church of His Satanic Majesty), but the academic criteria themselves ought to be most precisely spelled out. What is being counterbalanced is not the Protestant *man* or his Protestant *methodology*, but rather the *material* to which he restricts himself. One wants the *matter* of Catholicism well taught, according to a method appropriate to the university. In bringing in a Catholic, then, a department can and should appoint with an eye to freedom in the future. Rather than reinforce the categories of the old preconceptions, we should look for a man in Catholic studies who has transcended methodological parochialism and whose real method and discipline have relevance far beyond the boundaries of the Catholic material to which he happens to apply it. Above all, we should avoid anyone who *does* a Roman Catholic *thing*. Such a man will not be so easy to find as the sharp Jesuit or the Catholic moral theologian; but rather than settle for a reinforcement of present patterns, I should personally prefer that the whole notion of a Catholic counterbalance be abandoned and with it the temporary stopgap measure of Catholic studies as such, in the hope that a growing imbalance and categorical irrelevancy within departments of religion might more quickly bring on the revolution.

One further question must be raised. If it were possible without methodological compromise to have Catholic material taught in the department of religion with the same competence and scope that is now generally reserved for Protestant material, ought one to set up a program in Catholic studies? Should there be students or concentrators in Catholic studies as such? In one sense, at least, the answer would clearly be "Yes." There is no reason why a student working in the phenomenology or the history of religions ought not to be a student of Catholic studies in the same way as his colleague might be a student of Hinayana Buddhism—but *only* in the same way. So also a psychologist or philosopher of religion might concentrate on Catholic material, but only within his real specialty, philosophy or psychology. It might be argued that a specialty or program in Catholic studies as such—apart from considerations of a larger discipline—would have contingent historical value in producing capable scholars able to extend the happy counterbalancing function of Catholic studies in other universities. If this were—on contingent grounds—allowed, it would have to be clearly recognized that its ultimate purpose would be to produce such favorable conditions in the field at large that the program itself might safely dissolve itself and cease to exist (and, I should say, the sooner the better). The continued existence of a "program in Catholic studies"—the serious recognition of the rubric "Catholic" as an appropriate means of defining a major, independent slice of the departmental pie—would operate against everything that I have maintained about the broad disciplinary structure of an *aufgehoben* department and would produce men who might not be able to take their places in some broader discipline. To me that danger overrides the present contingent need and suggests that, even if we must bring in men specifically to *teach* Catholic studies, in order temporarily in the person of one man to counterbalance more than one manifestation of Protestant zeal, we ought not to allow a program as such to be established under that temporary rubric.

Throughout this paper I have used the word *aufgehoben* quite freely. In fact, my view is more Marxist than it is Hegelian, which is to say that I am not so sure that neat methodological categories can ever or should ever control the actual future development of departments of religion. What is wanted is openness to change. I should like to call into question my own imperious-sounding claims and demands for the future by citing and agreeing with the following Marxist commentary on man's thought and the actual goals of history:

> Being a man is an incarnation, a self-realization. This self-realization follows a certain path, and its history is leading to a certain point somewhere. But the path which this history is following is not planned beforehand in the theoretical consciousness of man. On the contrary, the path is worked out in the very process of living, in what men do and don't do.

Modes of Jewish Studies in the University[1]

JACOB NEUSNER

LEARNING constitutes a central religious category in Judaism. From the earliest days of Pharisaism almost to the present time, "study of Torah" predominated, in various forms, in shaping the values of the Jews. The present-day academies in which "Torah" is studied claim descent from schools first founded in Palestine well before the third century B.C. and in Babylonia in the second century A.D. The books written in those schools and the conventions and canons of inquiry originally laid down there continue to occupy students in traditional schools. Among the intellectual traditions which took shape in the Middle East in late antiquity, the Jewish one thrives much in the old way, as well as in new forms, and represents one of the longest unbroken chains of learning among men, along with Confucianism and the study of philosophy.

The advent of the study of Judaism in American universities must be seen from this perspective. Judaism is no parvenu in the world of the academy. The scholar whose main task is the study of Judaism may be a relative newcomer in the American university, for until the late 1950's only a few faculties provided for appointments in the subject of post-biblical Jewish learning. But there is nothing at all novel about scholarly study of, or within, Judaism.

[1] I have derived great benefit from the extensive criticism of the several drafts of this paper by colleagues. My hearty thanks go to Professors Baruch Levine, Brandeis University, Hans H. Penner, Bernard Gert, Fred Berthold, Jr., and Robin Scroggs, Dartmouth College, Morton Smith, Columbia University, Thomas Sanders, Brown University, Willard G. Oxtoby, Yale University, Jonathan Z. Smith, University of Chicago, Victor Nuovo, Middlebury College, and Rabbi Eugene Wiener, Jewish Theological Seminary of America, as well as to the editors of this volume. They have all given very generous amounts of time and thought to this paper, for whose limitations I am, of course, solely responsible.

If a scholar has received sufficient training in the classical tradition, its sources and methods, then he has become a new representative of a very old discipline. I stress this point, not because antiquity by itself confers any great prestige, but rather because today some Jews celebrate their "acceptance" by the universities of America, as if they had done little or nothing to deserve it. Given both their reverence for learning and veritable awe of the learned man, and also the persistence of these religious traits in cultural and secular forms, they bring to the university a rich appreciation of its central tasks, and their tradition makes its contribution as well. But the university as we know it is only the most recent, and at present not by any means the most important, setting for the enterprise of the Jewish intellect.

My purpose here is not to argue the thesis that Jewish studies belong within the university curriculum, but rather, first, to analyze briefly what these studies comprehend, second, to distinguish between modes of Jewish learning in universities and in Jewish schools, and finally to adumbrate the place I believe appropriate for Jewish studies within the study of the history of religions. A second, equally important place, in Near Eastern studies, is not under discussion here.

Definition: What Is Included in University Studies

We must first carefully define the various modes of Jewish learning so that we may be able to distinguish those germane to universities and those most useful in parochical, Jewish schools. It is clear that the wide range of Jewish studies exhibits a mixture of presuppositions, methods, and topics of interest. Not all of these would contribute to university studies of religion. Furthermore, it is obvious that, when Jews study themselves and their own traditions, they naturally rely upon unarticulated assumptions and exhibit implicit attitudes which require specification. After examining the several definitions for Jewish learning, we shall then be in a position to separate the aspects of Judaic studies appropriate for universities from those best cultivated in Jewish seminaries.

What do we mean by Jewish studies? To answer this question, one must define "study of Torah," *Wissenschaft des Judenthums*, "Hebraica," "Hebrew studies," "Judaica," "Jewish learning," and other terms used to denote the subject under discussion. Of these terms, the broadest is "Jewish learning," which includes the systematic study of the beliefs, actions, and literary and cultural products of all persons who have been called, or have called themselves, "Jews" (of which more below). Within "Jewish learning" one may discern several fairly distinct categories. First is "study of Torah," the traditional, religiously motivated activity, developed over the centuries and focused upon study of the Talmud, commentaries, legal codes, rabbinic interpretation of the Hebrew Bible, and similar sacred sciences pursued in classical Jewish academies and seminaries. Second is "Hebraica" or "Hebrew studies," the study of the Hebrew language, biblical, cognate, and, more recently, modern literature, and related subjects, which was undertaken in American universities and Protestant divinity schools from the very beginning, and now continues in departments of Near Eastern languages and literatures, linguistics, or comparative literature. Third is "Judaica," the systematic study of Judaism, its history and theology, law and practices, and of the Jews as a group, generally carried on in departments of religion or in the social sciences. Of these modes of Jewish learning, the third is the one that will be discussed here. The divisions within "Jewish studies" are rarely demarcated by such clear-cut boundaries as those I have suggested. In general, university programs in "Jewish learning" are divided between Near Eastern and religious studies.[2]

[2] For a survey of the existing pattern, see Arnold J. Band, "Jewish Studies in American Liberal Arts Colleges and Universities," in *American Jewish Year Book*, LXVII, ed. Morris Fine, Milton Himmelfarb, and Martha Jelenko (New York and Philadelphia: Jewish Publication Society of America, 1966), 3-30. Band compiled a list of 54 professors and 34 Hillel directors teaching courses at 92 Ameri-

Adequate definitions for the terms "Jew," "Jewish," "Judaism" and "Judaic" are required as well. The study of Judaism includes its philosophy and theology, religious literature, art, music, law, and history; a "Judaic" study focuses upon some aspect of Judaism as a religion. The study of the Jews concerns the culture, sociology, politics, languages, art, literature, and other artifacts of the distinct historical group of that name. That group is composed of people who were born of a Jewish mother, or converted to Judaism. I offer the definition of the Jew given by Jewish law. One may broaden it slightly by adding that a Jew is one who thinks he is, or is thought by others to be, Jewish, with the qualification that such belief is not based upon mistaken facts. Whether or not one may isolate qualities which are distinctively "Jewish" is not at issue here.[3]

In this definition one must stress the importance of change. Qualities or features which Jews borrowed from other peoples in one setting frequently became rooted in Judaism or Jewry, so that later on, or elsewhere, they came to be seen as peculiarly Judaic or Jewish. The Jewish calendar, that "unique" construction of Judaism, derives mostly from the Canaanites. It may be argued that the festivals were "monotheized" or "Judaized," but in fact different verbal explanations have been imposed on the

---

can colleges and universities. Among the top graduate and undergraduate schools (41), Band found that what he calls "Judaics" are offered in the following departments:

Near Eastern studies (including Oriental studies, etc.)–14
Religious studies–12
Classics–4
Foreign languages (including modern languages, linguistics)–5
German–2
Jewish studies (or Hebrew studies)–2
English–1
Philosophy and religious studies–1

The field seems mostly divided between departments of Near Eastern or Oriental studies, which stress language and literature, and departments of religion.

[3] See the very helpful comments of Raphael Loewe, "Defining Judaism: Some Ground-clearing," *Jewish Journal of Sociology* VII/2 (1965), 153-175.

same festivals celebrating the same natural phenomena of the same Palestinian agricultural year. In the early days of Reform Judaism, it was thought that, if one uncovered the "origin" of a practice or belief, he might then decide whether it was "essential" or peripheral. Nowadays there is less interest in "origins." The exposure of the "genetic fallacy" may have been part of the reason for this shift: it was quickly recognized that determination of the "origin" does not exhaust the meaning of a belief or practice. Yet there was another source as well. For it has been progressively more difficult, with the advance of scholarship, to discover *any* deeply "Jewish" or "Israelite" practice which was not in some degree the creation of some other culture or civilization. The Jews, over long centuries, have assumed as their own what was produced originally by others, and their infinite adaptability has been made possible by short memories and tenacious insistence on the mythic-Jewish origins of purely gentile or pagan customs. Whatever was or was not Jewish, a great many things have *become* so.

So far I have not alluded to peculiar Jewish disciplines or methods of study, although these exist, some people suppose, in Talmudic dialectic. That dialectic, however, is formed of Roman principles of legal codification and Greek principles of rhetoric. Probably one could find numerous parallels among contemporary Syriac, late-Babylonian, and Hellenistic traditions, if these were sufficiently well known to us, just as the Jewish academies have their parallels. Although a discipline may be peculiar to a tradition of learning and still be derivative, I doubt that Jewish learning can be associated over a long period of time with any particular discipline, in the sense that sociology has its methods, or physics its procedures. Obviously Jewish learning can lay no persuasive claim to exclusive possession of subtlety or cleverness, devotion to the intellectual life, dedication to "matters of the spirit," or any of the other traits—pejorative or complimentary—claimed for it by its religious and secular enemies or apologists.

"Jewish learning," broadly construed, is most nearly analogous, in university terms, to an area study, in which various disciplines, drawn from the humanities, such as philology, art history, musicology, or literary criticism, and from the social sciences, such as political science, economics, sociology, or the like, are brought to bear upon a certain region, or nation, or segment of society. "Jewish learning" does not necessarily fit into a special department, though "Judaica" appropriately belongs in a department of religious studies, "Hebrew studies" or Hebraica, in a department of Near Eastern languages, and "Jewish studies" pursued from a historical or sociological perspective in a department of history or of sociology and anthropology. Just as many methods may be profitably applied to the study of a geographical region, so also many methods may be used to elucidate aspects of the study of the Jews as a group or of Judaism as a religion. Specialists in various areas of Jewish learning may be located in different departments. In addition, *centers* of Jewish learning, in which specialists from several disciplines may be brought together to work on the Jewish and Judaic materials, ought to be created, where feasible, in some universities. Such "institutes of Jewish studies" would be analogous to the Russian Institute at Columbia and the Middle East Institute at Harvard. On the other hand, a *department* of Jewish or Judaic studies seems to me a misnomer, for departments normally take shape around particular disciplines or approaches to data. Even though departmental and disciplinary lines are breaking down, it is still important to structure Jewish studies in universities according to appropriate existing principles of academic organization.

So far as it is necessary in the beginning to select certain modes of Jewish learning for university purposes, I think two are primary: concentration in Hebrew language and literature for Near Eastern or comparative literature departments, and in the history of Judaism for departments of religious studies. I see no role whatever for the Judaica specialist in the study of contemporary philosophy, though of course studies in the history of philosophy will require his contribution. The social scientist normally makes use of all kinds of data, deriving them from many different cultures, traditions, and social groups, without specializing in any of them. I should suppose, therefore, that the various social sciences, especially anthropology, sociology, and psychology, would find the inclusion of a "specialist in the Jews" egregious and wasteful.

Whether history belongs to the social sciences or the humanities, I see a limited place for the Jewish historian *as such* in a history department. In the past, to be sure, general histories of the Jews have been written, and one might thereby be led to suppose that "the Jews," as a single entity (or "people") existing in various times and places, have had a single history, in the same way as England, or America, or China has had a history. It seems to me that the normal inquiry of historians proceeds on the assumption—whether upon geographical, or political, or sociological grounds—that what one is dealing with is a single entity which has had a history. To suppose that "the Jews" constitute such an entity or "people" requires, first of all, assent to a theological or ideological judgment. Once that step is taken, however, the morphology of one's further studies has been established. Whether or not it is congruent with that of historical studies is an open question.

A specialist in Jewish history presumably must be trained nor merely in historical *method*, but also in the data pertaining to his field, data which in the Jewish case extend over more countries, cultures, and centuries than most scholars are capable of mastering. The specialist in Jewish history who works in late antiquity has to reckon with Jews who spoke several languages and lived in several different political systems, who wrote many kinds of books, preserved afterward among many different and conflicting groups, each of which claimed to be "the Jews" or "Israel" from that time forward. When the Jewish historian proceeds to medieval studies, he must once again face the variety and breadth of Jewish data, and so too in the modern period. Whether or not a single historian can specialize in "the Balkans" or "the Middle East" and achieve the mastery of the many languages, literatures, and histories demanded of him, I think it unlikely that the same could be done in a thoroughly professional manner with the Jews. Both unarticulated ideological or theological and technical or methodological problems stand in the way of Jewish history.

If, on the other hand, a scholar working, for example, mainly in medieval European history specializes in Jewish materials, as another may stress Germany, or Italy, or Poland, he may make a very significant contribution. For he becomes acquainted at the same time with the broader cultural and social environment which shaped the lives of all people, including the Jews, in medieval Europe; he deepens his understanding of the various political and economic systems governing all groups in a given territory, including the Jews; and he learns about the literature, religion, and other aspects of the civilization of those among whom Jews lived over a period of several centuries. He is, in other words, dealing with a specialty within a broader field of historical research, just as others do. He is not expected to do more than anyone else can reasonably ask of himself. He can become an expert, and, reaching the frontiers of knowledge at a few specific points, he may cross over into unexplored territory.

I do not see how the thirty or forty centuries generally included under the rubric of "Jewish history" can be adequately studied by any one person, and I do not think professional scholarship can cope with so broad a temporal range of study, even within a relatively narrow frame of reference. The need to know the whole of a single period will prevent the historian from knowing the rest of the history of the Jews. In larger faculties, where several men may concentrate upon a single period, such as medieval or modern Europe, there should be a specialist in Jewish material, just as there is in French, Italian, or Russian. But, in general, Jewish history seems to me a less manageable field than the history of Judaism (of which more below). The contrary expectation supposes that the study of Jewish history may safely exclude careful attention to the affairs of the societies among which Jews were living. The presupposition is that these affairs had little or nothing to do with Jewish religion, culture, sociology, literature, and the like. From the Canaanites to the Americans, massive testimony to the contrary has accrued, with variation, but without exception. It is, moreover, a theological judgment to include in Jewish history the study of "normative Jews" and their culture and to exclude the history of others, such as various sorts of Christians, Karaites, and Sabbateans, who from their origins on have claimed to be "the Jews" or "Israel." Whether or not such a judgment can be made, it certainly ought not to be made—and then put into effect—by *historians.* So there is, or should be, no such field of specialization as Jewish history and, hence, no place in a department of history for a specialist in Jewish history. Places obviously should be found for a medievalist, or a modernist in European or even American studies, and certainly a specialist in ancient history, who works mainly, though not exclusively, on Jewish sources. All those who do specialize in the nonspecialty known as Jewish history in fact end up, as is entirely proper and necessary, concentrating on a particular time period and geographical region, and frequently on only one aspect of Jewish history of that circumscribed time and place.[4]

[4] I am well aware that one- and multi-volume histories of the Jews have been written. These are invariably highly theological (ideological), frequently homiletical treatises, in which given themes, such as the nobility of the Jews and the heartlessness of their (generally) Christian neighbors, the literary productivity ("culture") of the Jews and the benighted and narrow minds of their neighbors, and the like, are played upon. Before World War II such histories concluded at the climax of "the Enlightenment and Emancipation," which seemed then to be the happy ending of the long bloody story. Afterward, the State of Israel generally provided the dramatic conclusion for the narrative. I know of only one exception to the rule that a comprehensive "history of the Jews" is bound to be of less than professional historical quality, and that is Salo W. Baron's

JACOB NEUSNER

Modes of Jewish Studies Outside the University: Study of Torah

What is the relationship between university-based Jewish studies discussed above and studies in a Jewish school? The place of Jewish learning in universities is necessarily conditioned by the universe of discourse existing within the university. The university attempts to bring into relationship with one another many kinds of area studies and many sorts of disciplines, in both the humanities and the social sciences. In the context of this heteronomous discourse within the university, various bodies of knowledge contribute to the elucidation of questions of common interest. Under these circumstances Jewish studies are required to concentrate on those elements that are of interest to other disciplines or areas. But the classical tradition of Jewish learning contains many elements that are of no interest at all to outsiders. Pursued for their own sake, that is to say, as an autonomous body of tradition and knowledge dependent upon no other scholarly tradition and no other body of questions or perspectives for validation or relevance, Jewish studies have quite another type of existence. Seeing matters from this standpoint, we may come to a clearer understanding of the relationship between a given area study and those who actually *live* in the area which is under study.

Within the community of the faithful, Jewish studies from Pharisaic times onward have focused upon the study of the traditions regarded as having been revealed at Mt. Sinai to Moses (according to Pharisaic belief) in both oral and written form. The written revelation is contained in the Pentateuch and, beyond that, in the prophetic books and the writings supposed also to have been written under divine inspiration. The oral tradition was finally written down in the form of the Palestinian and Babylonian Talmuds, various collections of Scriptural exegeses known as

---

Social and Religious History of the Jews, 12 vols. (New York: Columbia University Press, 1952-1967).

Midrashim, and cognate literature. Other literature produced by Jews in the long period from Ezra to Mohammed, circa 440 B.C. to A.D. 640, was not preserved by the Pharisaic and rabbinical schools and was not therefore included within the scope of the term "Torah." From the Islamic conquest of the Middle East and the subsequent fructification of all fields of human thought, "Torah" expanded, even in rabbinical circles, to embrace the disciplines of philosophy and metaphysics. From the tenth century to the fifteenth, a vigorous philosophical tradition took shape under the impact of Moslem rationalism. Still a third mode of pre-modern Jewish studies existed in the form of Kabbalah, the Jewish mystical tradition, which conceived of "Torah" under a wholly new guise, as an arcane doctrine of metaphysical mythology. A fourth form was the legal and ethical tradition. This was pursued, first, through commentary upon the Babylonian Talmud, second, through legal research resulting in the issuance of a *responsum* (a letter in reply to a specific legal question), or in the provision of a court decision, and, third, through the construction of great codes of Jewish law, bringing up to date and organizing by specific principles the discrete corpora of laws then being developed in particular countries and by various authorities. A fifth form, which was liturgical and in a measure belletristic, resulted in the composition of a great body of poetry, both religious and secular, in the Hebrew language. A sixth was Bible study and commentary. Of the modes of Jewish learning in pre-modern times, biblical-Talmudic studies were by far the most common; the others existed in small and relatively isolated, uninfluential circles, except at specific times and for local reasons.

The birth of *Wissenschaft des Judenthums* among the nineteenth-century German Jews who had received both a classical Jewish and a university education added to the range of Jewish studies several modern sciences. These were, specifically, history, philology, textual criticism of the classical texts, and biblical studies in the modern mode.[5]

[5] Of special interest in this connection are N. N. Glatzer, "Begin-

New also, and of greater importance, were the attitudes of complete freedom of interpretation as well as, in Glatzer's words, of "freedom from the possible application of the results of scholarship to the conduct of life." A further change, Glatzer points out, was from the exegetical to the abstract mode of discourse. No longer were books called "contributions toward" or "comments on," but instead major comprehensive projects were undertaken. Most recently, sociology and contemporary history have begun to take root in a particularly Jewish academic environment. Furthermore, books formerly ignored by Jews but preserved by Christians, such as the biblical apocrypha and the New Testament, Josephus, Philo, and the like, have reentered the framework of Jewish learning in modern times.

What unites classical and modern sciences of Judaism are the convictions, first, that such an entity as a "Jewish people" exists, which permits one to study as a *unity* the literature, history, and other cultural artifacts of people who lived in widely separated places and epochs; second, that sufficient unity pervades the culture so that one may meaningfully write a history of Jewish (as opposed merely to modern Hebrew) literature, or a history of the Jews, or similar compositions; and, third, that scholarship concerning "the Jewish people," its culture and religion and history, even its languages, is intrinsically important and interesting. Most significant of all, Jewish studies carried on in an autonomous framework presuppose not only their own intrinsic interest and importance but also their worth in molding the values of the living generation, whether these be religious or secular. (*Wissenschaft des Judenthums* was not a university discipline—though it aspired

nings of Modern Jewish Studies," in *Studies in Nineteenth-Century Jewish Intellectual History*, ed. A. Altmann (Cambridge: Harvard University Press, 1964), 27-45, and N. N. Glatzer, "Challenge to the Scholar: A Judaic View," in *Judaism* XI/3 (1962), 210-220. I subscribe wholeheartedly to Professor Glatzer's theses in the latter article.

to academic status—but the creation of the early Reformers of Judaism who, despite disclaimers, intended through it to point the way toward the future development of the faith.) Jewish studies in Jewish institutions, therefore, are pursued not simply because they may illuminate some aspect of the humanities or social sciences but, especially and immediately, because they will help the Jewish student to form his beliefs and values by reference to the tradition of which he is a part, or, more descriptively, which shaped his forefathers' in various ways.

In my view, any cultural or religious tradition has the right to be taken seriously in its *own* terms, and especially by those to whom it addresses itself. It is not enough to study the traditions and lore of the Jews as aspects of humanity, or because they may provide significant insight into the human condition, as I once argued. The rhetoric may be appealing to some, but the results are disastrous to scholarship. All specificities, all boundaries, all possibility of commitment are quite properly destroyed when the particularities of Jewish learning are subsumed under, and then blotted out by, the perspectives of the humanities or social sciences. It is one thing to study Yiddish, Judaeo-Arabic, Judaeo-Persian, or Hebrew at various points in history because they represent interesting data for the linguist, a valid and important perspective. But it is quite another to study the various languages Jews have regarded as Jewish in order to come to a deeper understanding of their values or of the way their languages generate and interpret visions of reality, or even in order to learn to express oneself through them. The linguist may learn to make use of one of the many languages he studies; the philologist may penetrate into the deeper meaning of a word; but only the committed student and his equally devoted teacher want to *use* that language and find a deeper means of self-expression through that use. Yiddish or Hebrew may well be studied by linguists or Orientalists, respectively, but the value of studying them is quite different, more personal and, I think, more profound, when believing Jews in an autonomous and self-contained setting learn them. Jewish studies represent a heteronomous body of learning; but they also constitute an autonomous tradition, with its own claims and value statements. To ignore the latter is to render impossible the success of the former.

I argue, therefore, that certain kinds of Jewish studies belong within the university curriculum, others only within Jewish institutions of higher learning (such as seminaries and institutes for advanced study), and some in both. Rather than specify particular branches of Jewish studies appropriate for each setting, this essay will develop the particular criteria in terms of which judgments should be made. To take one example: the Talmud deserves to be studied—forever, I hope—in the classical, dialectical manner. It was composed with just such study in mind, and when deprived of the richness of commentary, scholastic disquisition, and the search for new insights in the perfectly traditional, old-fashioned modes, it loses its integrity. That is to say, study of the Talmud must be "study of Torah." But at the same time the Talmud is a historical document. Thus it may be viewed as a resource for philological and cultural studies, as evidence for the state of religion, economic life, sociology, and politics in ancient times, and as a repository of values which in various ways have continued to guide the life of the Jews. For social scientific purposes, the Talmud (as much as the Church Fathers) provides data of great interest for inquiry in the tradition of Max Weber and Ernst Troeltsch, to name only two sociologists of religion. I see no connection between classical Talmud study and the university curriculum, but many relationships between Talmudic literature and various university studies in both the humanities and social sciences. To generalize, potentially each branch of Jewish learning has a contribution to make to university studies, and the criterion for incorporation into the university curriculum will be the possibility of applying university methods of study to the particular subject matter(s).

I think it unfortunate that the success of Jewish studies

within the university rests, as it has for a century, upon that of Jewish studies outside it. The mastery of the necessary languages and classical disciplines required for advanced scholarship in Jewish materials cannot be acquired in a few years or in a few courses. Jewish learning demands too deep an education for advanced work to be undertaken upon a foundation presently existing in university curricula alone. Today, therefore, Jewish studies, both in the history of Judaism and in the languages, literature, and history and sociology of the Jews, depend upon extra-university resources. At the present time it may well be advantageous for the scholar of many Jewish subjects to be a Jew in origin and upbringing. The insufficiency of university facilities, and not the intrinsic character of the subject, is the cause. I think that the university must fully carry out its responsibilities, so that a person entering with no background in, or even contact with, the subject may within the normal period of years emerge as a suitably qualified scholar. Thus the university will preserve its own autonomy and achieve that self-sufficiency which in the end will protect and maintain its character. No subject taught in a university must ultimately depend upon foundations laid outside of it. Of course, university-based scholars of Judaica must make maximum use of the substantial achievements of modern scholarship, which has produced the translations, concordances, critical texts, and scientific commentaries needed to provide somewhat easier access to documents, mastery of which would otherwise require a lifetime of study.

On the other hand, one can hardly consign extra-university Jewish learning to the sterility or boredom of the old issues, forms, and procedures. The same problems which led to the development of contemporary humanities and social scientific scholarship within the university are just as troublesome outside of it. Indeed, the philological, historical, social scientific, and other methods hammered out in the past century provide as useful a tool for analysis of a text in a seminary classroom as in a university. One may, of course, continue to ask the old questions and carry out the old procedures. Proof of this possibility derives from the actuality of Jewish learning in more than a few Jewish institutions of higher learning. But the old questions seem less troubling, and the old answers of diminishing persuasiveness. If we find a key to treasures of insight, it should open many doors. The newer modes of learning need, therefore, to reshape the older ones.

The difference between modes of learning in a university and in other centers of study should be made explicit. Scholars in universities do not differ from their counterparts in Jewish-sponsored schools of higher learning in commitment, concern, or protagonism. But the focus of commitment and concern is radically different. The university scholar seeks understanding of structures, the parochial scholar (and I do not use the word pejoratively) seeks participation in them. In a university, commitment is to the scholarly method or result; in a parochial institution, to the content of what is studied. In a university, concern is for humanity or society first, to a particular segment or example of it second; in the parochial institution, concern is for the group first, mankind afterward. Protagonism in the parochial institution is taken for granted. In the university, one advocates scholarly alternatives; but the act of advocacy of a religion as such will impede the comprehension of a religion other than one's own, and I suspect it will also impede understanding of one's own religion. In the parochial center of learning, the significance of the opinion or perspective on the external environment, although one can hardly claim to ignore or exclude it, cannot be so decisive as the opinion and perspective on the tradition itself.

From the university perspective on "reality," it is impossible to locate "the Jewish people"; what comes into view are only various groups called "Jewish," a term bearing various meanings in diverse settings and serving particular functions within different societies. Thus, to one outside the tradition, the "Jews" as a group are best defined functionally and episodically. In the Jewish school, on the other hand, "the Jewish people" loses its quotation marks. From his own viewpoint the believing Jew cannot deny the reality of Jewish history. Indeed, in Jewish schools the Jewish people constitutes a central category of analysis, on a par with Jewish Law, the God of Abraham, Isaac, and Jacob, or the hope for the end of days and the advent of the Messiah. Thus Jewish history represents a vital field of study in Jewish seminaries, for in that context peoplehood as a construct serves to unify the otherwise discrete and disparate data concerning the Jews. Jewish history provides a chief source for the verification and validation of theological or ideological convictions in an institution so defined. The appeal to the past, together with the recognition of the authority of some men in it, is the presupposition of religious thought for those who are Jewish by identity.

Judaism Within the History of Religions

What is the role of Jewish studies in the history of religions? The techniques of the history of religions and its categories of analysis have been applied unflinchingly, mostly by scholars of Christian descent, to every religious tradition of mankind, both archaic and modern, except for two, Christianity and Judaism. Of the two, Judaism is still less studied than Christianity. To be sure, the Scriptures of ancient Israel have undergone religious-historical study, and the Jewish sectarian environment between the Maccabees and the first century A.D. (including the early Church) has been carefully examined from many perspectives. Yet practically no work has been done, except by a very few individuals, on the history of Judaism since that time. No subdivision within the history of religions known as "history of Judaism" has yet come into existence. The reason is that, for Christianity, "history of religions" was really meant to provide a means of studying the religions of the Orient. The history of Judaism was clearly to be subsumed within the "Judaeo-Christian tradition," which for theological reasons was not to be subjected to the same kind of analyses.

The "Judaeo" part of the Judaeo-Christian tradition, according to this conception, usually drops away about A.D. 70, but never later than A.D. 135. Similarly, in Protestant and nonsectarian schools, the "Roman Catholic" part of the "Western" Christian tradition (or, under secular auspices, "civilization") ends at the Reformation. Such extraordinary events in the history of Roman Catholicism as the nineteenth-century Renaissance somehow find little, if any, place in histories of Western "Judaeo-Christianity."

The truth is that the university has been basically *Protestant*—though nonsectarian, liberal, and kindly disposed toward Jewish and Catholic as well as Hindu, Buddhist, and Moslem students and their religions. It was the Protestant vision which determined American university perspectives until the most recent past. That vision is, admittedly, broader and more mature than the Jewish or Roman Catholic equivalents. The New Testament and the history of Christianity are not systematically studied in any Jewish-sponsored university, in this country or in the State of Israel, except in relationship to the history of Judaism, whereas great attention has been paid at notable nonsectarian, Protestant-oriented universities to the Jewish tradition. Philip Ashby points out that the history of the history of religions in America cannot be separated from the history of Protestant theological education.[6] I think one may fairly add that the history of all forms of the study of religion in secular American universities can be written in terms of the history of cultural, if not religious, Protestantism. Nevertheless, it is hard to see how others, of different religious traditions or of secular orientation, have improved upon the Protestant record.

With the growing maturity of the history of religions, however, I see no alternative to both the inclusion of Jewish data in that discipline and the application of the issues and methods of that discipline to the study of Judaism. These, I suggest, are the specific points at which Jewish studies

[6] "The History of Religions," in *Religion*, ed. Paul Ramsey (Englewood Cliffs, N.J.: Prentice-Hall, 1965), 1-49, *passim.*

have their most promising, best-integrated place within the university (outside of Near Eastern studies).

The history of religions, as I understand it, focuses upon the phenomena and the morphology of religions. It raises questions concerning the interpretation of the religious structures, including myths, ideas, theological attitudes, and rites and rituals, as means of perceiving reality, or organizing it, or construing it, used by men in diverse circumstances. The history of Judaism has already contributed considerable data to that inquiry, mainly through the researches, in our own day, of Erwin R. Goodenough and Gershom G. Scholem, each of whom has shown, the one with archaeological, the other with mystical sources, the possibilities of relating Jewish religious data to the broader patterns discerned in other religious materials. Goodenough was, and Scholem is, primarily a historian of religion, secondarily a historian of Judaism—though this ordering of interests affected not so much the result as the attitude, motivation, and focus of concern. Yet, although Goodenough and Scholem have contributed much, we are only just beginning to appreciate the potential uses to be made of Jewish data. When one considers, for example, that there is still no study of phenomenology of the rabbi, in his inseparable political, cultural, and religious roles, one wonders how the nature of religious leadership can as yet be fully and properly comprehended. The rabbi, no less than the shaman, ought to provide basic information about the nature of the religious virtuoso and what he represents to the minds of his followers.

More broadly, however, one may suppose that Judaism, which seems so remote and intellectual in its central value structure, is among the religions which have in past times laid the greatest stress upon the man-God in various forms, not only rabbinical but also Messianic and, certainly within Hassidism, mediatorial. In its struggle against modern Christianity, modern Judaism has insisted that Jesus "could not possibly have been accepted by normative Jews as the Messiah" because the Jews could not have believed in a man-God or in a spiritual Savior who was not a politician or a general. That denial, if correct, required the exclusion of Hassidism, only two generations behind the German Jewish scholars, of Frankism, three generations, and of Sabbateanism, four generations earlier. But it also excluded the possibility of comprehending the figure of the Talmudic rabbi himself.

A second interesting theme is surely the transmutation of religion with the desuetude of the ancient ways of perceiving reality. Descriptions of Archaic or so-called primitive religions normally omit reference to modern or contemporary religious phenomena except among still archaic peoples. But the great question in the history (not merely philosophy) of religion must be: What happens when archaic reality comes to an end and modernism begins? It is one thing to regret, condemn, look back fondly or sadly. It is quite another simply to ignore the fact that something called, and calling itself, *religion* has persisted into modern times in various ways and forms and therefore requires study. I can think of no more interesting example of a religion in the throes of transmutation into the modern idiom, better documented, with more variations in time and space and subtleties of definition, than the history of modern Judaism.[7] I have mentioned only two issues within the history of religions which cannot, I think, be satisfactorily discussed without considerable attention to the history of Judaism. There are many others.

It is therefore the history of *Judaism* which finds a most natural accommodation within the university curriculum. As a set of structures to be analyzed, and not as a set of theological (or other) propositions to be evaluated, Judaism becomes interesting in that setting. It is self-evident that the same principle holds for all religions, including Christianity. In particular, like the theologies of other traditions,

[7] I have tried to present one useful structure of interpretation of the history of modern Judaism in "From Theology to Ideology: The Transmutations of Judaism in Modern Times," in *Churches and States*, ed. K. H. Silvert, (New York: American Universities Field Staff, 1967), 13-48.

the study of Jewish theology, *except* when examined from a comparative or morphological perspective by historians of religion, and *not* as a self-validating system, has no place in the university curriculum. It is where Judaism, among other religious traditions, provides evidence of a particularity in which broader categories or issues may be exemplified, or find expression, that Judaism becomes relevant to the curriculum of the university. I think it likely that Judaism will make its contribution toward the definition of larger structures of analysis. Eliade's work on archaic religions, Hinduism, and Christianity quite naturally provided him with particular data, out of which generalities or categories of analysis emerged. Given somewhat different data—a religion mostly without cathedral or temple for thousands of years, for example—he might well have raised different issues to begin with. Judaism focuses, in the terms of analysis proposed by Professor Jonathan Z. Smith, upon the following structures: holy people, the structure of election; Holy Land, the structure of sacred space, Zion and exile, Temple and synagogue; holy days, the structure of sacred time, the Sabbath, the feasts, the daily service; holy rites, structures of initiation; holy law and holy book, the cosmic law, personal piety, the law and interpretation; holy men, rabbi and student, the philosopher, the magician, the mystic, the Messiah, and the Hasid. These "structures" illustrate the viability of Eliade's basic scheme of analysis, but they also suggest ways in which particular Jewish data might modulate those categories.

I look forward, too, to the revivification of comparative studies of religions. In this the history of Judaism will both benefit and contribute. For example, taken in isolation, the rabbinical academy may be studied from antiquity to the present day, but without a significant awareness of what it really was, or what gave it its particular shape and method at a given time or place. When, however, one asks how the rabbinical school compared to the Hellenistic academy or to the Christian monastery, how it functioned in society and in the faith, as contrasted with the equivalent structures in Manichaeism, Buddhism, or Islam, much new insight may result. And it was the rabbinical academy which was the apparently unique leadership-training institution of Judaism. Similarly, the comparison of the rabbi and the mandarin has yet to be undertaken. How much other central institutions, structures of belief or ritual or myth, and the like may be illumined by contrast or comparison with those of other religious traditions, we may only surmise. So while the history of Judaism has much to contribute to the history of religions, the issues of the wider field may raise wholly new questions, and provide quite novel perspectives, for the narrower one. Indeed, the richness of Scholem's perspectives derives in the end, not from his grand study of Kabbalah, the science of which he himself founded, but rather from his ability to ask broader questions concerning the structure of Kabbalistic experience and thought.

We may turn, finally, to some issues confronting any aspect of the history of religions. First, what is to be the relationship between the historian of Judaism and the historian of religions? It is not unreasonable to expect the former to become familiar with the methods, issues, and ideas of the field as a whole and to see his task as part of a larger undertaking. But the other side of the coin is this: can a historian of religions make use of the history of Judaism without first becoming a specialist in Judaism? It is a painful and difficult question, for if, as I suggested above, Jewish studies must now depend to a significant extent upon the resources of Jewish, and not university, curricula, then how can a non-Jew hope to make a contribution to the history of Judaism or, through the history of Judaism, to the history of religions? On the one hand, it is difficult to conceive that anyone could acquire a genuine mastery of Judaism without a close study of the texts which for the most part preserve it. Judaism has few monuments outside of books, and the "native speakers" of the tradition, those who embody one or another aspect of the tradition in their own lives, are with few exceptions either not interested in addressing themselves to those outside the limited community of the faithful or incapable of doing so. Hence texts, almost alone, constitute the available evidence. To read them, one must know Hebrew and know it well. And to read them well, one must have undergone a long apprenticeship in mastering texts which represent a fundamentally *oral* tradition that has been transcribed. Talmudic studies in particular cannot be mastered without a teacher or, better, several teachers in both the old and modern manners.

Can Judaism be studied by one who has no personal relationship to it? I think so. Many useful inquiries can be made by the historian of religions. First, since most of the major rabbinic texts of classical times exist in good English translations, the scholar who comes with particular issues or questions in mind may well locate what he feels is relevant and proceed to restudy the classical text in the original. Second, and more important, the historian of religions should be able to depend upon the results of the scholarship of others—philologists, text critics, commentators, historians, historians of law, art, music, and theology, sociologists, and other scientists—and not have to repeat the processes which originally yielded their results. In every field of intellectual endeavor one customarily depends in some measure upon others, either predecessors or colleagues in cognate fields. Jewish learning does not present an arcane and remote exception. The contrary view, that the true scholar is only one who has gone through the traditional processes of learning in the traditional modes and then rejected them for modern scholarship, predominates in many circles of Jewish scholarship. It reveals the latent mandarinism of Jewish learning (itself a datum for the history of religions). The mastery of specific texts, mastered in ancient ways, through the old commentaries upon the old questions, constitute the primary qualification for scholarship. What is important is not what one can do with what one knows, but what one has "been through," as if exposure to the texts magically transformed and therefore qualified the student.

Modern scholarship adds a second qualification, namely, disenchantment with the old methods after such exposure to them. It is no less a magical view of learning, but one which elevates to a norm the experience of alienation.

The question of studying a religion not one's own generally depends upon the supposition that one's own religion plays a central part in one's capacity to comprehend some other. I do not see this as a serious classroom problem at the outset. Professor Jonathan Smith's syllabus opens with the words: "In this course, we will survey some of the basic religious structures of Judaism, using categories derived from the discipline of the History of Religions. Your task will be to try to interpret a representative sample of Jewish religious expressions—not in order to judge them as 'true' or 'false,' or to ask questions as to their contemporary or personal 'relevance'—but rather to strive to understand what they have meant and mean to a group who have expressed themselves, and the meaning of their existence, who have constructed and interpreted their world and their history through these religious myths, symbols, and rituals." In my view, that sentence partially lays to rest the ghost of "personal involvement." (But see below.)

This is not to say that the study of the history of Judaism is not likely to raise certain broader questions about the nature of religion or the "science" of religion. After the tasks of description, interpretation, and understanding have been undertaken, the further responsibility of reconstituting the data into the raw material for philosophy of religion has yet to be carried out. But I do not see how that work can be done in the narrow framework of the history of Judaism, as it is studied in the university classroom. Rather, it is to be done in two ways and for two different purposes: first, in the Jewish seminary, for theological purposes; and, second, in the philosophy of religion, for phenomenological purposes.

One can hardly overestimate, moreover, the importance *for* Jewish learning of the study of the history of Judaism within the context of the history of religions. Ashby quotes Kitagawa as follows:

> The expert in one religion must also be cognizant of the nature, history, and expressions of religion beyond the one religion he seeks to understand. Adequate understanding of one religion is seldom, if ever, achieved by knowledge about that religion only. The historian of religions needs to possess wide knowledge of his subject in its universal expressions if he is to fathom one religion in depth.[8]

So far, with the major exceptions of Scholem and Goodenough, historians of Judaism have not taken comparative approaches very seriously. It is true that they have conjectured about "influences" of one thing upon something else—for example, Iranian influences upon Qumran; but only rarely have they transcended such narrow, positivistic questions.

Most scholars of Jewish subjects would, moreover, accept Kitagawa's statement if it were phrased in any terms other than religion. It is recognized that one must have command of several languages, literatures, histories, and cultures in order to study various aspects of the Jews or Judaica. Jewish scholarship was born in the age of positivism, however, and has remained ever since the last refuge of fundamentalist, naive, positivistic thinking. It has, therefore, not even bothered to apply its reductionist presuppositions to Judaism as a religion but, instead, has by and large ignored it from the start. So very little effort is devoted to the study of the history of Judaism that it is not even included in the curriculum of the Jewish Theological Seminary or in the programs of most other institutions of Jewish learning. If it were possible, some scholars of Judaica would deny that Judaism has existed as a religion in any sense, regarding it only as a law, a culture or "civilization," a nation (people), or something—anything—other than a "religion,"

[8] "The History of Religions," 44.

or religious tradition. Others will go so far as to deny that Judaism, if it is a religion, has had any theologies. An examination of the pages of Jewish scholarly journals will uncover remarkably few articles about Jewish religion, though there are a great many which contribute in some way to the study of Jewish religion. But those contributions take the form of intellectual or social history, philology, sociology, and textual criticism. The central contribution to the study of Judaism now emerging in the universities will be a methodology appropriate to the study of the history of Judaism joined with concern for that study.

We therefore have a provisional task at hand: to learn what are appropriate issues and methods and to bring these issues and methods to bear upon a rich and practically untouched, almost unknown religion. Since that religion has entered a new age in its history, with the general decay of pre-modern forms in the West, it should be clear that few Jews are in the situation of the Buddhist who comes to the West to study Buddhism. Similarly, since the effort to convert the Jews seems finally to be concluded, except as an eschatological hope to be left for the eschaton, Christians normally do not come to the study of Judaism in order to master the information necessary to undertake a mission to the Jews. Normally atheists are less bothered by the absurdities of Judaism than by those of Christianity, which impinge more readily upon their consciousness. One's personal emotional condition can play no role of consequence in the study of a religion which few in the West have held in its classical forms for at least a century. Accordingly, whatever engagement of feeling we find may be of two kinds. First, it may be similar to the engagement of the classicist or the antiquarian, namely, a fondness for the dead past and its glories. Since it is dead, one may speak of its glories. So far as it is alive—and in its many modulations Judaism is very much alive—one cannot yet know what these glories may be, or what they are not. But the history of Judaism extends backward in time far, far beyond the nineteenth century, to at least the destruction of the first Temple, and I see sufficient grounds for many far-reaching investigations long before "feelings" and "involvements" pose much difficulty. Since Eliade refers to problems of aesthetics, it may be useful to draw an analogy from the study of the history of art. One may penetrate very deeply, I think, into the art of Rembrandt without for a single minute intending to paint in his fashion. One may similarly penetrate deeply into the understanding of Jewish religion on its own plane of reference, or on the plane of reference of religion as a phenomenon in human history, without intending to adopt that religion or any other. The "modernization" of Judaism, therefore, is what may make possible the study of its history.

Nonetheless, I think I err on the side of optimism. There is a second form of engagement of feeling not to be ignored or denied. The very involvement of Jewish scholars in the study of Judaism is bound to operate as a personal factor. The influence of Yehezkel Kaufman's *History of the Religion of Israel* upon biblical scholars of Conservative Jewish origin cannot be explained entirely in terms of the persuasiveness of Kaufman's case, if only because he has made very little headway elsewhere. Kaufman supplies, rather, a peculiarly satisfying way for biblical scholarship in a supposedly modern form to coexist with a very traditional, indeed primitive, formulation of Jewish theology, especially for people who want to continue to study the Bible as revelation. Having abandoned the classical faith in the Pentateuch as revealed by God to Moses on Mt. Sinai, the Conservative Jewish scholar finds comfort in Kaufman's arguments leading to much the same faith, but on a much more positivistic basis, in the "Mosaic revolution" of monotheism within Israelite culture. It would, moreover, be a misunderstanding of the modernization of Judaism to suppose that modern Jews see themselves as discontinuous with the past. On the contrary, the very stuff of their modernism is the effort to restructure or re-form inherited, archaic beliefs, attitudes, and patterns. Whether this is quite self-consciously undertaken, as in Reform and Conservative

Judaism, or quite unself-conscious to begin with, as among so-called Orthodox and secular Jews, is not at issue here. What is important is that the modern proceeds from the archaic, and their relationships are subtle and difficult to comprehend. Hence the Jewish scholar of Judaism, however secular or objective he may think himself, must still conscientiously attempt to meet Kitagawa's conditions, just as other historians of religion must, and for much the same reason: "First is a sympathetic understanding of religions other than one's own; second is an attitude of self-criticism, or even skepticism, about one's own religious background. And third is the 'scientific' temper."[9] In the beginning the Jewish historian of Judaism must see both himself and his enterprise as themselves constituting data in the modern history of Judaism. So, as elsewhere, the very act of scholarship affects what is under study.

Conclusion

The broad range of Jewish studies may contribute to the university curriculum at many points, but the particular point at which a specialist in Jewish studies most nearly approximates the university's needs is in the field of the history of Judaism. This is not to suggest that specialists in the Hebrew language and the study of Hebrew literature do not belong in departments of Near Eastern languages and literatures, for they do, even though before recent times Hebrew literature was hardly a Near Eastern creation at any single, significant stage in its history after the tenth century. Specialists in the sociology of the Jewish community may well make a noteworthy contribution to the social sciences. Specialists in a given period and locale of Jewish history obviously have their appropriate place in a history department, so long as they are adequately trained to make a contribution to the broader interests of that department. Specialists in medieval Jewish philosophy or in

[9] "The History of Religions in America," in *The History of Religions: Essays in Methodology*, ed. Mircea Eliade and Joseph M. Kitagawa (Chicago: University of Chicago Press, 1959), 1-30. Quotation is on 15.

modern Jewish "thought" may join in the discussions of the history of philosophy, or even in modern philosophical discourse pursued in old-fashioned ways (where these still persist). But so far as Jewish studies cover an *area* by means of many *disciplines*, there can be no place for a department of Jewish studies, though a center involving disciplinary specialists of many kinds obviously would serve a useful purpose. And so far as a university offers a strong program in the study of religions, it is in *that* program that its primary appointment in Jewish studies should quite naturally find its place, but not to the exclusion of an appointment in Hebrew language and literature. Given the predominant content of those studies, I think this is the only appropriate way of handling the matter.

There is one final point to be made: the development of Jewish studies in universities must not be shaped to meet the parochial interests of the Jewish community, the synagogue, or Judaism. Jewish community groups in recent times have discovered that the future of the community is being decided upon the campus. They have therefore chosen to strengthen programs aimed at influencing the Jewish college student to come to an affirmative decision upon basic issues of Jewish identity and commitment. As chaplaincy, or Hillel programs, such efforts are wholly unobjectionable. It is, however, quite natural for Jewish community groups to look upon professors in the field of Jewish learning in general, and of the history of Judaism in particular, as allies in the "struggle." They are widely expected to continue in the classroom the advocacy of Judaism which begins in the synagogue schools and continues in the pulpit. Secular Jewish organizations, interested in recruiting future leaders for their fund-raising and other programs, similarly turn to the campus and therefore to the professor of Jewish studies, particularly when he is a Jew to begin with, for support. Jewish studies certainly belong in parochial settings as well as in universities. When in universities, however, neither such studies nor those responsible for pursuing them must be used for propagandistic purposes of any kind. It is not the duty of the professor of the history of Judaism, or of Hebrew, to interest himself in the state of the souls of his students, whether Jewish or gentile. It will render his true task impossible if he does so, except insofar as he sees himself, and his students, as themselves constituting data for the study of the history of Judaism. It is certainly not the task of any professor to serve other than university commitments. It may, therefore, be wise for universities to avoid dependence upon Jewish community funds in the creation and maintenance of programs in the field of Jewish learning. I am not suggesting that the Jewish community and synagogue are more dangerous as a pressure group than any other, but only that they are no less so. In any event, rabbis and others who have achieved considerable mastery of Jewish traditional learning are not on that account appropriate candidates for full or, more especially, part-time university posts, any more than are local priests or ministers. Nothing will so endanger the healthy development of Jewish learning in its various modes within the university as the exploitation of that development for other than strictly and narrowly defined university purposes.

Judaic studies, that is, the study of the history of Judaism, and Hebrew studies, the study of Hebrew language and literature, together belong within the university curriculum of the humanities, the latter to serve the interests not only of linguists or Semitists but also of students of religion. If, as G. E. von Grunebaum said, "A humanistic education will essay to evoke the widest possible range of responses to the stimuli of civilization,"[10] then within it the history of Judaism provides a number of important perspectives. It is the account of the development of a world religion from almost the very beginnings of human history up to the present day. Its history includes the most varied forms

[10] G. E. von Grunebaum, "Islam in a Humanistic Education," in *The Traditional Near East*, ed. J. Stewart-Robinson (Englewood Cliffs, N.J.: Prentice-Hall, 1966), 36-68 (reprinted from *The Journal of General Education* IV [1949], 12-31). Quotation is on 36.

and expressions of that world religion, its organization into several sorts of political systems, its narrowing into essentially salvific forms, its broadening into a whole civilization (in Central and Eastern Europe), and then its renewed development in a series of complex and subtle responses to the modern situation. In the development of Judaism, foreign cultural traditions were absorbed, modified, eliminated, illustrating the processes of cultural interaction and transformation.[11] Finally, the history of Judaism contains a number of unifying elements, shared by other Western religions yet in some ways quite unique. Judaism is, as von Grunebaum said of Islam, "both close enough to the Western view of the world to be intellectually and emotionally understandable and sufficiently far removed from it to deepen, by contrast, the self-interpretation of the West."[12]

[11] Paraphrase of von Grunebaum, *ibid.*, 37.
[12] *Ibid.*

The Character and Contribution of the Sociology of Religion

PAUL M. HARRISON

DURING THE last two decades, eight major articles have been written in this country on various aspects of the history, theory, and method of the sociology of religion. In order of publication, the authors were Milton Yinger, Talcott Parsons, Charles Glock, Gerhard Lenski, Yoshio Fukuyama, Louis Schneider, Harvey Cox, and David Moberg.[1] Parsons' essay was a contribution to the Hazen Foundation series on *Religious Perspectives of College Teaching*.[2] In addition to sociology, the series included essays on history, English literature, economics, philosophy, classics, music, anthropology, experimental psychology, physical science, biology, and political science.

The extent of the disciplinary coverage of the series indicates that those scholars of religion fully respected the character of their subject. Religion is a complex, multifaceted, universal, human-social phenomenon. It is more complex than our language, more multifaceted than our

[1] J. Milton Yinger, "Present Status of the Sociology of Religion," *The Journal of Religion* xxx/3 (July 1951); Talcott Parsons, *Religious Perspectives of College Teaching in Sociology and Social Psychology*, (New Haven: Edward W. Hazen Foundation, 1952); Charles Y. Glock, "The Sociology of Religion," in *Sociology Today: Problems and Prospects*, ed. Robert K. Merton, Leonard Broom, and Leonard S. Cottrell, Jr. (New York: Basic Books, 1959); Gerhard Lenski, "The Sociology of Religion in the United States: A Review of Theoretically Oriented Research," *Social Compass* IX/4 (1962); Yoshio Fukuyama, "The Uses of Sociology: By Religious Bodies," *Journal for the Scientific Study of Religion* II/2 (Spring 1963); Louis Schneider, "Problems in the Sociology of Religion," in *Handbook of Modern Sociology*, ed. Robert E. L. Faris (Chicago: Rand McNally, 1964); Harvey Cox, "Sociology of Religion in a Post-Religious Era," *The Christian Scholar* XLVIII/1 (Spring 1965); David O. Moberg, "Some Trends in the Sociology of Religion in the U.S.A.," *Social Compass* XIII/3 (1966).

[2] Parsons, *Religious Perspectives of College Teaching in Sociology and Social Psychology*.

politics and economics, more universal than our own culture, more human than our social scientists sometimes allow, and more social than our humanists often admit. It exceeds the grasp of its most honored students and easily eludes the comprehension of those who persistently observe that "organized religion" is paltry and corrupt when compared with the glory of their own ideal religious expressions.

Therefore, religion deserves more comprehensive treatment than is usually given it by the liberal humanists, by the scientists of the social division, or by the seminary divines. Perhaps Roy Battenhouse was seeking to express this point when he said "that religion should be considered a *field* of study—not precisely a department, on the one hand, not merely an interdisciplinary concern on the other hand." In addition to what he called "the basic faith" (which in itself is a topic of endless complexity), the study of religion involves the customs of historical periods, the secular and canon laws, the lay and priestly institutions, religion's humanitarian projects, the parochial service institutions and mission societies, and religious architecture and art, including painting, sculpture, drama, and dance. Each of these sacred expressions possesses its own vast history.[3]

If religion is too complex to entrust to a single discipline or even a core of disciplines, it is probably too intricate to remain the exclusive possession of a single type of educational institution, be it a church, a seminary, a denominational college, or a university. Church-school teachers, seminary theologians, and university professors may operate from different perspectives and possess different intentions, but all share an inescapable inclination to reduce religion to terms they can comprehend, control, and define. The inclination is inescapable because it is a necessary preliminary to the establishment of meaningful discourse between the scholar and his colleagues and students.

[3] Roy W. Battenhouse, "A Strategy and Some Tactics for Teaching in Religion," in *Religious Studies in Public Universities*, ed. Milton D. McLean (Carbondale, Ill.: Southern Illinois University Press, 1967), 29f.

Sociology of religion is one of the major disciplines that has contributed to our understanding of religious behavior. It has much in common with several of the disciplinary approaches we have mentioned. Demerath and Hammond, who have published the most recent volume in the field, say that "the sociological analysis of religion has four distinctive characteristics worth identifying here": its concepts have empirical referents; it radically abstracts from the particular to the general; it focuses on socially structured or group behavior, rather than on individuals as psychology of religion does; and it seeks to relate religion to other aspects of social experience.[4] It would be more correct to say that the discipline is distinctive in utilizing all four characteristics than to speak of the characteristics themselves as distinctive, since scholars in other disciplines, most notably historians, have also applied these methods in their studies of religion. The primary contribution of the sociology of religion, however, is probably achieved when the focus is on structured religious activity and the relationship it has to other aspects of social life.

I shall not attempt to defend the sociology of religion against the accusations of its cultured despisers. Rather, I shall discuss some of the problems that confront it in the present religious situation. There is a series of dilemmas arising from the split that sociology of religion has undergone as a result of having been torn between communities of scholars, one group situated primarily in the universities and conceiving the discipline in "scientific" terms, the other group located in the seminaries and receiving its orientation from Christian theology. Another serious division among sociologists, most recently observed by Moberg in his essay, is represented in the contrast between European and American schools. The European philosophical sociologists had an important influence on Harvey Cox at the time he wrote his article severely criticizing the American

[4] N. J. Demerath III and Philip E. Hammond, *Religion in Social Context: Tradition and Transition* (New York: Random House, 1969), 4f.

school. This factor would be less critical if only journeymen sociologists were affected by it. But professors of religion in general and theologians in particular have been becoming increasingly interested in sociological work, and for various reasons they are likely to be most deeply influenced by the European and the American seminary sociologists, both of whom have been less empirically and more ideologically oriented than their American university counterparts. Many of the "theological sociologists," for example, are powerfully moved by the new forms of theology that appear, it seems, about every five years. I shall attempt to demonstrate that this division not only obscures valid sociological issues but distorts sociological theory and method in such a way that sociology of religion often becomes a polemical device rather than a scholarly endeavor.

Milton Yinger assessed the status of sociology of religion in 1951.[5] He noted that, "after the highly auspicious beginnings in the work of such men as Robertson Smith, Max Weber, Emile Durkheim, Georg Simmel, Ernst Troeltsch, and many others, it has . . . failed to move very far in the direction of greater theoretical adequacy."[6] By 1962 Yinger had changed his view. Sociological theories of religion, he thought, were still in need of development, but some efforts were being made again in both Europe and America, so that sociologists no longer regarded the study of religion as a bizarre specialty. "To study the sociology of religion is to work with most of the major areas of current interest in the analysis of society and culture," he said. "Without careful attention to religious groups and behavior, one leaves serious gaps and weaknesses in his study of social stratification, social change, intergroup relations, political sociology, bureaucracy, community studies, social consensus and dissensus, the sociology of conflict, and the developmental processes in newly formed nations. . . ."[7]

[5] Yinger, "Present Status of the Sociology of Religion."
[6] *Ibid.*, 194.
[7] J. Milton Yinger, *Sociology Looks at Religion* (New York: Collier-Macmillan, 1963), 7f.

It will help us understand some of the present problems of sociology of religion if we develop a historical perspective. The articles by Fukuyama and Lenski both provide a survey of what has occurred since the Civil War.[8] Fukuyama observes that in the period from 1865 to 1915 the first courses in sociology were taught by ministers who drew no clear lines between descriptive and normative work, who divided their time more or less equally between sociological observation and preaching the social gospel or teaching social ethics. The second period from 1915 to 1945 witnessed a slackening of interest in the study of religion on the part of the university sociologists, but it was then that the seminary sociologists, especially at Chicago and Yale, made their significant contribution. Research methods became increasingly sophisticated, and the demands on the resources of time and money increasingly heavy. The Institute of Social and Religious Research was established in 1921. Financed by John D. Rockefeller, Jr., it was to engage in "unbiased studies in the realm of religion and religious organizations." It published over ninety volumes during its thirteen-year history and supported many important projects, such as the work of the Lynds in Middletown.[9]

In this period the church became a consumer as well as a producer of sociological knowledge. But then, as now, the churches had great difficulty taking seriously the findings of the research for which they had contracted. It was this circumstance, it is said, that led Rockefeller to withdraw his financial support from the Institute.[10] The most prominent men on the Institute's staff were H. Paul Douglass

[8] Fukuyama, "The Uses of Sociology: By Religious Bodies," 195-203. In his article on sociology of religion in the United States, Gerhard Lenski (see note 1) conceives the development of the field in almost precisely the way envisaged by Fukuyama. According to Lenski, the first period from 1865 to 1915 was the time of "grand theorizing" when Spencer and Ward engaged in their speculations. The second period from 1915 to 1945 was characterized by empirical and scientific endeavors in which people like the Lynds and W. Lloyd Warner set the pace. From 1945 to 1965 Lenski, like Yinger, sees an effort under way to synthesize theory and research.

[9] *Ibid.*, 197. [10] *Ibid.*, 198.

and Edmund de S. Brunner, who published *The Protestant Church as a Social Institution* in 1935. Both men were deeply disappointed at the reaction of the churches. Committed to the validity and value of studying the church as an institution by methods used for studying other kinds of institutions, Arthur E. Holt later observed that "those who held the church to be a supermundane entity were shocked that such a holy thing could be examined and compared with other institutions and social systems. . . . Others, who to a greater or less degree admitted the mundane aspects of the church as a divine institution, were extremely sensitive that the Institute studies might exhibit the shortcomings of the church and its professional leaders in such a way as to harm the pursuit of its spiritual mission."[11]

By 1945 the breach was virtually complete between university-based sociology and the study of religion in the church-related schools and seminaries. University sociologists had by that time become infamous among the theologians and ecclesiastical sociologists for being dominated by the philosophies of positivism, reductionism, and determinism.[12] Therefore, in marked contrast to the intimate alliance between sociology and the church and seminary that was typical of the first era, "today, the institutionalized religious researcher is unlikely to have specialized academically in sociology at the graduate level. With few exceptions, he is more likely to have majored in 'social ethics' at the seminary or to have taken a few courses in sociological methods along with his theological education."[13] As interest progressed in the sociology of religion in the universities, it declined in the seminaries. Some evidence of this trend is found in the bibliographical notes at the end of Yinger's chapters in the 1965 edition of *Sociology Looks at Religion*.[14] There he mentions more than sixty sociolo-

[11] Quoted by Fukuyama, *ibid.*, 198. Editorial in *The Christian Century* LI, May 2, 1934, 587, and May 9, 1934, 623.

[12] William Kolb, "Images of Man and the Sociology of Religion," *Journal for the Scientific Study of Religion* I/1 (Oct. 1961).

[13] Fukuyama "The Uses of Sociology: By Religious Bodies," 200.

[14] See note 7.

gists, only six of whom teach in seminaries. It is clear from this and many other indicators that the traditional scholars of religion, most of whom have been educated in parochial institutions, have not been avid consumers of sociological information and theories about religion.

In the move from the seminary to the university, sociology of religion did not locate in departments of religion. Indeed, there are fewer sociologists of religion teaching in departments of religion than there are in the seminaries. The institutional shift of the field has been rather from the theological schools to the social science division of the universities. Today there are no more than three or four departments of religion in the United States that possess the services of a competent sociologist. One reason is the difficulty of attracting graduate students into a department that has a single sociologist. Another is the problem involved in developing interdepartmental programs in fields each of which requires a minimum of three-years' residence for a doctorate. James Gustafson recently expressed the opinion that the sociological study of religion belongs in both the sociology department and the religious studies department because "the gap between such departments can be very large," especially when they are affiliated with different colleges or divisions of the university.[15] But if this view is shared by very many who teach in the field of religion, it is a matter of low priority.

In the list of articles mentioned above, there are three types. Theoretical essays were written by Parsons, O'Dea, and Yinger, each of them describing religious belief and behavior in terms of structural-functional theory. Functionalism seeks to explain the persistence of religion, or any other uniform social behavior, in relation to its utility for society, that is, by reference to its fulfillment of essential human social needs. It is one of the fundamental purposes

[15] James M. Gustafson, "Comments," on Thomas F. O'Dea, "Sociology and the Study of Religion," *A Report on an Invitational Conference on the Study of Religion in the State University* (New Haven: The Society for Religion in Higher Education, 1965), 20.

of sociology to develop theories that suggest why society works in the way that it does. Such theories have been advanced by Parsons, Robert Merton, Marion Levy, and many others, on the basis of "functional-structural requisites." Despite the criticism that has been forthcoming in recent decades, functional theory has proved to be a remarkably flexible sociological instrument, perhaps primarily because it can be adapted to a vast array of philosophical theories and research methodologies. It does not necessarily preclude the possibility of alternative explanations of religious reality. Religion, therefore, may arise to fulfill basic social needs, even though its ultimate impulse and source may be transcendent.

It is possible for an empirical sociologist to operate on the pragmatic level without explicit reference to functional theory, or to any other theory. A considerable amount of American sociology is of this kind; it describes what people do without making any effort to explain why they do it, which is what forces the theoretical questions. The second type of article on the sociology of religion fits into this category. Emphasis there is upon what has been done in the past, what is being done in the present, and what must be done in the future to fill in gaps in our knowledge at both the theoretical and research levels. This type is represented by the essays of Glock, Fukuyama, Schneider, Lenski, and Moberg.

The third type of article was written by Harvey Cox. It stands alone, as does Cox himself in this instance, since he is the only author on our list who is teaching in a seminary. He argues that sociologists of religion in America are doing nothing of any real importance and that the future will be gloomy if his suggestions are not followed.

But before I critically analyze his remarks, I should like to review the contribution of Charles Y. Glock, a more orthodox member of the sociological fraternity. The focus of his research for the past fifteen years has been religion and religious institutions. He is one of the prominent figures among the university sociologists who have led the way to a renewal of interest in the study of religion. He wrote his article in 1959, stating that he hoped "to encourage the study of religion and religious institutions in contemporary Western society through the application of modern empirical research wherever possible."[16]

Glock begins his essay by mentioning the contribution made by functional theory to the understanding of religion and by quoting Kingsley Davis at length. Generally speaking, he points out, religion sustains devotion to communal goals and limits the exercise of private interests. Specifically, this effect is achieved in four ways: religion justifies the primary ends and values of the society; it provides ritualistic means for renewal of commitments to the community; it supplies a concrete set of symbols as a communal rallying point; and it serves as a vehicle for the application of reward and punishment, that is, social control. Then offering some criticism of functional theories of religion, Glock contends that they do not account fully for the place of religion in modern society and that they have not been sufficiently elaborated to take care of this matter. Nor, he adds, do they provide an adequate theoretical basis for identifying functional alternatives to religion and for showing how the fundamental socio-psychological needs that are fulfilled by religion in accord with functional theory can be fulfilled by other social means. Functional theorists have been content to make this point without devising procedures for describing and explaining the phenomenon.

In the next section of his article Glock cites the research that has been done on religious organization. He commends the contribution of O'Dea on the Mormons[17] and Sklare's work on the Jews.[18] He indicates a need for inquiry into the relationship between religion and bureaucratic organization, and he also recommends that an analysis of decision- and policy-making procedures within the churches

[16] Glock, "The Sociology of Religion," 153-177.

[17] Thomas F. O'Dea, *The Mormons* (Chicago: University of Chicago Press, 1957).

[18] Marshall Sklare, *Conservative Judaism* (Glencoe, Ill.: The Free Press, 1955).

and their relation to polity and theology be undertaken. By the time Glock's article was published, religious bureaucracy had already been made the subject of several studies, which suggested that even the most cherished and sacred theological beliefs and moral commitments could be sabotaged by expediency and transformed by the pressures of organizational and secular necessity.[19] Sociologists demonstrated greater interest in this sort of minutia than churchmen or theologians.

The following section of Glock's article provides another view of the kind of contribution that sociology makes to the study of religion. Referring to the work already carried out by Weber and others on the problems of religious leadership and authority, Glock observes that there is still more to be done in analyzing the character of the ministry and the social and religious factors involved in defining the profession. He asserts that we lack a conceptual framework for studying any of the professions, and he also cites a need for analysis of the value conflicts that exist between the seminary and the parish. Next he discusses "the individual and religion," pointing out that sociology up to that time has had to get along with instruments that permitted only the crudest measures of the nature and extent of religious commitment and participation. (His own subsequent work in this field and the research of Fukuyama and others have broken through persistent barriers to our understanding of the character and depth of religious affiliation.[20]) Finally, Glock calls for further investigation of the relation between religion and the specific social spheres of politics, economics, the family, education, social welfare, law, and medicine.

Although many useful studies in this field have been made

[19] Paul M. Harrison, *Authority and Power in the Free Church Tradition* (Princeton: Princeton University Press, 1959).

[20] Charles Y. Glock and Rodney Stark, *Religion and Society in Tension* (Chicago: Rand McNally, 1965), esp. Chap. 2; Yoshio Fukuyama, "The Major Dimensions of Church Membership," *Review of Religious Research*, Spring 1961; N. J. Demerath III, *Social Class in American Protestantism* (Chicago: Rand McNally, 1965).

since that article was published (including contributions by Bellah, Berger, Demerath, Fichter, Fukuyama, Hadden, Hammond, Lenski, Luckmann, O'Dea, Schneider, Underwood, and Winter), one would never suspect that such studies exist from reading the critical article written in 1965 by Harvey Cox, entitled "Sociology of Religion in a Post-Religious Era." Cox's basic assumption is that what theologians are doing should have a prescriptive effect on what sociologists of religion do. This assumption is debatable, since at least one task of social scientists is to discover the social sources of religious ideas and behavior, including the ideas of theologians.

Cox opens the article by asking how sociologists of religion should interpret such ideas as "the non-religious gospel," the "post-religious era," and "the secular gospel." This is a fair question, and Cox offers some hypothetical answers. First, he suggests, sociologists of religion could simply "close the store" on the assumption that this is really an age beyond religion because the theologians have said so. Cox recognizes the inadequacy of this notion. Second, the new theology could be interpreted as one more effort by theologians "to slip away into some kind of magical inaccessibility." Third, sociologists could dismiss these ideas as attempts by the theologians to prove the superiority of Christianity over other religions.

Cox rejects all of these alternatives and issues a warning to the sociologists that "to dismiss the entire post-religious era thesis and the non-religious interpretation discussion as timidity, arrogance, or charlatanry would be a serious mistake."[21] To my knowledge, however, no sociologist has proposed that emotions like timidity and arrogance could be used as categories of sufficient explanatory power to illuminate a social movement as complex as the new theology. Cox must know that those who most often accuse the radical theologians of engaging in a trivial charade are their own offended theological brothers, not the sociologists. It is a theologian who commented that "the current hulla-

[21] Cox, "Sociology of Religion in a Post-Religious Era," 10.

baloo about the death of God is, of course, largely an affair of religious journalism. . . . Our secular city boys, with their demands for the desacralization of culture . . . are actually lapsed animists who want to save us from the *false* spirituality from which they have just been rescued." Albert Outler, who wrote those words, describes an animist as one who "misconceives the spiritual as something spooky and unnatural and so misconstrues the 'supernatural' as the antithesis to nature."[22]

That is a nice blend of theological interpretation and anthropological theory, but these remarks would do Harvey Cox a disservice if they were to be construed as directly applicable to every aspect of his work, because he is better at sociology of religion than his article on that subject permits him to appear. In the same collection of essays to which Outler contributed, Cox offered a competent sociological interpretation of the death-of-God phenomenon, maintaining, in accord with the theories of the sociology of knowledge, that the death of God "represents a crisis in our language and symbol structure. . . ." It "can occur only where the controlling symbols of the culture have been more or less uncritically fused with the transcendent God. When a civilization collapses and its gods topple, theological speculation can move either toward a God whose being lies beyond culture (Augustine, Barth), toward some form of millenarianism or toward a religious crisis that takes the form of 'Death of God'."[23] This is a sophisticated fusion of theological interpretation and sociological theory in which Cox cryptically developed an analysis of what may appropriately be called the *social sources of the death of God.*

Cox, however, is not interested in pursuing the pedestrian paths of the sociological analysis of formal religion. His more ambitious goal is to redefine the nature of the disci-

[22] Albert C. Outler, "Veni, Creator Spiritus: The Doctrine of the Holy Spirit," in *New Theology No. 4*, ed. Martin E. Martin and Dean G. Peerman (New York: Macmillan, 1967), 201, 207.

[23] Harvey Cox, "The Death of God and the Future of Theology," *ibid.*, 245, 246.

pline. "What is needed," he writes, "is a recasting of the theory, objectives and scope of what once was called sociology of religion so that the renovated discipline, whatever it may be called, can address itself to the cultural reality of the 20th century."[24] In the future, "sociology of religion must turn from the outward, even crumbling, crust of 'religious institutions' and 'religious behavior' and move toward the rich world of human meanings, the 'Lebenswelt,' as its object of study. As sociology of religion makes its Exodus it may meet a theology which has also begun to take 'this world' more seriously. Together they may write a new chapter in the history of human consciousness."[25] Apparently, the field of sociology of religion is capable of experiencing redemption, a total reorientation of its interests and goals because, Cox says, "the basic category to be used by such a reborn sociology should not be religion but 'orientation,' or "identity.' "[26]

Cox appears to be suggesting that sociologists of religion should join hands with the radical theologians who have discovered that religion is a cultural residue that for years has had more social than religious significance. Now that virtually all honest people know this to be true, however, religion is losing even its sociological importance. Cox correctly disapproves of the functional theorists who hold that only institutional forms of religion serve to integrate society,[27] but he later affirms the functionalists' procedures himself when he says that the primary aim of the new sociology of religion will be to discover what it is that integrates society in the new era. Thus he writes: "If the 'post-religious era' thesis makes any sense at all, it is a theory about the emergence of a very different style of social integration in our epoch, a type of integration which lacks certain of the characteristics previously thought integral to religion. This thesis entails also the emergence of a 'post-religious' or at least 'post-Christian' man whose personal identity and self-image vary in important respects

[24] Cox, "Sociology of Religion in a Post-Religious Era," 17.
[25] *Ibid.*, 26. [26] *Ibid.*, 17. [27] *Ibid.*, 16f.

from his predecessors." Hence we see that the only "new" thing that the new sociology of religion will do is to describe in terms of functional theory what the new religion is doing. That Cox invariably uses quotation marks to set off phrases like "post-religious" shows clearly that he believes the "non-religions" of the future will be essentially religious in character, in the sense that they will only slough off the irrelevant and anachronistic elements of antiquated Christian forms while retaining, and perhaps recrystallizing, the pure and the best religious values. In order to increase the chances that this process will occur in the coming age, a new man will be born, termed by Cox the "post-Christian man." The advent of this new man most assuredly will be necessary, since it is clear that the old sinner could neither create nor enjoy the "non-religious religion" of the future without corrupting it.

Cox's article is rendered more significant by the support he has received from some sociologists who share both his discomfiture with established religion and his hope for a more effective social integrator than the contemporary church, which reinforces our domestic patterns of segregation and blesses our civic religion.

Thomas Luckmann is a sociologist of considerable stature who has done important work in both empirical research and theory.[28] Yet his recent book, *The Invisible Religion*, seems to be informed more by the prescriptions of some form of philosophical theology than by the scientific canons of the university sociologists.[29] It reflects the idealistic hopes and the affirmative views of the nature of man and society that are found among the newest Pelagians. There also appears to be underlying it an implicit asociological assumption that existing institutional structures are the

[28] *A Comparative Study of Four Protestant Parishes in Germany* (New York: Research Division, New School for Social Research, 1955). Luckmann and Peter Berger recently coauthored a favorably reviewed study in the sociology of knowledge entitled *The Social Construction of Reality* (Garden City, N.Y.: Doubleday, 1966).

[29] Thomas Luckmann, *The Invisible Religion* (New York: Macmillan, 1967).

root of all evil and that, if religion will assume new forms, or if it can exist without any differentiated social form at all, the world will probably be a better place.

It is true, of course, that religion is not exhausted by any of its existing forms. But the title of Luckmann's book suggests that the essence of historical and social religion cannot be perceived. The idea of an invisible social reality is more likely to offend orthodox sociologists than orthodox theologians, who are accustomed to conceptions like the oneness and indivisible nature of the Invisible and Visible Church. Luckmann, however, is not interested in bowing to the views of the majority of sociologists. He believes that recent sociology of religion is theoretically inadequate because it tends to identify religion with its institutional form.[30] He argues that contemporary sociologists are in error because they assume that religion "is amenable to scientific analysis only to the extent that it becomes organized and institutionalized."[31] Thus Luckmann considers it important to distinguish between sociologists who define or describe religion exclusively as an institutional phenomenon and sociologists, like himself, who claim that religion can achieve social reality and maintain social viability without assuming institutional form. Contemporary sociology of religion, Luckmann says, "is exclusively concerned with church-oriented religiosity";[32] he, on the other hand, is more interested in the noninstitutional forces that function to integrate society. As he puts it, the central question for sociology of religion is "what are the conditions under which 'transcendent,' superordinated and 'integrating' structures of meaning are socially objectivated?"[33] If we assume this is a meaningful sentence,[34] then we can reasonably suggest that Luckmann is not concerned with religion in the sense in which this term is understood by traditional sociologists, by priests, by laymen, and by the atheist on the street.

[30] *Ibid.*, 18, 22.
[31] *Ibid.*, 22.
[32] *Ibid.*, 26.
[33] *Ibid.*
[34] Cf. "Two Currents in the Sociology of Religion," *Theology Today*, Oct. 1967, in which I offer a fuller discussion of Luckmann's views.

"Integrating structures" does not necessarily denote religion. What he and Cox and some of the radical theologians are actually talking about is a nonreligion of the future that should not be set off by quotation marks, a civil humanitarian ideology, perhaps, that is not a religion by any definition except that which equates religion with integrating society and giving comfort to the individual. It represents what the sociologists have for years called a "functional alternative"; and for an even greater number of years some of them have been speculating that the society of the future may be able to survive without any form of religion.[35]

Luckmann almost achieves this stance when he writes that "religious institutions are not universal; the phenomena underlying religious institutions or, to put it differently, [the phenomena] performing analogous functions in the relation of the individual and social order presumably are universal."[36] We are faced here with a complex sentence that is full of ambiguity. To say that the "phenomena underlying" religious institutions are universal is not necessarily to say that anything religious is universal, or even present at all. The underlying phenomena may simply be psychological needs shared by all men, crudely fullfilled by religion in the past, but met by some other social mechanism in the present and future. Therefore, Luckmann seems possibly to be in agreement with those sociologists who believe that religion is a social residue and that something else is now appearing that will perform analogous functions.

But as one reads the radical theologians and sociologists like Cox and Luckmann, it appears that there is an *a priori* character to their fundamental argument, for they never define key terms like "religion" and "institution," and so there is no limit to what they can claim or disclaim, affirm or deny. On *a priori* grounds, Luckmann *may believe* that there are human needs and social requisites that are specifically religious in character and that can, therefore, be

[35] See, e.g., M. Guyau, *The Non-Religion of the Future* (New York: Schocken, 1962—original edition published in 1897).

[36] Luckmann, *The Invisible Religion*, 43.

fulfilled only by religious structures. If so, religion is assured a place in every society, at least in covert form, and it is the sociologist's task to discover and identify it. Or he may believe, again on *a priori* grounds, that the same needs are not religious and that it is only by the accidents of history that they have been thus far satisfied by religion. The radical religionists and sociologists have as much right to *a priori* reasons and definitions as anyone else, but it would clearly facilitate discussion if they would tell the world what they mean by "religion." As it is, we can only know that they believe what is usually called religion will not exist in the future in institutional forms or, if it does, the world will be the worse for it.

The center of Luckmann's concern is apparent when he expresses the opinion that all institutional forms of religion are declining and then declares that there is a strong possibility "that a new religion is in the making."[37] No empirical evidence to support this idea is offered, but Luckmann's positive interest in the possible event is indicated by his effort "to raise [this] from a purely speculative status to the status of a productive hypothesis in the sociological theory of religion."[38]

His first step in raising his speculation to the level of a productive hypothesis is imaginative, but it probably will not prove useful for future work in the sociology of religion. He proposes that we "regard the social processes that lead to the formation of Self as fundamentally religious." "It is in keeping with an elementary sense of the concept of religion to call the transcendence of biological nature by the human organism a religious phenomenon."[39] Thus we can see the positive attitude that Luckmann has toward whatever he believes to be the true forms or the essence of religion. The process of socialization is good since it raises the man-animal to the status of being human, and perhaps because this is "good" he calls it the basic religious act. What happens in the socializing event is that a person

[37] *Ibid.*, 40.
[38] *Ibid.*
[39] *Ibid.*, 49.

internalizes a world view.[40] The world view is always the product of a specific historical people. It provides both the integrative and creative power of the people; therefore, it "performs an essentially religious function," and we may "define it as an elementary social form of religion."[41]

Within the world view there is a narrower realm of meaning which Luckmann calls "the sacred cosmos." He deviates from Harvey Cox when he says, in accord with Durkheim, that the world view always clearly differentiates the realms of the *sacred* and the *profane*. The "ultimate significance" of everyday life is to be found in the sacred cosmos.[42]

Luckmann said his purpose in *The Invisible Religion* was to seek for a redefinition of the nature of individual existence and of the relationship between the individual and society.[43] The critical role of religion can now be understood because the elementary relationship between the individual and society is religious; but Luckmann, unfortunately, does not begin to explore the implications of his idea that the development of the self in society is a religious event. For example, is it a process that begins and ends relatively early in life, or is it a continually experienced process terminating for the individual only at death, but continuing externally and everywhere in the experience of the living? Does the socializing religious process have demonic as well as creative and positive qualities, so that individual nature, or the nature of social groups and nations, is sometimes distorted by the socializing experience?

Luckmann neither asks nor answers these kinds of questions. There is no reason to suppose that they occurred to him. His positive view of the socializing process and his equating of it with the essence of elementary religious experience are similar to Harvey Cox's elemental faith in the essential virtues of the Secular City. In the case of Luckmann, we can only speculate that the process of socializing the individual may appeal to him as something closer to God's primal creative event than anything that occurs at

[40] *Ibid.*, 51.

[41] *Ibid.*, 53.

[42] *Ibid.*, 58.

[43] *Ibid.*, 9-11.

the more complex and rationalized levels of the relationship between man and society. The basis for his negative evaluations of organized religion is clearly stated throughout the book, but the reasons for his positive assessment of the elementary socializing processes and identification of these with elementary religious forms are not given. "Elementary" religion is identified with these processes, and apparently it is always creative and always functions positively for both society and the individual. Given these presuppositions, it is quite correct to say that "religion is present in nonspecific form in all societies and all 'normal' (socialized) individuals." There even exists, he writes, "a religious dimension in the 'definition' of individual and society but [it] is empty of specific empirical content."[44]

Two important things have happened. First, an ordinary and universal social process has been identified as the elementary form of religious life. Second, since it is devoid of specific empirical content, it cannot be amenable to empirical sociological procedures. Therefore, it can be identified by the sociologist as a religious phenomenon only on *a priori* grounds. In this way alone can Luckmann determine the essentially religious character of the creative process of the development of the social self.

One can fully agree with Luckmann that religious phenomena are not exhausted by *official* or *traditional* institutional types. It is clearly important, as Luckmann says, to discover and to analyze "the world views of contemporary industrial societies," to discover the "sacred cosmos" of these societies and to analyze the religious values and assumptions resident in nonreligious social institutions.[45] Luckmann's fundamental error is to presuppose that, since religion is manifested in social forms other than the *official* and *traditional* institutions (churches, sects, and so on), these alternative social manifestations are not necessarily institutional. This is tantamount to saying that the religious ideas of the politicians, the industrialists, and the laborers, and the forms that these religious ideas assume as they are

[44] *Ibid.*, 78.

[45] *Ibid.*, 91.

expressed in the secular social structures, are not institutionalized in *any* way. In my view, this amounts to maintaining that these ideas will disappear with the death of the individuals who believe them. Obviously, they do not.

The majority of sociologists take "institutional" in broad terms to signify "a stable property of groups" that enables a group to maintain its basic character and beliefs "even though the personnel of the group continues to change."[46] If this definition is accepted, we can argue that the nonecclesiastical, social, religious representations are as institutional as the ecclesiastical forms, even though their religious aspects are less formal and more covert. We can further argue that religion does *not* have the same function in its formal ecclesiastical manifestations as it does in its "secular" or "elementary" expressions. Analysis of the nature of these various functions is a continuing aspect of the sociologist's task, but we can briefly suggest that religious expressions in the political or economic realms probably have social effects (that is, functions) different from those which they have in the ecclesiastical sphere. In other words, the nonpriestly use of religion differs from the priestly. The primary function of civic religion is to sustain the social order; the function of traditional religion is to sustain the religious community in general, the priestly traditions and orders in particular, and to sustain the stability of the secular community as a by-product. To the extent that we have entered the post-religious age, we have lost the countervailing political power of the priestly order and are confronted by the monolithic power of the quasi-religious totalitarian nations and by the new "civil religions" of the pluralistic societies.

No religious expression, whether it is ecclesiastical or nationalistic or civil, is consistently motivated by devotion to God or by love of neighbor. Nor is any of these religious expressions perfectly autonomous. For years sociologists of religion have been content to demonstrate that the secular order is dependent upon religion. Now we are beginning to

[46] Glock and Stark, *Religion and Society in Tension,* 4.

realize with full force how dependent religion is upon the integrity and vitality of the civil order.[47] The "world view" and the "sacred cosmos" of every society is expressed through its social institutions, both ecclesiastical and secular. The tremendous theoretical contributions of Durkheim and Weber were rooted in their effort to discover the relationship between the ways religious ideas were expressed in traditional religions and the ways they were expressed in secular institutions. Weber was interested in the relationship between organized religion and economic institutions and ideologies; Durkheim was concerned with the basic social function of *organized* religion, for as he wrote, "in all history, we do not find a single religion without a Church."[48]

Perhaps Durkheim was wrong in his understanding of the nature of religion and the relation of religion and society. It may be that Luckmann is more correct and that future religion will operate without specifically differentiated religious institutions. But a more radical state of affairs than either Durkheim or Luckmann envisioned is also possible for the future. The most interesting questions for sociology of religion today arise out of the basic query whether a society can survive at a creative human level without religion *in any form.* Is the frightening anomie that plagues our society a permanent or a passing condition? What is its relation to the development of religious tolerance and pluralism and the lack of ultimate answers provided by a society with no dominant, official religion? There is considerable evidence that individual men can lead constructive and meaningful lives without being religious, that is, without being *ultimately committed* to God or *anything* under God,[49] but can a whole society exist without possessing the faith that the society and its destiny is in accord with transcendent

[47] Robert N. Bellah, "Civil Religion in America," *Daedalus*, Winter 1967, 14ff.

[48] Emile Durkheim, *The Elementary Forms of the Religious Life* (Glencoe, Ill.: The Free Press, 1947), 44.

[49] C. Conrad Cherry, "The Atheistic Humanism of Albert Camus: A Challenge to *Homo Religiosus*," unpublished MS.

power and purpose? When the priests of the "official religion" break the faith and proclaim the death of religion, will an informal folk religion spring up to sustain the people and their society?

The utility of these questions depends upon the degree of clarity that is achieved with respect to the subject at hand. As Glock and Stark have observed, "the necessary starting point for studying any phenomenon is to establish criteria by which it may be identified and distinguished from all other phenomena."[50] The contribution that could be made by the radical theologians and their compatriot sociologists is seriously restricted by their refusal to confine themselves by definitions. This procedure has the advantage of indicating that the subject matter, in this case the complex phenomena of "religion," is not conceived to be limited by the feeble efforts of its discussants; but it has the disadvantage of producing something more akin to poetry than to science. Many theologians are accustomed to working at the level of mythological explanation. When a theologian turns sociologist or a sociologist turns to the specialty of religion, however, he must content himself with working in the circumscribed, prosaic, and nonpoetic realms of rational definition and explanation. The power of sociology resides in great part in being responsibly obedient to the self-imposed limitations of the field. Sociologists fail when they ignore the restrictions incumbent in the empirical method and seek to compete with the theologians. We cannot require of any sociologist that he develop the definitive definition of religion, or even that he be in agreement on this matter with the majority of sociologists; but we do need to know what he means when he uses the fundamental terms, especially when he clearly deviates from the accepted standards, for there is no other way of being reasonably certain that the author's subjective conceptions of religion correspond to any reality.

When the radical theologians and sociologists discuss the religion of the future, they do not appear to be referring

[50] Glock and Stark, *Religion and Society in Tension*, 1.

to a phenomenon that corresponds to what we ordinarily call religion. They often affirm that it is something much different from our conceptions without, however, describing the specific nature of the new "religionless religion." Their penchant for paradox may enhance their status among philosophers, but it clearly detracts from their contributions as sociologists.

There is a difference, however, between paradox and bald contradiction or misuse of standard terminology. The community of scholars, no less than the community of man in general, depends upon a necessary minimum of cognitive agreement, so it is very likely that what is meaningless for sociology is also meaningless for theology. When the radical theologians recommend that we seek, not for a theology of God, but for a theology of man, this proposal must be as theologically nonsensical as it is sociologically incomprehensible. When the theologian or theological ethicist asserts that modern secular man "can neither understand nor use the term *God* meaningfully,"[51] he is straining the boundaries of credibility. As Harmon Holcomb correctly and acutely observes, "In my experience, modern man is capable of believing almost anything and my own neighbors believe all of them."[52] If modern man can believe *anything*, this raises more serious questions about *everything* he believes than the secular theologians and radical sociologists have yet dared to ask. Let us venture one possible question of remarkably reactionary proportions. Could it be that modern man still believes in God but that, like the radical theologians, he is so embarrassed by his own moral guilt or so troubled by the theological inadequacy and pretentiousness of his fathers that he is reserving publication of his humble beliefs until a more propitious season, a time perhaps when the theologians have regained their composure and presented us once again with a constructive perspective?

[51] Harvey Cox, *The Secular City* (New York: Macmillan, 1965), 241.

[52] Harmon R. Holcomb, "The Language of Worship in a Secular Age," *Colgate Rochester Divinity School Bulletin,* July 1967, 65.

Until that day, the sociologists of religion can best contribute to the enterprise of scholarship in religion by working apart from or beside the theologians and philosophers, not by seeking to replace them. The central task of sociology of religion is not to redefine and transform the nature of religion and society, but to discover and explain by means of adequate theoretical construction and empirical labors the relationships between religion and society. Both Luckmann and Cox reprove contemporary sociologists of religion for failing to follow the lead of Durkheim and Weber. It is not necessary to examine their own fidelity in this matter. The wise sociologist will simply accept this advice.

Durkheim has been an anathema among many sociologists of religion and theologians because he reduced the idea of God to a social projection; religion he described as a collective representation of society. The reductionism was an error he shared with men like Feuerbach and Marx, but as so often with people of that stature, his errors have proved more useful than our own highest achievements.

In examining the relationship between religion and society, the sociologist can say with Durkheim that the concept of God is *at least* a projection of man's subjective idealizations of his own community. In a day when men believed in God, the idea that He was in any sense a social projection was unsettling or even repugnant. But, ironically, in a time when the theological professionals inform us that God is dead, the suggestion that negative theology may be socially conditioned appears to be a positive contribution.

One of the most impressive chapters written in the sociology of religion in the last decade was presented by Peter Berger in his presidential address in 1966 before the Society for the Scientific Study of Religion.[53] He observed that the ideas of the radical theologians "did not spring from nowhere."[54] Following the procedures of the historian of ideas he showed that there is nothing new in their procla-

[53] Peter L. Berger, "A Sociological View of the Secularization of Theology," *Journal for the Scientific Study of Religion* VI/1 (Spring 1967), 3-16.

[54] *Ibid.*, 3.

mations. A shift from a transcendental to an immanental perspective occurred as early as Schleiermacher and was sustained by Harnack, Bultmann, Bonhoeffer, Gogarten, and Buri. These men share with the contemporary secular theologians credit for the discovery that traditional religion is not philosophically or scientifically tenable or that it is not in accord with the modern world view.[55] This stands as the usual sufficient explanation for the skepticism of modern man. But from the perspective of the sociologist of religion, this is only a partial explanation. As Luckmann and Berger point out in their recent coauthored work, the sociology of religion and of knowledge stand in a close dialectical relationship because religious ideas are, in great part, rooted in secular structures.[56] Berger made the same point in his presidential address: "It would be naive sociologically to think that there are not also practical, specifically social roots for the theological developments."[57] He cited the disintegration of Christendom itself as the most obvious example. Closely associated with this in some crucial ways is the "pluralization of the social world," so that no longer is the church the sole or even the primary "reality-defining institution." "The traditional religious certitudes have become progressively less credible, not necessarily because modern man has some intrinsically superior access to the truth, but because he exists in a socio-cultural situation which itself undermines religious certitude."[58] This assertion is surely correct, but it might have been better if he had said that the Christian community was found totally un-

[55] *Ibid.*, 5.

[56] *The Social Construction of Reality*, 169: "The analyses of objectivation, institutionalization and legitimation are directly applicable to the problems of the sociology of language, the theory of social action and institutions, and the sociology of religion. Our understanding of the sociology of knowledge leads to the conclusion that the sociologies of language and religion cannot be considered peripheral specialties of little interest to sociological theory as such, but have essential contributions to make to it. This insight is not new. Durkheim and his school had it . . . ."

[57] Berger, "A Sociological View of the Secularization of Theology," 8.

[58] *Ibid.*, 10.

prepared for the multidimensional revolution of the modern world. This formulation makes it easier for sociologists to keep open the question of the validity of Durkheim's fundamental hypothesis that religion necessarily provides the dynamic for the human community. It is certainly true that the contemporary socio-cultural situation undermines religious certitude, but more precisely it may be that it undermines the bad faith, the lapsed animism, the parochialism of our priestly theologians, the provincialism of our secular priests, the indifference of our laity, and the cool detachment of our scholars. It may be, as Luckmann said, that a new sacred cosmos is developing that will creatively transform and thus transcend all of the old cosmic orders and provide the community of man with a new integrating religious power. But, in any case, the sociology of religion must not be asked to serve as an agent of redemption in the misguided hope that it can be more than a useful instrument for the analysis and partial explanation of the religious communities of man. The contribution of sociology of religion as a theoretical-empirical discipline resides in great part precisely in the capacity and willingness of its practitioners to recognize its limitations as well as its powers.

Comparative Religious Ethics

DAVID LITTLE

THE MATERIAL and the method that properly make up the study of "comparative religious ethics"[1] are by no means self-evident. At present the field, if it can be called such, lacks systematic rigor, even though there are some hopeful signs in certain quarters. Many people, from many points of view, do make comparative statements about religious ethics, but only very few stop to reflect critically on what is meant by "ethics," "religious," and "comparative." Clearly, the understanding of these terms and of their relations to each other will shape and direct specific investigations.

A review of three or four of the conventional ways of dealing with comparative religious ethics makes the instability of the field obvious. In one group there are the "apologists," who propose to defend a particular view of ethics over against other religious or nonreligious views. Apologists, of whatever religious or nonreligious persuasion, tend to make some unexamined assumptions about the comparative relation of "religion" and "ethics." They tend to hold, first, that concepts like "religion" and "ethics" have fairly firm and clear meanings and, second, that there are more or less determinate relations between the concepts in various historical contexts. Thus Hendrik Kraemer, a Christian student of comparative religion, can argue that "all ethics in the world, except the Christian ethic, are some form of

[1] In ordinary English usage there is no clear distinction between the words "morals" and "ethics." Both terms appear in this essay, though I would more or less hold to Ladd's working distinction: "moral statements" make specific prescriptive or evaluative judgments; "ethical statements" reflect on and justify moral statements. John Ladd, *Structure of a Moral Code: A Philosophical Analysis of Ethical Discourse Applied to the Ethics of the Navaho Indians* (Cambridge: Harvard University Press, 1957), 82-83.

eudaemonism."[2] What makes the Christian ethic so different, and so much better, is that it is "radically religious." It is concerned to obey God's Will and not to realize some highest good.

Interestingly enough, this way of understanding "religion" and "ethics" has been adopted by the philosopher P. H. Nowell-Smith,[3] though he uses it to discredit, rather than defend, religious ethics of any sort. Nowell-Smith argues that the trouble with religious ethics (say, Hebraic or Christian) is that they are "heteronomous" or deontological, rather than "autonomous" or teleological. They postulate a divine authority as the source of morality, instead of relying on the individual to determine his own end and direct his action in accordance with it. Drawing on Piaget's work, Nowell-Smith suggests that religious authorities necessarily cultivate a dependent or childish ethic and for this reason ought, in due time, to be dispensed with.

Kraemer and Nowell-Smith are using the relevant concepts for partisan purposes. There is hardly much refinement or sophistication in either treatment. Is it really so evident that religion always fosters a heteronomous ethic or, for that matter, any ethic at all? Are there only deontological elements in the Christian tradition,[4] or is there a rich variety of "ethical implications," depending on the kind of religious belief and the kind of ethical situation at hand? These questions are either left unanswered or badly muddled by arguments like those of Kraemer and Nowell-Smith.

A second group, the "grand theorists," has been slightly more responsible about its use of basic terms, even though

[2] Hendrik Kraemer, *Christian Message in a Non-Christian World* (Grand Rapids, Mich.: Kregel Publications, 1956), 86-88.

[3] P. H. Nowell-Smith, "Morality: Religious and Secular," in *Christian Ethics and Contemporary Philosophy*, ed. Ian T. Ramsey (New York: Macmillan, 1966).

[4] Nowell-Smith admits he is indulging in a "serious oversimplification" when he makes this charge, but he gives no warrant for so indulging. His attempts to classify religious systems according to Piaget's terminology are very confused. See *ibid.*, 99.

figures such as Edward Westermarck[5] and L. T. Hobhouse[6] developed a broad cross-cultural theory of ethics at the expense of analytical precision and intensive empirical investigation. Both Westermarck and Hobhouse did help to advance the comparative study of ethics by beginning to make some necessary distinctions between "religion" and "ethics." Westermarck sharply formulated an issue that is still vigorously discussed by philosophers and theologians today. He contended that, when a religious believer claims, as Christians usually do, that God's Will is good and ought to be obeyed, the believer has made a prior judgment about God's Will that is logically independent of his religious assumptions. Consequently, Westermarck set out to discover the nonreligious source of ethical belief. From his wide-ranging comparative inquiry he concluded that ethical judgments are "really generalizations derived from approval or disapproval felt with regard to certain modes of conduct."[7] That is, he espoused a version of emotivism, which led him in turn to view the "radical diversity" among the ethical codes of societies as unresolvable by any objective ethical method. In short, Westermarck was a relativist as well as an emotivist.

Hobhouse accepted the idea that "religion" and "ethics" are analytically independent of each other. And, like Westermarck, he embarked on an enormous comparative study of different societies and their ethical codes. In contrast to Westermarck, however, he proposed a theory of ethics that was rationalist and absolutist. Under the influence of T. H. Green's neo-Hegelianism, Hobhouse discovered a grand evolutionary pattern at work throughout all societies. Societies moved, he believed, from kin-bound particularism and

[5] Edward Westermarck, *Origin and Development of the Moral Ideas* (London: Macmillan, 1906), I, 12-13. See also Morris Ginsberg, "Life and Work of Edward Westermarck," *Essays in Sociology and Social Philosophy* (New York: Macmillan, 1960), II, 76-77.

[6] L. T. Hobhouse, *Morals in Evolution* (New York: Henry Holt, 1916), 575.

[7] Quoted in R. B. Brandt, *Ethical Theory* (Englewood Cliffs, N.J.: Prentice-Hall, 1959), 167.

ethnocentrism toward universalism and individual responsibility, or "self-realization . . . in the consciousness of a common humanity with a common aim."[8] On the basis of this rational universal standard, Hobhouse thought it was possible to resolve ethical disputes among different cultures. He also used this standard to classify and compare religious beliefs. Some beliefs retard and some encourage the evolution of the "common purpose," though, for him, the principle of harmony ultimately transcends all religious belief.

Apart from the philosophical problems with these approaches,[9] neither one contains a clear distinction between descriptive and normative ethics.[10] It is one thing to describe how different ethical codes do in fact function; it is another to propose how ethical judgments ought to be made. Westermarck and Hobhouse jumbled these discrete activities in such a way that their descriptive work too quickly became the servant of their respective normative theories. As a result, neither man was sufficiently sensitive to the extreme complexity of describing just how ethical convictions actually function in various societies. As we shall see, re-

[8] *Morals in Evolution*, 596.

[9] I touch on some of the problems below. For a critical discussion of Westermarck, see Brandt, *Ethical Theory*, 166-169. For a critical discussion of Hobhouse, see J. Kemp, *Reason, Action and Morality* (New York: Humanities Press, 1964), 144-147.

[10] As will be obvious, I want to broaden Frankena's definition of descriptive ethics to bring it in line with Ladd's work. Frankena distinguishes between descriptive and normative ethics in the following way. *Descriptive ethics* is "empirical inquiry, historical or scientific, such as is done by anthropologists, historians, psychologists, and sociologists. Here, the goal is to describe or explain the phenomena of morality or to work out a theory of human nature which bears on ethical questions." *Normative ethics* "may take the form of asserting a normative judgment . . . and giving or being ready to give reasons for this judgment. Or it may take the form of debating with oneself or with someone else about what is good or right in a particular case or as a general principle, and then forming [a] normative judgment as a conclusion," *Ethics* (Englewood Cliffs, N.J.: Prentice-Hall, 1964), 4. For Ladd, " 'descriptive ethics' may be defined as a scientific meta-theoretical inquiry into the ethical discourse of a specified informant or group," *Structure of a Moral Code*, 30. It is the inquiry into the structure of ethical reason that I also consider important.

cent work in the field has made important advances beyond both men in this regard.

A third group, consisting of anthropologists and sociologists, has made undeniable contributions to the study of comparative religious ethics. Nevertheless, many in this group have hindered as much as they have helped theoretical progress in the field. Some social scientists, for example, have been more successful than others in maintaining the distinctions between descriptive and normative theory.[11] The "functionalist" school, whose members, like Emile Durkheim, Bronislaw Malinowski, and A. R. Radcliffe-Brown, have been so active in comparative social analysis, has had a particularly hard time remembering this distinction. Durkheim, for one, hoped to construct a "science of morals" out of cross-cultural inquiries that would not only adequately describe the origins and function of ethical experience but would also indicate how ethical judgments ought to be made in the contemporary world.[12]

Functionalism has several problems. One of them is to try, as Durkheim did, to justify a way of doing ethics by explaining how ethical practices function in social life. But explaining is one thing, justifying another. Even if ethical behavior is universally "conducive to the survival and coherence of a society," that is no sufficient reason to recommend that ethical obligation always means preserving and

[11] Max Weber, for one, had a much better grasp of this matter than most. In his words, "One can only demand of the teacher [as scientist] that he have the intellectual integrity to see that it is one thing to state facts, to determine mathematical or logical relations or the internal structure of cultural values, while it is another thing to answer questions of the value of culture and its individual contents and the question of *how one should act* in the cultural community. . . . These are quite heterogeneous problems." "Science as a Vocation," *From Max Weber: Essays in Sociology*, ed. H. H. Gerth and C. Wright Mills (New York: Oxford University Press, 1958), 146. But perhaps even Weber oversimplified this problem. See W. G. Runciman, *Social Science and Political Theory* (Cambridge: At the University Press, 1965), 156ff.

[12] See, e.g., *Sociology and Philosophy*, tr. D. F. Pocock (Glencoe, Ill.: The Free Press, 1953). Cf. the penetrating criticisms by W. D. Ross in *The Right and the Good* (Oxford: Clarendon Press, 1955), 12-15.

unifying one's society. Obviously, a number of other questions remain to be asked. But, beyond that, the purely explanatory power of functionalism is far from established. As Runciman puts it, "to show how something is useful [conducive to social survival and coherence] is not to explain how it originated or why it is what it is."[13] Moreover, it is a truism that social patterns and institutions often continue to exert influence even after they have outlived their usefulness (become "dysfunctional"). Ethical patterns do so every bit as much as other conventions. Apparently, the functionalist has no way to explain such phenomena without introducing other considerations into his theory.

The problem of confusing description and justification is further illustrated in some of the work of Clyde Kluckhohn in the field of comparative ethics.[14] Kluckhohn contends that the existence of "ethical universals" in every known society—ethical proscriptions within the ingroup against unjustified killing, stealing, and lying as well against arbitrary activity in matters of property and sex—counts against the ethical relativism of theorists like Westermarck. But the empirical discovery of cross-cultural ethical constants (descriptive conclusions) does nothing to show us whether those constants are "right" and "ought to be obeyed" (normative conclusions).[15] It is logically possible to be a descriptive relativist and a normative absolutist, or vice versa. These positions vary independently.

The relation of "religion" to "ethics" is still another recurrent problem in social scientific studies. These concepts

[13] Runciman, *Social Science and Political Theory*, 112. Cf. R. B. Brandt, *Hopi Ethics* (Chicago: Chicago University Press, 1954), 293, and Clyde Kluckhohn, *Culture and Behavior* (Glencoe, Ill.: The Free Press, 1964), 292-294, for similar criticisms.

[14] Kluckhohn, *ibid.*, Chaps. 15 and 16; cf. his "Common Humanity and Diverse Cultures," in *The Human Meaning of the Social Sciences*, ed. D. Lerner (New York: World, 1959), 279; "Values and Value-Orientations," in *Toward a General Theory of Social Action*, ed. T. Parsons and E. Shils (New York: Harper & Row, 1962), 418.

[15] See Paul W. Taylor, "Social Science and Ethical Relativism," *Journal of Philosophy* LV/1 (Jan. 2, 1958), 32-44. Cf. Ladd, *Structure of a Moral Code*, 322-328.

are not clear, for example, in the work of Max Weber.[16] Nor are they related with much clarity or consistency by very many of the functionalists. Malinowski tells us at one point that "all the morality of primitives is derived from religious belief."[17] But, as MacBeath demonstrates, Malinowski's own conclusions contradict this statement.[18] On the ordinary rules of individual and social morality among primitive peoples, Malinowski comments: "They in no way have the character of religious commandments . . . but [are] provided with a purely social binding force."[19] An adequate theory will obviously have to overcome glaring inconsistencies of this sort.

From this cursory review of work in the field, it is clear we shall not make much headway until we begin to straighten out some fundamental difficulties. Fortunately, we are not without help. Moral philosophers and anthropologists have started to examine critically the problems we have mentioned—the nature of a theory of comparative ethics, the relation between descriptive and normative inquiry, the bearing of ethical theory on social theory, and the connection between concepts like "religion" and "ethics." It will be useful now to pull together some of the suggestions for dealing with these problems made by R. B. Brandt, John Ladd, Alexander MacBeath, Christoph von Fürer-Haimendorf, and others.[20] We shall touch, first, on the issue

[16] Weber overemphasized, I believe, the dependence of ethical reason on religion; for instance, see his comments in "The Social Psychology of the World Religions," in *From Max Weber*, 286-287. Throughout this essay Weber's reference to these matters is neither precise nor consistent.

[17] Quoted in Alexander MacBeath, *Experiments in Living: A Study in the Nature and Foundation of Ethics or Morals in the Light of Recent Work in Social Anthropology* (London: Macmillan, 1952), 308-309.

[18] *Ibid.*, 314.

[19] *Loc. cit.*

[20] See Brandt, *Hopi Ethics* and *Ethical Theory*, esp. Chaps. 5 and 11; Ladd, *Structure of a Moral Code*; MacBeath, *Experiments in Living*; Christoph von Fürer-Haimendorf, *Morals and Merit* (Chicago: Chicago University Press, 1967), and "Morality and the Social Order among the Apa Tanis," in *Gods and Rituals*, ed. John Middleton (Garden City, N.Y.: Natural History Press, 1967), 1-19. Dorothy Emmet has some interesting things to say on the relation of ethical

of a theory of comparative ethics, second, on religion and ethics, and, third, on ethical theory and social theory.

A Theory of Comparative Ethics

Although we are hardly in a position to provide a developed theory, we can outline considerations that, it appears, must be taken into account in beginning the task. In order to avoid some of the grosser difficulties in which anthropologists and sociologists sometimes become entangled, it is necessary, when studying human action, to make a good deal of the distinction we mentioned earlier between explaining and justifying. As we said, it is one thing to explain action by referring to psychological, social, or economic causes. This is properly the business of social science. It is, however, quite another thing to explore the "reasons" or justifications an agent himself gives for his action. Ladd points out that much confusion results because anthropologists who treat moral rules are not always clear "whether they are reporting the informant's justifying arguments or the authors' own explanatory interpretation of these rules."[21] These two kinds of examination are analytically discrete, and whatever else it may be, the study of ethics consists in attending to the reasons men offer to justify their actions.

Accordingly, as Ladd and others[22] have suggested, we shall need to investigate the logical structure of ethical reasoning, as it functions in justifying the prescriptions and evaluations of a given ethical system. This will be a large part of the job of "descriptive" ethics. There is no implica-

---

theory to anthropological study in *Rules, Roles and Relations* (London: Macmillan, 1966). See also May and Abraham Edel, *Anthropology and Ethics* (Springfield, Ill.: Charles C. Thomas, 1959). In *Ethical Judgment: The Place of Science in Ethics* (Glencoe, Ill.: The Free Press, 1955) Abraham Edel attempts to advance the general discussion. In my view, his book is hopelessly fuzzy.

[21] Ladd, *Structure of a Moral Code*, 47. Cf. Ladd, "Ethics and Explanation," *Journal of Philosophy* XLIX/15 (July 17, 1952), 499, 504.

[22] Ladd's study is nicely complemented by Paul W. Taylor's *Normative Discourse* (Englewood Cliffs, N.J.: Prentice-Hall, 1961). Many of my own suggestions are stimulated by Taylor's helpful study.

tion that other explanations (for example, historical or economic) for the emergence of a given ethical system are not relevant. It simply means that these explanations can never provide a complete account. To "understand"[23] an ethical system is to allow for the structure and substance of its own justifying reasons, as Ladd's reconstruction of the Navaho system so admirably shows.

When that task is done, we begin to have a basis on which to make careful cross-cultural comparisons. To know that there are several universal prescriptions, such as Kluckhohn refers to, is not uninteresting in itself, but we must come to see how these prescriptions operate in different ethical systems. Are the prohibitions against murder and stealing justified in the same way among the Navahos as among the Gahuku-Gama of New Guinea? Do they serve the same avowed purposes in various societies? Only when these questions are answered do we have a sophisticated way of beginning to deal with descriptive relativism.

My own reaction is that Ladd has put his finger on one "descriptive universal" among ethical systems—namely, a similar formal structure of justification—though we need further empirical confirmation. It is at least a reliable hypothesis that ethical discourse in various cultures proceeds according to an "appellate" pattern, from relatively specific prescriptions and rules to broader standards and principles of validation and, finally, to ultimate "reasons" by which the entire system is vindicated or justified.[24]

I think we can go on to extrapolate from the work of Ladd and others some further examples of descriptive universals. These we can deduce from the observation that

[23] My argument is closely related to what Weber appears to have had in mind when he defined "human action" as all behavior "to which a subjective meaning is attached by the agent." See Weber, *Theory of Social and Economic Organization* (Glencoe, Ill.: The Free Press, 1947), 88. Weber's well-known concept of *Verstehen* is obviously relevant here. See Runciman's interesting discussion of this point, *Social Science and Political Theory*, 11ff.

[24] For extensive treatments of what I call the "appellate" pattern of ethical reasoning, see Ladd, *Structure of a Moral Code*, and Taylor, *Normative Discourse*.

men do universally "give reasons" to justify their moral actions. The matter of giving reasons is *a priori* an *intersubjective* act; that is, it is impersonal or "social" rather than private or arbitrary.[25] William Frankena puts this point well: ethical language, he says, is *public language*; when one uses it, he must "depart from his private and particular situation and must choose *a point of view, common to him and others*. . . . [Subjectivism] cannot assert itself in the public arena, as it has and does, unless it inconsistently talks in just the manner it condemns."[26]

This fact about ethical reason is especially pertinent since ethical language has invariably to do with *relational action*, that is, with the relation of ego's conduct to that of alter ego. Unlike aesthetic justification, for example, ethical justification is a matter of ego's either giving or being prepared to give reasons to alter ego regarding action that has a bearing on alter's wants and interests.[27] The presence of ethical reason among men further implies that there is an underlying (or necessarily assumed) *respect for* the other's wants and interests. Giving reasons for action that bears on another entails an appeal for the other's acceptance or consent. This sort of respect is implied in what philosophers refer to as the principle of reversability, according to which ego applies to himself the same standards he applies to alter.

I conclude that the basic problem around which ethical systems are organized is what we may call *the problem of cooperation*, or the problem of harmonizing ego's wants and interests with those of alter. As Mary Warnock well says, ethics is "the theory of how people should live *to-*

[25] Ladd, *ibid.*, 105.

[26] William K. Frankena, "Decisionism and Separatism in Social Philosophy," in *Rational Decision-Making*, ed. C. J. Friedrich (New York: Athernon Press, 1964), 22-23.

[27] For a trenchant analysis of "moral language" in relation to the problem of relating wants and interests, see David P. Gauthier, *Practical Reasoning* (Oxford: Clarendon Press, 1966), esp. Chaps. 8-10. Cf. Kurt Baier, *The Moral Point of View* (New York: Random House, 1966), Chaps. 5 and 6. At critical points my own sentiments lie more with Gauthier than with Baier.

gether."[28] To put it another way, ethical reason is by definition in the business of "ruling out" arbitrary or "antisocial" behavior, that is, behavior in which ego disregards alter though his action affects alter's interests. Incidentally, it is probably no accident that Kluckhohn discovered the particular ethical universals he did: they are more or less indispensable guarantees against arbitrariness in any social relationship.

I want now to suggest that there is a determinate range of general patterns for handling the problem of cooperation and that ethical systems can be analyzed and compared according to this range.

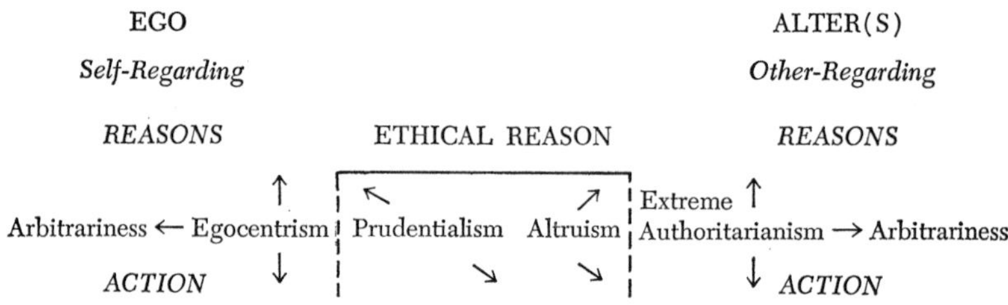

First, we distinguish between the *action* engaged in and the *reasons* given for the action. Second, we distinguish between a *self-regarding* pole and an *other-regarding* pole on the spectrum. These distinctions are important because, for example, an action considered "other-regarding" may be justified for "self-regarding" reasons ("kindness pays off"). At either end of the spectrum we have placed "arbitrariness," or action that is (according to our definition) "unethical" or "immoral." Arbitrary action is that for which no reason can be given. Either ego or alter satisfies his desires vis-à-vis the other simply because he "wants to." In this regard one of the most fascinating aspects of *Moral Judgment of the Child* is the close relationship Piaget finds between the heteronomous authority of the adult (alter)

[28] Mary Warnock, *Existentialist Ethics* (London: Macmillan, 1967), 38. Cf. Kemp, *Reason, Action and Morality*, 140-141.

and the egocentric self-understanding of the child (ego). I wish to call attention to the proximity of both "egocentrism" and "extreme authoritarianism," as I call it, to arbitrariness on our spectrum. Whereas egocentrism, in Piaget's sense,[29] is radically self-regarding, respecting both the action and the reasons given by the agent, extreme authoritarianism, as in the case of the brainwashed individual, is radically other-regarding. In such a case the agent (if he can be called that) acts in a totally servile way, doing whatever is commanded simply because it is commanded by the authority. The arbitrary component in both egocentrism and extreme authoritarianism indicates why I place them outside the range of "ethical reason." They are "pre-ethical" (as Piaget considers the egocentric child to be).[30]

In contrast to egocentrism and extreme authoritarianism, "prudentialism" and "altruism" represent different ways of resolving conflicts between ego and alter(s) on the basis of reasoned justification. Although prudentialism shades into egocentrism, there are some important differences. Prudence implies rational foresight and rational assessment of one's "true interest" or welfare, and it calculates action on that basis.[31] So long as members of a given society ac-

[29] As Piaget argues, thought in the young child takes place almost exclusively "from the ego's point of view": "the child thinks for himself without troubling to make himself understood [by others] nor to place himself at the other person's point of view." Jean Piaget, *Judgment and Reasoning in the Child* (Totowa, N.J.: Littlefield, Adams, 1966), 1. In our terms, alter is almost completely ignored.

[30] See Jean Piaget, *The Moral Judgment of the Child* (Glencoe, Ill.: The Free Press, 1965). Piaget's central thesis is that "ethical reason" develops only as the child develops the capacity for cooperation and mutual respect. In his words (95-96): "Cooperation is really a factor in the creation of the personality, if by personality we mean, not the unconscious self of childish egocentrism, nor the anarchical self of egoism in general, but the self that takes up its stand on the norms of reciprocity and objective [impersonal] discussion, and knows how to submit to these in order to make itself respected . . . . Cooperation being the source of personality, rules cease, in accordance with the same principle, to be external. They become both the constitutive factors of the personality and its fruit . . . . In this way autonomy succeeds heteronomy."

[31] For accounts of the rational component in the concept "pru-

cept the notion that serving one's welfare constitutes a good reason for justifying a prescription, then that society may be said to have a "prudential" ethical system, as, for example, Ladd says of the Navahos.[32] Ladd shows that in Navaho society even prescriptions regarding self-sacrifice are justified by a prediction of unpleasant personal consequences if the prescription goes unheeded. This same sort of appeal is made in proscribing murder, stealing, quarreling, and so on.[33]

Other-regarding action is prescribed for self-regarding or "egoistic" reasons. It must be remembered that our spectrum is an analytical device and that a given system may not be limited to one pattern. For example, Navahos do not completely restrict themselves to self-regarding reasons for their action. "The general Navaho presumption [is] that the welfare of others is a necessary condition of one's own welfare."[34]

Ladd himself notes the Hobbesian element in Navaho prudentialism, that is, the emphasis upon rewards and punishments in justifying an ethical code. The same pattern is widespread in primitive ethical systems. In fact, my intuition is that prudentialism is the predominant pattern among pre-literate societies. K. E. Read gives evidence for this point in his essay "Morality and the Concept of the Person among the Gahuku-Gama":

> The prudent individual is truthful because "lying makes people angry; it causes trouble," and most people wish to retain the good opinion of those with whom they are in close daily association. . . . To lie and to be deceitful may be regarded as bad, but almost in the same breath

---

dence," see H. J. N. Horsburgh, "Prudence," *Proceedings of the Aristotelian Society*, Supp. Vol. 36 (1962), 65-76; and A. Phillips Griffiths and R. S. Peters, "The Autonomy of Prudence," *Mind*, April 1962, esp. 175-176. See also Geoffrey Russell Grice, *The Grounds of Moral Obligation* (Cambridge: At the University Press, 1967), esp. Chap. 1.

[32] Ladd, *Structure of a Moral Code*, 309.

[33] *Ibid.*, 228-248.

[34] *Ibid.*, 297.

> people joke about the manner in which they have either misled others or have escaped the consequences of some of their actions.[35]

Again, prudentialism is found as a recurring pattern among the various peoples of Southeast Asia analyzed by Fürer-Haimendorf.[36]

Examples of "pure altruism"—other-regarding action for other-regarding reasons—are not, so far as I know, easy to come by among primitive and non-Western ethical systems.[37] Western systems themselves, including Christianity, may be understood as an unstable mixture of prudentialism and altruism.[38] I agree with Ladd that Kant pre-

[35] Read's essay appears in *Myth and Cosmos*, ed. John Middleton (Garden City, N.J.: Natural History Press, 1967), 203.

[36] *Morals and Merit*, e.g., 78ff., 114ff. Cf. "Morality and Social Order among the Apa Tanis," 18.

[37] Again and again prudentialism seems to appear among primitive groups, though I am in no position to be very confident about this observation. Concerning literate, non-Western religions my knowledge is severely limited. One helpful study of Theravada Buddhism, Winston L. King's *In the Hope of Nibbana* (La Salle, Ill.: Open Court, 1964), draws out a number of prudentialist elements, particularly with respect to what is known as "Kammic justice," or the pursuit of material rewards and the avoidance of deprivations in the sequence of rebirths through which an individual passes. Merit, according to this scheme, "is the totality of one's accumulated or stored-up goodness, which will manifest itself in good fortune of various kinds, both in this life and lives to come. Pleasures, success, health, friendships . . . are the direct consequences of meritorious deeds" (50). King goes on to emphasize what we would call an "egoistic" emphasis within the Theravada system: "one's merit is one's own . . . . Both responsibility for, and fruitage of, merit rest squarely upon each individual in himself and by himself" (though this view is not held with complete consistency).

Interestingly, the Five Precepts of Buddhism parallel, with one exception, Kluckhohn's ethical universals. They prohibit taking life, stealing, illicit sexual relations, lying, and taking intoxicants (140ff.). At the level of Kammic justice, the Precepts are justified prudentially. A person who lives by them will gain "great wealth and possessions," "great fame and reputation," a happy rebirth, etc. (43ff.).

[38] Within the New Testament these patterns appear to be present. Jesus' references to rewards and punishments seem a clear instance of prudentialism (though that is by no means all there is to Jesus' ethic); and Paul's statement in Romans 9:3 has always seemed to me a striking example of altruism: "For I could wish that I myself were

sents as clear a case for pure altruism as there is. For him respect and concern for alter's wants and interests are theoretically divorced from ego's own wants and interests. Ethical prescriptions are never justified *because* they are in ego's interest, but simply because the process of giving reasons for action (practical reason) *itself* rules out arbitrary lack of respect for alter. Action which takes life or property or otherwise disregards alter's interests "without reason" is contrary to ethical reason by definition.[39]

By means of these illustrations I simply wish to suggest the usefulness of this scheme as a descriptive method for identifying root elements in comparative ethical experience and for beginning to sort these elements out in empirical work in the field. I am, of course, aware that these are but the bare bones of a theory of comparative ethics and that much remains to be done in refining and elaborating it. Nevertheless, we do have enough of the foundations, I believe, to enable us to speak of descriptive ethics as a determinate field and to assume that ethical systems do have some universal features and are organized around a central problem (of cooperation) according to one of several characteristic patterns. These conclusions will in themselves make us suspicious of loose talk about descriptive relativism in ethics.

With respect to normative relativism, I should be inclined to think on the basis of what we have already said about ethical reason that, if ego acts so as to frustrate or deprive alter of his wants and interests and yet can point only to his own desire as the sole reason for the act, then ego is guilty of gross arbitrariness, which must always and everywhere be considered morally wrong. The point is that ego's "reason" is no reason at all, as we have analyzed the concept. Interestingly, even egoists or prudentialists

---

accursed and cut off from Christ for the sake of my brethren, my kinsmen by race."

[39] For an interesting recent attempt to develop this argument, see R. S. Peters, *Ethics and Education* (Glenview, Ill.: Scott, Foresman and Co., 1967).

(like the Navahos) undertake to *argue* and *to gain public assent* for the principle that "every man has a right to seek his self-interest." Moreover, the principle is generalized (as in Navaho society) so that the same "right" is extended to each member.

In the dispute over relativism illustrated by Westermarck and Hobhouse, I should accordingly find the absolutist (or objectivist) position more promising, though, of course, on quite different grounds from those Hobhouse offered. Anyone who takes seriously the place of reason in ethics will find Westermarck's emotivism unpersuasive. There is something patently unsatisfactory about trying to justify a moral judgment by stating "I know I'm right because I feel myself approving what I'm saying." Normally one wants to know *why* or for what "reasons" he finds himself approving or disapproving an action. Despite these observations, however, I do not mean to give the impression that the issue over relativism is settled. I only submit that the relativists have by no means carried the day.

Certainly, to assume there is a particular structure to ethical reason, as we have, prevents a number of blunders often committed by zealous relativists. That Eskimos believe it right to put the elderly to death, whereas the Romans believed it wrong, does not necessarily prove the case of the ethical relativist, as Brandt has cogently pointed out.[40] It may rather be that *both* groups operate under some such prescription as "Do others a favor, whenever possible," and that each group simply construes the prescription differently. The Eskimo judges that, given the aches and pains of old age, the fact of an afterlife, and so on, he is doing his elders a favor by putting them to death. The Romans, viewing the matter in terms of different beliefs, regarded it as a favor to let the old live on. The action of each group, however, is determined according to the same rule of fair treatment under the terms of its shared beliefs. I doubt that all ethical conflicts can be accounted for in this way, but students of comparative ethics should

[40] Brandt, *Ethical Theory*, 100.

be very careful in identifying what is variable and what is not among different cultures.

So far as the study of Christian ethics is concerned, it will be necessary to come to some conclusions about the relativism-absolutism controversy on philosophical and anthropological grounds before arguing about the status of Christian prescriptions vis-à-vis non-Christian ones. This will be necessary, not so much to "prove" or "disprove" Christian ethical convictions by philosophical means, as to determine how Christian ethics should be understood and communicated. If there are (or can be) ethical absolutes, then Christian ethical prescriptions must be seen in relation to them. And the Christian who communicates his ethics may, presumably, assume some common moral experience to which he can appeal. If, on the other hand, there are no absolutes in ethics, then the Christian's understanding of his own ethical claims, and his way of going about communicating them, will necessarily be quite different.

The Relation of Religion and Ethics

This topic has not been reviewed with clarity and consistency in the relevant literature. The reason is partly that the subject is intrinsically difficult, but also partly that it lends itself so easily to partisan purposes. Before any substantial work can be done in the field, we should need to come to a more subtle and coherent understanding of what "religion" is and how it functions in ethical discourse than exists among the "apologists," the "grand theorists," or most of the social scientists.

Again, we are not without guidance. The contributions of MacBeath, Ladd, and Fürer-Haimendorf provide some good beginnings. On the basis of extensive analysis and comparison, MacBeath rejects the notion (found—inconsistently—in Malinowski, as well as in Weber) that ethical convictions depend on, or are derived from, religious beliefs, or at least that religious belief and ethical experience are universally inseparable. "My contention is simply that whatever its presuppositions and implications and whatever support it may receive from or give to religion, morality is autonomous, containing its authority, the grounds of its goodness and rightness, within itself."[41]

Definitions of "religion" are notoriously open to debate, but there is no need, I think, to throw up one's hands in despair.[42] For our purposes, MacBeath's effort will suffice. "Religion," he says, is comprised of an element of belief regarding the supernatural (whether personally or impersonally understood), an emotional element of awe in face of the sacred, and ritualistic practices which dramatize man's relation to the sacred realm. "Ethics," on the other hand, consists of its own three elements: ends or ideals regarded as good or worthy of pursuit; moral rules or principles according to which actions are judged right or wrong; and motives or sentiments or attitudes of mind which find expression in the pursuit of ends and obedience to rules.[43] MacBeath argues that, so understood, these are quite distinct matters that bear no necessary or empirically consistent relation to one another.

Rather, MacBeath contends that we have many examples of primitive societies in which the members do not rely upon any nonmoral (say, religious) convictions in order

[41] MacBeath, *Experiment in Living*, 295. In this connection see Ninian Smart's discussion of "moral discourse and religion" in *Reasons and Faiths* (London: Routledge and Kegan Paul, 1958), Chap. VII. Smart also argues for the "autonomy of ethics" from religious discourse, but he goes on to show the various ways in which they relate to each other. For a discussion of one way in which "social ethics," as they are called, relate to "religious ethics," see A. H. Somjee, "Individuality and Equality in Hinduism," in *Equality*, ed. J. R. Pennock and J. W. Chapman (New York: Athernon Press, 1967).

[42] Ninian Smart is correct, I believe, when he says that "there are at least family resemblances between religions, and the phenomenologists of religion have not been utterly frustrated in their attempts to adduce similarities" ("Gods, Bliss and Morality," in *Christian Ethics and Contemporary Philosophy*, 16). The suggestions made by William A. Christian toward a "theory of religion" are also significant. See *Meaning and Truth in Religion* (Princeton: Princeton University Press, 1964), esp. Chaps. 3 and 4.

[43] MacBeath, *Experiments in Living*, 298-299.

to justify or even define their ethical rules and principles. In general, primitive men "understand the rules, which are the conditions of effective cooperation with their fellows, and therefore, the requirements of social well-being, as clearly as they understand the rules for building a canoe or growing crops. The moral rules involved in the former are as much the results of experience and experiment and, therefore, as rational as the technical rules involved in the latter."[44]

There is support for this view in the findings of Ladd and of Fürer-Haimendorf, particularly in the latter's examination of village clan life in Southeast Asia. Ladd shows that, although religious beliefs among the Navahos are not inconsequential for ethical ideals and practices, Navaho prescriptions are "this-worldly" and "are not based upon supernatural authority."[45] Likewise, Fürer-Haimendorf says of two village groups: "the Daflas and Apa Tanis subscribe to a world-view which, being basically utilitarian and prudential, is directed towards 'this-worldly' goals, and lacks a belief in any link between moral and [religious] concepts."[46] These conclusions about the logical as well as empirical separability of religious from ethical discourse reinforce our earlier argument about the "autonomy of ethical reason."

MacBeath does not go so far as to say that religion and ethics do not have mutual influence upon one another, in particular instances and in particular ways. And, certainly, Fürer-Haimendorf does not deny mutual influence either.[47] But the essential point is, religion and ethics are distinct phenomena, and *the peculiar relations between them must be studied case by case.* MacBeath suggests some general ways in which religion *may* influence ethical ideals and practices, though he also stresses that "a man's ideas about what is right and good may exercise as much influence on

[44] *Ibid.*, 326. This may be a bit overstated. But the basic point appears to stand.

[45] Ladd, *Structure of a Moral Code*, 268.

[46] Fürer-Haimendorf, *Morals and Merit*, 82; cf. 23.

[47] *Ibid.*, 95-96.

his conception of the supernatural as his ideas about the supernatural exercise on his moral conception."[48] Religious beliefs may impinge upon ethics in some of the following ways: they may add extra incentive or extra authority for doing one's (independently defined) ethical duty; they may add extra hope and confidence in the fulfillment of obligations in face of adversity; religious rituals (more or less as the functionalists hold) may have important integrative effects upon the individual and the society at large; training in religious discipline may lead to greater moral discipline; religion may present a society "with the conception of a supersensible reality which . . . is regarded as the embodiment of moral perfection and purity,"[49] who is, in effect, both holy and morally good.[50]

It seems to me that the second and fifth points in particular need elaboration, for they touch on the place of "beliefs about reality" and "standards of value" in religious and ethical discourse. Ladd supposes one element in ethical justification to be some sort of appeal to "reality" or "the nature of things," including, possibly, supernatural reality.[51] It will obviously matter greatly in ethical reasoning what the circumstances of action ("the nature of things") are believed to be. If the world is seen as about to pass away, as the early Christians perceived it, then one sort of prescription would make sense. If, on the other hand, the world is considered to have a long future ahead of it, another choice is implied. R. M. Hare recently stressed the importance of hope and confidence—recurrently religious concepts—for ethical behavior.[52] If there is no belief in

[48] MacBeath, *Experiments in Living*, 295.

[49] *Ibid.*, 348.

[50] For other discussions of the connection between the concept of God and moral goodness, see H. R. Jones, *Concept of Holiness* (London: Allen & Unwin, 1961), esp. Chap. 8, and Burton F. Porter, *Deity and Morality* (London: Allen & Unwin, 1968). Porter, in particular, is attempting to answer the charges of Kai Nielsen ("Independence of Religion from Morality," in *Christian Ethics and Contemporary Philosophy*, Chap. 8) that judgments about the goodness of God's Will rest on prior ethical judgments.

[51] Ladd, *Structure of a Moral Code*, 106; cf. 166.

[52] In an address at Yale Divinity School, Winter Semester, 1968/69.

the general reliability of the future, whether understood naturally or supernaturally, it is hard to imagine how moralists can go on. Thus can religious concepts influence what we may call "the definition of the ethical situation."

Furthermore, as observation of numerous primitive cultures makes clear, just who is considered a "human being," and hence is entitled to moral treatment, often depends on a group's beliefs about the world. John Layard speaks of certain tribes of central Australia for whom an outsider is not "human" in the tribal sense and therefore "must be killed."[53] And H. I. Hogbin states that among the Busama of New Guinea outsiders are often killed (in a significant phrase) *"for no reason at all."*[54]

Second, religious figures (such as Jesus or Buddha), religious events (such as the Exodus), and religious images or symbols (such as Nirvana) become standards of value that function as standards of validation in ethical argumentation. In discussing the notion of Nirvana and ethical values, Winston L. King comes to some interesting conclusions:

> We shall find that there are some values, states of consciousness, and related modes of conduct that can be called *intrinsically good because they themselves partake*

[53] John Layard, "The Family and Kinship," in E. E. Evans-Pritchard et al., *The Institutions of Primitive Society* (Glencoe, Ill.: The Free Press, 1954), 55.

[54] H. Ian Hogbin, "Pagan Religion in a New Guinea Village," in *Gods and Rituals*, 74 (italics added). Cf. the fascinating essay by Manning Nash, "Witchcraft as a Social Process in a Tzeltal Community," in *Magic, Witchcraft and Curing*, ed. John Middleton (Garden City, N.Y.: Natural History Press, 1967). Nash points out that justification of a killing often rests on determining whether the victim was in fact a witch or not. Here "beliefs about the world" are obviously decisive. As Nash states it (130): "The crucial factor . . . is that a man, together with a small number of his friends or kinsmen, have decided to kill another man as a witch. The problem facing the community is *was the killing justified*? That is, did a witch get destroyed, and therefore a source of potential evil removed, or did a man indulge a personal grievance, or a drunken impulse?" (Italics added.) The relevance of this sort of data to all we have been saying should be plain.

> *of the nature of Nirvana.* Naturally such consciousness and conduct characterize the higher ranges of saintly attainment. But there are also what we may call *instrumental* and *analogical* goods, or those deeds and attitudes that lead to Nirvana, or are more like Nirvana than their opposites. . . . The basic drive in the Buddhist ethico-religious discipline of effort is, of course, to rise from the analogical and the instrumental goods to the intrinsic goodness of Nirvana itself.[55]

The comparative function of these standards in religious-ethical discourse needs extensive analysis. I am doubtful that these standards—for instance, the concept of Nirvana or the life and death of Jesus Christ—are necessarily justified "heteronomously," as Nowell-Smith argues. Buddhists and Christians are just as likely to argue that these standards are good because they enable one to "see the point" of life and to understand "what it's all about." Especially in the appeals to Nirvana in Theravada Buddhism, the notion of heteronomous authority appears to make no sense at all. This is not to deny that some religious standards may be justified heteronomously, but only that there is either logical or empirical evidence to suggest that they always are.[56]

Third, and closely related to this second point, it appears that religion functions by providing a definition of benefits (and of harm). In the words of G. J. Warnock:

> I suspect that religious views [of ethics] differ from "humanist" views [and, I would add, other secular views] not by denying the essential moral relevance of human benefit or harm, but rather by incorporating *very different beliefs as to what is really good or bad for human beings.* The religious believer finds in a supernatural order a whole extra dimension of preeminently important gains and losses, benefits and harm; his difference with the non-

[55] King, *In the Hope of Nibbana,* 89.

[56] In addition, see the arguments of Porter, *Deity and Morality,* esp. Chaps. 7-10. I am not completely persuaded by Porter's point of view, however.

believer is not on the question whether these are of moral significance, but simply on the question whether they are real or chimerical.[57]

That is, the substantive character of ethical systems may vary widely according to the definition of the benefits sought. For example, among the Nagas, a community of headhunters, there is "a strong belief that the spirits of the slain enemies . . . could be added to the community's store of vital force, and thereby contribute to the wealth and fertility of the village."[58] Such a belief obviously leads to a set of ethical prescriptions that may not be formally different from those of other systems (seek good and avoid evil), but which are very different substantively.[59] One way to distinguish Christian ethics from other sorts of religious and nonreligious ethics, then, would appear to center in what the Christian believes the benefits of his action to be.

Another aspect of this same point is the definition of rewards and punishments for ethical behavior. The function of supernatural rewards and punishments in ethics varies widely across cultures, but it is of great importance in some ethical systems.[60]

Finally, at least one more way in which religious and ethical types of discourse become interrelated and mutually influential is by means of the concept of social role. Various religions single out particular role conceptions (king-subject, father-son, promisor-promisee, and so on) and confer on them sacred status. These roles then shape the ethical thinking of a given group. There seems every reason to expect that the fruitful use being made of role

[57] G. J. Warnock, *Contemporary Moral Philosophy* (London: Macmillan, 1967), 79, note 27 (italics added).

[58] Fürer-Haimendorf, *Morals and Merit*, 100.

[59] See Brandt, *Hopi Ethics*, 278-279: "There can be little doubt that considerations of good or ill, for the public or for the individuals involved, are important for the stability and modification of Hopi ethical convictions."

[60] See, e.g., Hogbin, "Pagan Religion in a New Guinea Village," 74; and Raymond Firth, *We, The Tikopia* (Boston: Beacon Press, 1965), 287.

analysis within the Christian tradition can be broadened for comparative purposes.[61]

It is hoped these comments will serve to alert the student of comparative religious ethics to the complexity of the problems involved in relating religion and ethics. Above all, we need more empirical studies that are analytically precise, and fewer sweeping efforts, at least to begin with.

With respect, specifically, to the study of Christian ethics in a comparative perspective, the work of MacBeath, Ladd, and others ought to point up how utterly undisciplined and incontinent are many Christian apologetic approaches, such as Kraemer's. If one wants to claim that Christian ethics is absolutely different from all other ethics because of its religious beliefs, at the very least one is going to have to *argue* that, and not simply assert it. One will have to show, for example, that there *is* a unified "Christian ethic," as well as how and why this ethic allows for no independent ethical reasoning whatsoever. Furthermore, one will need to puzzle over the consequences for a pluralistic world of confining ethics exclusively within a confessional framework. Can the believer make moral appeals on *no* other grounds than his religious beliefs? Surely, there is something odd about arguing that way. MacBeath, I believe, gives us a clue why: it is doubtful that moral experience is collapsible without remainder into religious experience.

Social Theory and Ethical Theory

We have, at several points, called attention to the distinction between explaining modes of social conduct and justifying them, and we have hinted that social theory has to do mainly with the former and ethical theory with the latter. This distinction implies that there are at least two kinds of discourse, one that describes and another that evaluates,[62] and that these ought not to be confused. Natu-

[61] See Donald Evans, *The Logic of Self-Involvement* (London: SCM Press, 1963); John P. Reeder, "Ethics and Divine Commands" (Ph.D. diss., Yale University, 1968); and Emmet, *Rules, Roles and Relations*, esp. Chap. 7.

[62] See Taylor, *Normative Discourse*, Chap. 9.

rally, we do not mean that theories relating to the different kinds of discourse are not relevant to each other, but simply that they do importantly different things.

Let us try to make as clear as possible the distinction as well as the mutual relevance between explaining and justifying by examining reflection on one nearly universal feature of human social experience, the prohibition against incest. The incest taboo provides an appropriate case study because there is such a wide variety of both social scientific and ethical theorizing on the matter.

Several theories about the origins and continued existence of the incest taboo illustrate the dire consequences of forgetting our distinction.[63] Westermarck, for example, tried to explain the development of the taboo as the result of a natural emotional reaction against sexual relations by members of the same family.

> There is a remarkable absence of erotic feelings between persons living very closely together from childhood. Nay more, sexual indifference is combined with the positive feeling of aversion when the act is thought of. This I take to be the fundamental cause of the exogamous prohibitions. . . .[64]

Westermarck proposes to explain (give "the fundamental cause" for) the origin of the taboo as well as to expose the underlying basis on which the taboo is justified among all peoples. As we would expect, given his general social and ethical theory, the key is *psychological feeling.*

There are extraordinary problems with this theory. As an explanatory device it can account neither for the kind of thing a taboo is nor for the place the incest taboo appears to occupy in most societies. As Freud saw, the exist-

[63] The problems with a number of theories of the incest taboo are concisely stated in S. Kirson Weinberg's *Incest Behavior* (New York: Citadel Press, 1966), 236f.

[64] Quoted *ibid.*, 237, from Westermarck, *History of Human Marriage* (New York: Macmillan Co., 1921), 192-193; cf. *Origin and Development of Moral Ideas*, II, 364-378, for some additional thoughts.

ence of a taboo is proof in itself that people experience a strong desire for the prohibited object or act. "For what nobody desires to do does not have to be forbidden, and certainly whatever is expressly forbidden must be an object of desire."[65] Furthermore, much empirical work shows that incest is not nearly so infrequent as Westermarck's theory would have to imply.[66] In short, taboos arise at points of intense conflict of desires or "ambivalence of emotions," as Freud put it. An adequate explanatory theory will have to start from that fact.

Likewise, Westermarck's theory is ineffective in dealing with the character and quality of ethical justification, which centers on the incest taboo in most societies. The reduction of all justifying reasons to a "positive feeling of aversion" dismisses far too quickly the kinds of justification various peoples themselves actually give for the taboo.[67] What is most striking from a survey of the literature on incest is the recurrent appeal among many societies to what we would call "prudentialist" reasons. Among the Tikopia, for instance, "the idea is firmly held that unions of close kin bear with them their own [supernaturally enforced] doom";[68] and, as in many groups, the predicted misfortune is very serious, for the sin of incest is understood as an attack on the foundations of the society itself. Westermarck conceded that this sort of prudentialism is widespread, but he felt the belief in misfortune is simply a rationalization for reinforcing the feeling of aversion. The problem is that Westermarck has no way of showing *why* the incest taboo

[65] Sigmund Freud, "Totem and Taboo," in *Basic Writings of Sigmund Freud* (New York: Random House, 1938), 860.

[66] See, e.g., Weinberg, *Incest Behavior*, Chap. III. Cf. Russell Middleton, "A Deviant Case: Brother-Sister and Father-Daughter Marriage in Ancient Egypt," in *The Family: Its Structure and Functions*, ed. Rose L. Coser (New York: St. Martin's Press, 1966), 74-89.

[67] See Lloyd Warner, *Black Civilization* (New York: Harper, 1937), for an excellent account of the mythical elaborations of the incest-taboo theme; cf. Raymond Firth, *We, The Tikopia*, 278-297, for a similar account.

[68] Firth, *ibid.*, 287. Cf. Ladd, *Structure of a Moral Code*, 230-231, and Weinberg, *Incest Behavior*, 239.

holds such a central place in the "rationalizations" of peoples across the world. Presumably, there are many feelings of aversion. Why single this one out and show such concern to reinforce it? An ethical theory will have to provide a more adequate account of these facts than Westermarck has done.

Finally, a theory like Westermarck's does not appear to aid the person who is himself faced with the normative task of justifying or rejecting the proscription against incest. Confronted with individuals in our own society, for example, who see nothing wrong with incest,[69] is it of any help to point out to them that many people have a positive feeling of aversion to sexual relations among members of the same family? There is no ethical force at all to such an observation.

In sum, in the case of the incest taboo, Westermarck is guilty on three counts: (1) bad social science, (2) bad normative analysis, and (3) deficient grasp of the proper points of contact between social scientific and ethical inquiry. Let us try to show how Westermarck might be improved upon at each of these three points.

1. A scientific theory must provide some lawlike generalizations that are empirically testable about a given phenomenon.[70] Thus any general explanation of the incest taboo will need to show at least (a) that the taboo functions similarly in all known societies and (b) that it is related to certain constant features of human behavior. Short of meeting these two conditions conclusively, a "theory" is, at best, a hypothesis, or a candidate for empirical verification. To my knowledge, the most promising "theories" of the taboo are still very hypothetical. These include the related proposals of Weinberg[71] and Parsons,[72] neither one of

[69] See Weinberg, *ibid.*, 124ff.

[70] Richard S. Rudner, *Philosophy of Social Science* (Englewood Cliffs, N.J.: Prentice-Hall, 1966), 10.

[71] Weinberg, *Incest Behavior*, 249ff.

[72] Talcott Parsons, "The Incest Taboo in Relation to Social Structure," in *The Family: Its Structure and Functions*, 48-70.

which has been subjected to systematic cross-cultural testing. Until they are, of course, the social scientific questions cannot be considered finally resolved.

Nevertheless, on the basis of what information we do have, the proposals of Weinberg and Parsons are intriguing. Both men found their suggestions on Freud's insight that a taboo signals the presence of severe ambivalence of emotions. Essentially, they argue that the search for erotic gratification, which generates incestuous impulses between two members of the same nuclear family, creates an acute distributional dilemma. First, it appears impossible for intense sexual attachments (with spouse and children) to be shared without rivalry and jealousy. Second, and perhaps more important,[73] failure to frustrate incestuous impulses in the child (toward his parents or his siblings) appears to retard socialization and personality development, whereby the child learns to "diffuse cathexis," or relate to and cooperate with others in the broader society. In short, according to Parsons, the incest taboo "constitutes a main focus of the *regulation* of the erotic factor."[74] And, in the words of Weinberg, the incest taboo is "essential to personality development, to family integration and to societal cohesion."[75]

Parsons acknowledges that this is essentially a functionalist explanation. But it is unobjectionable on those grounds so long as its limitations are recognized[76] and it can survive further empirical verification. As a beginning, Weinberg

[73] See Reo F. Fortune, "Incest," in *The Family: Its Structure and Functions*, 70-74. Fortune states (73): "In practically all societies . . . penalties upon incest are not motivated by the damage done within the incestuous group by the incest. The penalties are imposed upon the offenders by the wider society as a protest against the offense of disturbing social cooperation; there are usually no such penalties imposed on other analogous provocations to jealousy in families."

[74] Parsons, "The Incest Taboo in Relations to Social Structure," 68.

[75] Weinberg, *Incest Behavior*, 258.

[76] Parsons acknowledges that this "explanation" does not account for the empirical origins of the taboo ("The Incest Taboo in Relations to Social Structure," 68-69). And Weinberg makes a plea for a multicausal approach to the problem (*Incest Behavior*, 243).

has conducted extensive investigations in the United States and has drawn as well upon the results of some European social scientists. With amazing consistency the data bear out Weinberg's predictions that infringement of the incest taboo results in, or is a symptom of, personality or family disorganization.

2. It is not hard to see how our earlier suggestions for a theory of comparative ethics, based on an analysis of ethical reason, are particularly congenial to the hypotheses of Parsons and Weinberg. That is, if ethical reasoning develops around the problem of cooperation, and if incestuous relations threaten the foundations of social cooperation, then it is not surprising that the incest taboo should become a central feature of ethical systems across cultures.

Nevertheless, our reflections on ethical theory do not rest on social scientific explanations. Parsons and Weinberg might be wrong about the incest taboo without necessarily altering our conclusions about ethical reasoning. Furthermore, whatever the status of the scientific explanation of the incest taboo, ethical analysis must still attend to the kinds and patterns of reasons people themselves give for such a taboo. Here, it is suggested, our spectrum of types of ethical reason may be an appropriate guide.

3. The hypotheses of Parsons and Weinberg provide an interesting occasion for reflecting on how explanatory theories are useful in ethical argumentation. *If* the suggestion is correct that the probabilities of a correlation between incest and personality/social disorganization are high, then that is clearly knowledge any moralist would want to have in evaluating incest. This knowledge would even give a factual core of truth to the prudentialist arguments in different societies, that something disruptive is likely to happen if incest occurs.

But there is nothing logical about these connections. One must first have a prudential position (or some other ethical position) before these alleged facts about incest take on evaluative significance. One must first "give reasons" why personal and social disorganization of the sort predicted is bad, and, according to our earlier argument, this process of justifying and evaluating can never logically be based on empirical observation. Thus do we distinguish, and yet show the mutual relevance of, social theory and ethical theory.

The History of Religions: Some Problems and Prospects

H. P. SULLIVAN

WRITING nearly twenty years ago, Professor George Thomas observed that the history of religions experienced mixed fortunes in the first half of this century.[1] The spirit of religious liberalism which pervaded many college and seminary curricula accorded the history of religions a somewhat favored place in programs of study during the first two to three decades of the century. As a science, the history of religions was considered able to examine man's religions—including Christianity—with total impartiality. Such neutrality appealed to those liberals who, disdaining Christian theology, preferred a philosophical approach to religion, judging Christianity, not with reference to its dogmatic assertions, but by "a careful empirical analysis of all the data furnished by the History of Religion."[2]

During the thirties the theological climate changed. Historical and systematic theology came into new prominence, and the uniqueness of Christianity was asserted against the former view of the continuity of Christianity with other religions. This change was reflected in a rather great decrease of interest in the history of religions. Colleges and seminaries focused their attention almost exclusively upon the Judaeo-Christian tradition, relegating the study of non-Christian religions, if any, to the area of missionary theology. Since the end of World War II, however, there has been a renewed interest in the history of religions. Especially within the past ten years or so, the discipline has experienced a dramatic growth in this country, in terms both of general academic interest and support and of numbers of people studying and teaching in the field. There are at least

[1] George F. Thomas, "The History of Religion in the Universities," *The Journal of Bible and Religion* XVII/2 (April 1949).

[2] *Ibid.*, 103.

three important and related reasons for this new good fortune.

First, the Second World War and subsequent Asian wars (in Korea and Vietnam) have brought to an end the insularity of the West, particularly the United States. Hundreds of thousands of Americans in military and civilian service have had contact with the ancient cultures of Asia. Many have responded positively to them and, in returning to this country, have prepared the ground for what has amounted to a virtual cultural invasion from the East. Oriental arts and crafts have become available all over the country. Significant American subcultural movements (such as the Dharma bums and hippies) have taken much of their inspiration from the East: sitarists nearly rival guitarists in popularity; "Zen," "*satori*," "*nirvana*," and other once exotic terms are now fairly commonplace in the American vocabulary, and for little more than the price of a pack of cigarettes one can buy paperback editions of the *Upanishads*, the *Bhagavad-gita*, or the *Tao-te-ching*.

Second, there has been a widespread development of "area studies" dealing with the nations and cultures of the non-Western world. Major universities and small colleges alike have established a variety of programs in which the important aspects of non-Western cultures—including their religions—are considered. The growth of these programs has been stimulated both by an academic interest in the dramatic economic, social, and political changes in these areas and by government support of such strategic study.

Finally, the spirit of ecumenism has awakened Christian theologians to the need for consideration not only of denominations other than their own but of non-Christian religions as well. "Encounter" and "dialogue" are key words in the search for universal religious and cultural understanding and community as well as in the quest for Christian unity.

All these developments have played a part in producing the great growth within recent years of the history of religions as an academic discipline. Yet the discipline is still very much in the process of defining itself, its tasks, and its contribution, not simply to the academic consideration of religion, but to a deeper understanding of man himself. In this essay I hope to consider some of the problems rising out of this process and to suggest some prospects for the future of the discipline.

A FUNDAMENTAL problem facing the discipline in this country is that of identity. As Kitagawa observes:

> The term the "history of religions" means different things to different people. To some it is a sort of Cooke's tour in world religions, in the sense that various aspects of religions are depicted and studied, using the comparative method. To others it is essentially a philosophical study of "religion" as it underlies all historical phenomena of various religions. To still others it is a historical discipline, analogous to church history, dealing with not only one religion but a number of religions.[3]

According to a recent survey, there are 575 teachers of Asian religion in the United States and Canada. Many—possibly most—teach courses which, in one fashion or another, may be called "history of religions." Yet many are really mavericks in the field, having come to it from other fields with little or no formal training in the method or content of the history of religions. The reason for this situation is understandable in terms of the academic history of the field.[4] Until recently there were few graduate degree programs in the history of religions, and those few were rather modest. Moreover, apart from these programs graduate study in non-Christian religions was usually done either

[3] Joseph M. Kitagawa, "The History of Religions in America," in *The History of Religions: Essays in Methodology*, ed. Mircea Eliade and Joseph M. Kitagawa (Chicago: The University of Chicago Press, 1959), 14.

[4] For excellent résumés of the development of the history of religions in America, see *ibid.*, and Philip Ashby, "The History of Religions," in *Religion*, ed. Paul Ramsey (Englewood Cliffs, N.J.: Prentice-Hall, 1965).

in a theological context or as part of philological or historical research. Hence, when the post-war boom in non-Western studies took place, philosophers, theologians, biblical scholars, and general historians were called upon to teach courses in the religions of the world in order to expand curricula and to meet growing student demands for this instruction. Their chief credentials were personal interest in the material and good intentions, plus a certain amount of self-education. It is only gradually, as the number and quality of graduate programs in the discipline increases, that trained historians of religions are becoming available. This situation has resulted in a crisis of identity for the history of religions.

The different names used to designate the general field are symptomatic of this crisis: "world religions," "comparative religion," "history of religions," "phenomenology of religion." For those for whom "world religions" (a fairly recent term) is the preferred designation, the study focuses attention chiefly upon the contemporary world religious situation, particularly of the "great" or "living" religions. The emphasis is upon grasping the significance of religious faith for the believer in these traditions, rather than upon knowing the history and formal institutions. Thus the orientation seems to be a theological one, and its purpose interfaith dialogue. "Comparative religion"[5] now often denotes the same sort of inquiry, but its original intention was, of course, a specific methodological orientation—namely, comparative study. But even this comparative study is only one aspect of the total investigation of religious phenomena, and the same may be said of the "history" and the "phenomenology" of religions.

No one of these terms adequately expresses the tradition of the comprehensive study of religions known as *allgemeine Religionswissenschaft*. Because its English translation—"the

[5] The term "comparative religion" is really an unfortunate and imprecise one. I believe that it was Archbishop William Temple who observed that, whereas some people are undoubtedly comparatively religious, there is no such thing as "comparative religion."

general science of religion"—is both awkward and somewhat incomprehensible, the term "history of religions" has come to be a synonym for *Religionswissenschaft* and, when used as such, to mean a well-defined discipline with a specified method. Although the work of individual scholars of course reveals differences in the emphasis placed on one or another aspect of the method, the "history of religions" has meant the systematic investigation of man's religious life in terms of both particular religious traditions and the comprehensive morphology of religion.

It cannot be too strongly stressed that the approach of the history of religions is—or ought to be—first and foremost an empirical one.[6] Unlike so-called normative studies, the aim of the history of religions is not to say what *ought* to be, but rather what *is*. It does not begin with or attempt to posit norms (what men *ought* to believe or to do religiously); its concern is not to judge the "truth" or "value" of a religious pronouncement or performance or even the validity of religious knowledge.[7] For example, whether

[6] It would be beyond the intention of this essay to do more than summarize some aspects of the method of the discipline. There are several important statements in print: e.g., Joachim Wach, *Religionswissenschaft: Prolegomena zu ihrer Wissenschafts-theoretischen Grundlegung* (Leipzig: Hinrichs, 1924), and *The Comparative Study of Religions*, ed. Joseph M. Kitagawa (New York: Columbia University Press, 1958); G. van der Leeuw, *Religion in Essence and Manifestation*, tr. J. E. Turner (London: George Allen & Unwin, 1938), esp. "Epilegomena," 671-695; Mircea Eliade, *Patterns in Comparative Religion*, tr. Rosemary Sheed (Cleveland: World, 1963), esp. Chaps. I, XII, XIII, and "Methodological Remarks on the Study of Religious Symbolism," in *The History of Religions: Essays in Methodology*.

[7] For a fuller statement of the differences and the relationship between the history of religions and theology, see Joachim Wach, *Types of Religious Experience: Christian and Non-Christian* (Chicago: University of Chicago Press, 1951), Chap. 1, "The Place of the History of Religions in the Study of Religion"; and Joseph M. Kitagawa, "Theology and the Science of Religion," *Anglican Theological Review* xxxix/1 (1957). As for the philosophy of religion, see the brief but excellent statement by van der Leeuw, *Religion in Essence and Manifestation*, 687; also Jean Daniélou, "Phenomenology of Religions and Philosophy of Religion," in *The History of Religions: Essays in Methodology.* Although it is not a normative study,

Jesus was really the Christ or whether Mohammed was indeed the last Prophet of God are not questions that the historian of religions, *as* a historian of religions, asks or attempts to answer. Assessments of the morality of the ancient practices of temple prostitution in India or of human sacrifice and cannibalism among certain archaic and "primitive" peoples are not his task. His work as a historian of religions is rather to grasp the *religious* intentions of these practices, no matter how bizarre or repelling they may seem to him ethically, theologically, sociologically, historically—or personally. In other words, as an investigator of religious facts, the historian of religions must put aside or suspend his own value judgments as much as possible in order to let religious phenomena "speak" for themselves. There is no question here of the investigator's having to be "neutral" in matters of religion, without opinions, preferences, or commitments of his own, any more than there is for the political scientist or the art historian in his field. (On the contrary, it can be argued that a religious man is better able to understand religious phenomena than one who is antipathetic or apathetic.)[8] What is required is that the historian of religions be aware of his value judgments and commitments and avoid imposing them upon the religious facts he is considering whether by way of offering an apology for religion, for example, or of advocating a particular religious position.

It would be naive to suppose—and some historians of religions have been guilty of so supposing—that total objec-

---

the history of religions can provide theology and philosophy of religion with the basic materials for their reflections.

[8] "The study of religion presupposes congeniality. The general hermeneutical rule that some likeness is necessary for all understanding has to be applied to the special case. There is nothing more painful than the helpless attempt at the interpretation of religious documents or monuments by one who does not know what 'awe' is or to whom these testimonies to man's search for communion with ultimate reality are just the dead records of experience of 'sick-minded' or backward people." Joachim Wach, "On Teaching the History of Religions," *Pro Regno, Pro Sanctuario* (Nijkerk: Callenbach, 1950), 529.

tivity or purely "scientific" examination is possible in describing and interpreting religious phenomena.[9] No matter how intellectually cognizant one is of one's own religious position, there still remains the subtle play of emotions and temperament on one's perspective and understanding. But not just irrational or nonrational factors may intrude. For there are also the effects of some basic philosophical presuppositions to take into account—not simply personal ones, but those of one's culture. One has only to survey the development of the scientific study of religion—in the social sciences as well as *Religionswissenschaft*—over the last fifty years to see changes in the *Weltbild* of successive generations reflected in significant changes in the sorts of questions raised by investigators. The questions asked regarding religion, the particular phenomena focused upon, the manner in which the data are classified and structured —all these activities are affected by one's own historico-cultural identity.

Especially prominent today is the awareness that the questions which the history of religions has been posing and the categories it has been employing are largely Western ones, conditioned by Western conceptions of man and religion. Indeed, *Religionswissenschaft* was itself a child of the Enlightenment, and although many of the great historians of religions have been men intimately familiar with Oriental thought, the fact remains that the basic assumptions and operating concepts of the discipline—and the very notion of "conceptualization" itself—have been products of Western minds. As Kitagawa rightly observes, "Even those concerned with Eastern religions have asked, unconsciously if not consciously, "Western" questions and have expected Easterners to structure their religions in a way which was meaningful to Westerners.[10]

[9] For an excellent discussion of the factors which condition the understanding of religious data by the historian of religions, see Joseph M. Kitagawa, "*Gibt es ein Verstehen Fremder Religionen?*" *Joachim Wach-Vorlesungen* (Leiden: E. J. Brill, 1963), esp. 53-56.

[10] Kitagawa, "The History of Religions in America," 22.

It would be methodologically deceptive, then, to deny that the understanding of the investigator is somehow and to some degree *conditioned* by his own history—the social factors of his existence. On the other hand, to say that his understanding is completely *determined* by his social environment would be to commit the error Scheler rightly called "sociologism." Against this extreme relativism it must be insisted that the historian of religions does not—or ought not—*impose* religious intentions on the phenomena he encounters; if the phenomena have religious intentions, they are already there. But the investigator's ability to grasp them, as indeed his prior selection of the materials to be understood, will be qualified to the degree that he is unable to set aside for the moment—to suspend, not deny—his metaphysical, theological, and even commonsense commitments and value judgments and to enter into an empathic relationship (*Einfühlung*) with the materials. It is here we encounter the well-known insistence of phenomenological description (or descriptive phenomenology) that one must begin with the givenness, the objects. Or, as Husserl's famous slogan puts it "Back to the facts themselves."[11]

Although the historian of religions can never completely escape his cultural endowments and personal commitments and prejudices, he can at least be conscious of them and strive to achieve what Wach called a "relative objectivity."[12] This does not mean that his perspectives will no longer be conditioned, but it does mean that he can avoid the extremes both of a naive objectivism and of historical rela-

[11] The basic assumption here is, of course, that there are objects "out there" to be seen and that, in fact, one is capable of seeing them. If this assumption—or something like it—is not granted, then the history of religions has nothing to do and may as well close shop.

[12] See, e.g., Wach, *Types of Religious Experience*, Chap. 3, "The Concept of the 'Classical' in the Study of Religions"; also "Religionswissenschaft," *Religion in Geschichte und Gegenwart* (Tübingen: J.C.B. Mohr, Paul Siebeck, 1930): "Das Prinzip der 'relativen'—d.h. grösstmöglichen—Objectivität hat wie für alle geisteswiss. Forschung, so auch für die rel-wiss. massgebend zu sein," 1956-1957.

tivism and can seek an understanding of religious facts remote from him in time and place.

ALTHOUGH the approach of the history of religions is an empirical one, its total task clearly involves more than a simple cataloguing or description of facts. The historian of religions begins with historically given religious facts and directs his inquiry to the meaning of these facts in terms both of their history (that is, particular traditions) and of their morphological significance. He seeks to discern in these facts the types and structures of religious experience and expression and then to understand their essential—that is, their specifically religious—meanings. For example, sacrifice was the center of Vedic religion. The meaning of Vedic sacrifice as *Vedic* sacrifice can be grasped through an examination of the texts and traditional interpretations (that is, of its *particular* history). Its full significance can be grasped, however, only when it is seen in the light of the general morphology of sacrifice as a religious act. Likewise, certain of the religio-magical fertility practices associated with planting ceremonies of the Ashanti must be understood in terms of their contemporary significance as well as of their place in the history of Ashanti religion as embodied in the tradition, but their *full* meaning will not be known until they are viewed as part of the larger structure of fertility rites in the history of man's religions. Thus the historian of religions "is attracted to both the *meaning* of a religious phenomenon and to its *history*; he tries to do justice to both and not to sacrifice either one."[13] Yet there is always the possibility that justice will not be done to both, especially to history. And herein lies a major problem for the work of the history of religions: the balance between *history* and *phenomenology*.

The historian of religions must necessarily perform the phenomenological task of deriving "essences" (types, structures, patterns) from historical manifestations—or be con-

[13] Eliade, "Methodological Remarks on the Study of Religious Symbolism," 88.

tent with a clutter of historical facts or with pointless comparisons. These types and structures, however, are not "invented," in the sense that they are not—or at least ought not to be—*purely* subjective concepts of the investigator. They already "reside" in the phenomena (myths, rites, and the like) as definitive qualities, yet they have to be abstracted from the phenomena. As abstractions, types and structures are, as Wach cautioned, but heuristic concepts, "open to revision and correction in time."[14]

I think it important to insist that "types" are products of descriptive analysis. They arise out of an act of *integral* understanding, not just a simple, direct intuition, but a comprehension involving the total complex of the phenomenon—including its history. For the purpose of empirical investigation, at least, a particular structure cannot be said to exist apart from its concrete occurrences. (The structure has, then, an objective existence, but not necessarily a metaphysical reality). But what is seen of the total structure of a phenomenon may not be from one viewing to the next or from one investigation to the next the same. Hence two critical investigators of, say, the Hindu tradition—or more specifically within that tradition, a tantric ritual—possibly or probably may not see identically the same structure, since neither will have grasped the totality of the phenomenon's meaning. There is always something more to be seen. Yet what each has seen—that is, understood—may equally well be true of the phenomenon. Here conversation and exchange of insight between the investigators corrects and enlarges their respective decipherments. Furthermore, both must be open to the correction afforded by the discovery of new materials and by the external and internal criticism of existing materials.

What this all means is that, first of all, if the history of religions is to retain an empirical character, then phenomenology must be a methodological device, not a philosophy. To quote Bleeker:

[14] Wach, *Types of Religious Experience*, 57.

> Phenomenology in the sense of Husserl is a theory of the validity of human knowledge. A phenomenology of religion, however, intends to be an investigation into the structure and significance of facts drawn from the vast field of the history of religions and arranged in systematic order. . . . Therefore a phenomenology of religion is not a philosophy, but a *historic science* with a systematizing tendency.[15]

Its generalizations, then, must be referred constantly to historical situations for the revision and correction Wach urged. This return to the concrete is not a matter of having to wait until "all the facts are in" before a phenomenological judgment can be made; but neither is it simply a matter of "if you know one, you know them all." There is a real danger of methodological gnosticism here. Instead of allowing his concepts to mature through increasing contact with the facts, the historian of religions is apt to force a growing body of data into some rather slim conceptual scheme. In other words, his method can become prejudicial, the selection and interpretation of diverse historico-cultural facts being made to accord with some limited preconceptions. The historian of religions, then, can ill afford to rush to judgment in his phenomenological work; there must be careful historical preparation. All the pertinent details about a phenomenon must be considered. Here Max Mueller's dictum is of fundamental importance: "before we compare, we must thoroughly know what we compare."[16] Superficial examinations can be misleading; false clues may be given, and thus totally unsubstantiated phenomenological interpretations made. G. van der Leeuw, a pioneer in the phenomenology of religion, cautioned that without the control and constant correction of philological and archaeological research—that is, historical investigation—phenom-

[15] C. J. Bleeker, "Bulletin," *Numen* I/2 (1954), 147ff.

[16] F. Max Mueller, in a letter to Renan in 1883, quoted Wach, *Types of Religious Experience*, vii.

enological interpretation "becomes pure art or empty fantasy."[17]

Moreover, although it is important that the phenomenological interpretations be made on the basis of sound historical research, the historian of religions must remember that the paradigms which appear as a result of this research are methodological constructions, not (necessarily) metaphysical verities. While as phenomenologist the historian must speak of the "transhistorical" dimension of religious facts, he must with humility regard his structural abstractions as being such—namely, *abstractions.* The historical particularity of a phenomenon, even if it does not tell the whole story, certainly is every bit as definitive of the *reality* of the fact as is the transhistorical, structural significance. Indeed, the *history* of a phenomenon can be neglected only at the risk of distorting its full *meaning.* As the late Raffaele Pettazzoni asked:

> . . . is it allowable to declare that it [history] has nothing to tell us about the meaning of religious phenomena, and that historical development is fundamentally indifferent and totally negligible to phenomenological interpretation? Religious phenomena do not cease to be realities historically conditioned merely because they are grouped under this or that structure.[18]

In the last analysis, for the historian of religions as for any historian, "the understanding of individuality is the basic problem of hermeneutics."[19] Typologies and morphologies are invaluable aids in the understanding of the meaning of

[17] Van der Leeuw, *Religion in Essence and Manifestation,* 117. Van der Leeuw himself in his phenomenological investigations was not especially interested in the historical dimension of religion and overlooked the fact of historical conditioning. But, then, his personal example perhaps only underscores the importance of his warning.

[18] Raffaele Pettazzoni, "History and Phenomenology," *Essays on the History of Religions* (Leiden: Brill, 1954), 217-218.

[19] Joachim Wach, "On Understanding," in *Jubilee Book for Albert Schweitzer,* ed. A. A. Roback (Cambridge: Sci-Art, 1945), 139.

the individual phenomenon, but as in psychology, for example, they do not exhaust the *reality* of the fact.

> The endless variety of phenomena which the history, psychology, and sociology of religion provide us must be organized. Typological categories are designed to do that. "This construction of types is only intended for a better understanding of history from the point of view of life." (Wilhelm Dilthey, *Gesammelte Werke*, VIII, 100). As long as this is borne in mind there is no danger that concrete individuality and historical variety will be slighted in favor of a typological approach.[20]

History and phenomenology must go together with equal stress. In its rejection of *historicism* the history of religions can ill afford to throw out history, any more than it can afford to be preoccupied with it. The accent in the title "history of religions" ought to be equally upon *history* and upon *religions* (that is, structural meanings).[21] Again to quote Pettazzoni:

> Phenomenology and history complement each other. Phenomenology cannot do without ethnology, philosophy, and other historical disciplines. Phenomenology, on the other hand, gives the historical disciplines that sense of the religious which they are not able to capture. So conceived, religious phenomenology is the religious understanding (*Verständnis*) of history; it is history in its

[20] Wach, *The Comparative Study of Religions*, 25-26. Elsewhere Wach says: "Ein wichtiges Zwischenglied der ewiggleichen Natur und den historischen Unterschieden würden die Typen zu bilden haben. Alle Geisteswissenschaften arbeiten mit Konstruktion solcher Typen." *Religionswissenschaft*, 147.

[21] For Eliade, however, "the accent ought not to be upon the word *history*, but upon the word *religions*." (*Images and Symbols: Studies in Religious Symbolism*, tr. Philip Mairet [London: Harvill Press, 1961], 29). This view seems modified, though, by his later statement that the historian of religions "is attracted to both the *meaning* of a religious phenomenon and to its *history*; he tries to do justice to both and not to sacrifice either one of them." "Methodological Remarks on the Study of Religious Symbolism," 88.

religious dimension. Religious phenomenology and history are not two sciences but are two complementary aspects of the integral science of religion, and the science of religion as such has a well-defined character given to it by its unique and proper subject matter.[22]

ANOTHER aspect of the problem of the treatment of *history* of religions is the tendency of scholars to limit their studies either to archaic facts or to contemporary matters, rather than to deal broadly with the full range of religious history. For example, W. C. Smith suggests that the period of study of "primitive" and archaic religions is well past for the history of religions and "that progress in the study of religion can come when we can bring ourselves to forget about the *nature* of religion and attend rather to the process of its *contemporary* development."[23] Thus Smith urges a study of "living faiths" rather than the "externals of religion."[24] On the other hand, there are those who seem to regard the forms of religion in primitive and archaic settings as the only ones really worth studying, perhaps because of the belief, as Mircea Eliade states it, "that almost all the religious attitudes man has, he has had from the most primitive times . . . from the moment when man first be-

[22] Raffaele Pettazzoni, "The Supreme Being: Phenomenological Structure and Historical Development," in *The History of Religions: Essays in Methodology*, 66. See also Mircea Eliade, "History of Religions and a New Humanism," *History of Religions* I/1 (Summer 1961), 7: "In the past few years a number of scholars have felt the need to transcend the alternative *religious phenomenology* or *history of religions* and to reach a broader perspective in which these two intellectual operations can be applied together. It is toward the integral conception of the science of religions that the efforts of scholars seem to be orienting themselves today . . . . The results of these two intellectual operations are equally valuable for a more adequate knowledge of *homo religiosus.*"

[23] Wilfred Cantwell Smith, "The Comparative Study of Religion: Reflections on the Possibility and Purpose of a Religious Science," *McGill University, Faculty of Divinity, Inaugural Lectures* (Montreal, 1950), 49 (italics mine).

[24] Wilfred Cantwell Smith, "Comparative Religion: Whither—and Why?" in *The History of Religions: Essays in Methodology*, 34.

came conscious of the position he stood in within the universe. . . ."[25]

Both these positions—in different ways, to be sure—tend to depreciate history. Of the former it may be asked how profoundly we can understand the faith of contemporary men when we do not understand who these men are historically or what their faith is in terms of the community and tradition of which they are members. Surely, to achieve such understanding requires study of the so-called "externals of religion"—symbols, institutions, doctrines, practices—both in their *historical* presence and their *morphological* significance. Religious faith does not originate or exist in a vacuum; it is generated and shaped by the religious experiences of a community in its historical existence, expressed and reexpressed in myth, doctrine, ritual, and institution.

Moreover, it is questionable whether one can, as Professor Smith recommends, study "faith" in the sense of an interior quality of personal living, the profoundly intimate experience of relationship with the sacred. As van der Leeuw reminds us, in itself faith is not a phenomenon. Faith—or the religious experience in and out of which faith arises—is not the datum for historical investigation. What the historian of religions encounters are the *expressions* of religious experience in myth, symbol, ritual, and doctrine. In confronting religious expressions, the investigator seeks to understand the experience which prompted them, to delineate the structure of the experience and seeks also to devise a typology of such experiences; but the religious experience as such is not given.

[25] Eliade, *Patterns in Comparative Religion*, 463. It must be added that Professor Eliade does admit that man's changing historical situations have had an effect on his religious experience in that they have provided opportunities for "the discovery of new spiritual values" (464). Yet it is not clear how "new" these spiritual values really are, for Eliade also claims that man "is forever the prisoner of his own archetypal intuitions, formed at the moment when he first perceived his position in the cosmos" (433-434). Early (first?) man seems to have had it all; subsequent "history" simply repeats (or actualizes?) whatever was originally there.

So, in the last analysis, the "externals of religion" are all the data the investigator has to work with. The faithful assertion of a believer that "Jesus is the Christ" or that "Mohammed is the Prophet of God" is already such an external, employing not only the symbolic and conceptual language of a tradition but assuming the entire history of a community. It is difficult to see, then, how "a people's religious life"—that is, faith as an interior quality—can be set over against the several modes of expression of faith, at least for the purpose of empirical investigation. Perhaps an analogy can be made with the work of an art historian. What he examines and seeks to understand are not so many aesthetic experiences in themselves, but canvases on the walls of the Louvre or the National Gallery. Moreover, his understanding of the data entails the decipherment of a meaning which is not simply some pure experience transcending historical contingencies, but an encounter involving the flesh-and-blood reality of the artist, his time and place, his total situation. Likewise, the historian of religions has only the canvases of religious expression, and from these externals he seeks to grasp the experience which prompted them in all the complexity of its historico-cultural setting.

The second position—that of the archetypal approach—is more difficult to criticize, since its presuppositions seem to be based more on metaphysical predilections than on empirical analyses. There is no denying the especial value of archaic and primitive societies for the study of religion, since they are, in a sense, religious societies *par excellence.* In them the distinction between the sacred and profane dimensions of life is not so sharply drawn as in modern, more technologically developed societies. To restrict the significant forms of religious life to these societies, however, and to regard the *history* of religions simply as "the drama of the losing and refinding"[26] of primordial or arche-

[26] Eliade, *Patterns in Comparative Religion,* 465. The influence of Jungian psychology is undoubtedly very strong in such a view. The hypothesis of the "collective unconscious" and its "archetypes," however, is as unproven and unprovable as that of "primordial intuitions."

typal intuitions seems unwarranted. Moreover, there is something almost romantic about regarding archaic-primitive man as the *homo religiosus*.[27] This view is in a way akin to that of nineteenth-century scholars who, preoccupied with the question of the origins of religion, and thus for them its essence, looked to primitive societies for the supposedly "simplist" and hence earliest forms of religious life. In the modern approach the notion of "simplicity" and its equation with "earliest" are dropped, but "primitive" or "archaic" is still somehow taken to be synonymous with "essential" and provides the criterion for religiousness. On the basis of the universality of religion in human history and societies, it could perhaps be said with greater justification that, just as he is *homo symbolicus*, in a profound sense man—*every* man—is by nature *homo religiosus* and that the religious experience as an experience of ultimacy and completion, of reality and meaning, exists at least as a possibility of human existence.[28] "It appears," said van der Leeuw, "that 'homo religiosus' is to be found nowhere else than where 'homo' himself is found. . . . Only he who is not yet human, not yet conscious, he is no 'homo religiosus.' "[29]

[27] This view seems implicit in, for instance, Eliade's *The Sacred and the Profane: The Nature of Religion*, tr. Willard R. Trask (New York: Harcourt, Brace, 1959). In fairness to Professor Eliade, it must be said that in a number of places in his writings he does seem to accord a decisive significance to "history." Yet it seems to me that his several brilliant studies of religious phenomena and his remarks on methodology contain contradictory statements and leave the whole matter in some doubt.

[28] Such, in fact, seems to be the position of a number of anthropologists. E.g., see: Raymond William Firth, *Elements of Social Organization* (New York: Philosophical Library, 1951); David Bidney, "The Ethnology of Religion and the Problem of Human Evolution," *American Anthropologist* LVI (1954); Robert R. Marett, *Sacraments of Simple Folks* (Oxford: Clarendon Press, 1933). Marett even suggested that the title *homo religiosus* be substituted for *homo sapiens* (3).

[29] G. van der Leeuw, *De primitieve mensch en de religie* (Groningen-Batavia, 1937), 160-165, quoted in W. W. Malandra, "The Concept of Movement in History of Religions: a Religio-Historical Study of Reindeer in the Spiritual Life of North Eurasian Peoples," *Numen* XIV/1 (March 1967), 24.

Whether or not it is acceptable to assert that to be human means to be *homo religiosus*, clearly there are no empirical grounds for restricting religious man or religious meanings to some hypothetical archaic stratum of human culture or consciousness. To do so is to reduce arbitrarily virtually all of human history to the tedium of "losing and refinding" primordial intuitions. One detects in the preoccupation with the archaic and archetypal among contemporary historians of religions a fear of and overreaction to the excesses of the historicism of an earlier generation of investigators. Surely, however, the alternative to an arid historical relativism is not only an ahistorical reductionism.

As has been stated already, the historian of religions can ill afford to ignore or belittle the history of a phenomenon in his total comprehension of it. He needs to approach each historical event with an appreciation for both its uniqueness, its freshness, and the network of historical and cultural relationships in which and out of which it manifests itself. Such an appreciation of historical and cultural relationships must include, of course, the recognition that there is a sense in which every religious tradition is syncretistic, incorporating and being influenced by archaic elements in the process of historical development. Yet the significance of the historical development cannot be reduced finally to the deciphered meanings of the archaic survivals. Charles J. Adams has put the point well in speaking of the historical development of Islām: "Though it (Islām) may have sprung originally from a 'primitive' context and carried some signs of its origin with it (as what religion has not?), Islām is not a 'primitive' religion, nor is it the connection with its 'primitive' roots that constitutes its historical significance."[30]

What needs to be stressed is that the historian of religions should be interested in *all* religious phenomena, no matter where or when they occur; he cannot risk ignoring

[30] "The History of Religions and the Study of Islam," in *The History of Religions: Essays on the Problem of Understanding* ed. Joseph M. Kitagawa (Chicago: University of Chicago Press, 1967), 187.

any religious phenomenon if he is to achieve a total comprehension of man's religious life. The experience of Mohammed on Mt. Hira in circa A.D. 612 ought to be as valuable a datum as the paleolithic "art" of the Trois Frères cave or an initiation rite in a contemporary "primitive" society. His task is to investigate and understand the great diversity of religious facts which have constituted the history of man's religious life.[31] This means not only that he ought not to be preoccupied with a single cultural stratum or historical epoch but also that he cannot simply deal with a single aspect of religious experience and expression, neglecting other aspects. The historian of religions must strive to maintain a comprehensive, balanced outlook. Instead of reducing the study of religion to one type of experience or mode of expression (mysticism, symbol, myth, community), he must strive to deal with all forms—theoretical, cultic, and social.[32]

ANOTHER major problem for the history of religions is its relationship with those other disciplines which in one fashion or another are also engaged in the study of religious phenomena. One aspect of this problem is the claim of the history of religions to be an autonomous discipline, a claim not widely acknowledged. As Eliade remarks, "For nearly a century we have been striving to set up the history of religions as an autonomous discipline, without success: the history of religions is still, as we all know, confused with anthropology, ethnology, sociology, religious psychology and even with orientalism."[33] Those of us who actively profess our discipline in the academic community are painfully aware of this confusion; few of our colleagues seem to be aware that the history of religions does have "a well-defined character," to use Pettazzoni's words. In part this confusion is due to the historical "crisis of identity" already discussed, especially the association of the discipline

[31] See Wach, *Religionswissenschaft*, 21f.
[32] See Wach, *The Comparative Study of Religions*, Chap. 1.
[33] Eliade, *Images and Symbols*, 28-29.

with Christian apologetics and missionary theology, on the one hand, and philosophy of religion, on the other. (The placing of the history of religions in divinity schools and departments of religion, instead of by itself in the university, only reinforces the impression that somehow it is really a normative activity or an auxiliary of one.)

But perhaps the real fault lies with the historians of religions themselves in their failure to *practice* their discipline. Too often, for example, in the face of the rather enormous and evergrowing mass of religious data with which to some degree he must be familiar, the historian of religions retreats into the relative security and comfort of an area specialization. Eliade describes this situation well:

> A good many historians of religions are so absorbed in their special studies that they know little more about the Greek or Egyptian mythologies, or the Buddha's teachings, or the Taoist or Shamanic techniques, than any amateur who has known how to direct his reading. Most of them are really familiar with only one poor little sector of the immense domain of religious history.[34]

Indeed, this sort of specialization among historians of religions is a genuine threat to the growth and preservation of an *allgemeine Religionswissenschaft* today. A scholar may be an excellent Islamicist or Indologist or Sinologist, but he is not thereby a historian of religions. To quote Eliade again:

> Many excellent scholars . . . consider themselves "historians of religions" because they accept exclusively historical methods and presuppositions. They are in fact, however, experts on just one religion or one aspect of that religion. Of course, their works are of great value—indeed indispensable for the building of an *allgemeine Religionswissenschaft.* Nevertheless, the historian of religions, in the broad sense of the term, cannot limit himself to a single area. He is bound by the very structure of his

[34] *Ibid.*, 27.

discipline to study at least a few other religions so as to be able to compare them and thereby understand the modalities of religious behaviors, institutions and ideas (myth, ritual, prayer, magic, initiation, High Gods, etc.)[35]

What is distinctive about the historian of religions is not that he is an area specialist or a philologist—not even that he deals with religious facts, for social scientists often enough deal with such facts. What is—or should be—distinctive is *how* he deals with them, that is, his *religio-scientific method.* Indeed, it may be said that the history of religions is much more a matter of *method* than of content. But here, also, historians of religions have not always been faithful to their calling. Too often, instead of attempting to formulate their own generalizations on the nature of religion, historians of religions have relied heavily upon the theories of other areas of religious studies—philosophy of religion, theology, and especially the social sciences. The reason for this dependence may be, as Eliade suggests, a "philosophical timidity"[36] fostered, on the one hand, by the very nature of the discipline in its detailed historical researches and, on the other hand, by a "hang-up" with nineteenth- and early twentieth-century speculations. Whatever the reason, the fact is that the prominent theories of religion—the ones known to the general public and the ones which the historian of religions as teacher is constantly up against—are those produced by ethnology (usually outdated), sociology, psychology, and philosophy. Here the frustration for the historian of religions is great. For example, if he talks about myth, his listeners (especially undergraduates) have it already established in their minds that he means "disease of language," "pre-logical mentality,"

[35] Mircea Eliade, "The History of Religions in Retrospect: 1912-1962," *The Journal of Bible and Religion* XXXI (April 1963), 105.

[36] Eliade, "Methodological Remarks on the Study of Religious Symbolism," 91. Professor Eliade has done the discipline a great service in performing a sort of psychoanalysis of it in its historical development, illuminating its peculiar inhibitions, complexes, and scholarly neuroses. Moreover, he has in this country given it a new vigor by challenging historians of religions *to be themselves.*

"neurotic fantasies," "pre-scientific world views," or simply "fairy tales" and "fables." If he speaks of "primitive religion," they already know its nature is "animism," "pre-animism," "mana," "totemism," "collective sentiment," or simply the "superstitions of savages." But, then, the fault is mostly his, since for too long he has allowed others to "explain" religion.

In contrast to the methodological perspective of the social sciences on the history of religions, religion is a *sui generis* dimension of man's life, no matter how conditioned—historically, culturally, psychologically—religious experiences and expressions may be. Accordingly, religious facts need to be studied and understood in the first place as specifically *religious* facts, whatever else they may be. To approach a religious phenomenon in any other way is to miss "the one unique and irreducible element in it—the element of the sacred."[37]

It is in this insistence that the history of religions has encountered its greatest objections and misunderstandings, especially from social scientists. How can the religious phenomenon be investigated in itself? Must it not be considered in the context of economics or sociology or psychology, and so on? Of course, the Buddhist *samgha* or Islamic *ummah* or Christian church can be studied from the standpoint of sociology (for example, as a social institution) or of psychology (for example, as a source of a sense of individual and collective security and identification) or of economics (for example, as a factor affecting the production and distribution of wealth)—yet it still remains to say what it is as a *religious* community. In a similar fashion, the political institution (a state, a party) may be studied by the political scientist as a *political* institution, even though it also constitutes a body of historical, sociological, psychological facts.

The historian of religions seeks to understand the *nature* —the *religious* meaning—of a religious phenomenon, to understand it on its own terms and not in terms of any

[37] Eliade, *Patterns in Comparative Religion*, xiii.

secondary features or functions. The same may be said of the understanding of a work of art, such as Picasso's "Guernica" or Dostoevski's *Crime and Punishment.* No matter how completely it may be analyzed from the perspective of psychology, sociology, or political history, there still remains to be considered its essential (*definitive*) quality as an artistic creation. Religious expressions, like aesthetic expressions, Eliade reminds us, "exist on their own plane of reference"[38] and thus must be understood on their own plane of reference.

The history of religions cannot insist on this demand too greatly, especially in the face of the efforts by many social scientists to "explain" religion by reference to one or another "function" or "need." Such an "explanation" is, of course, no explanation at all, but only a description of an effect or secondary feature. Man does not "need" religion, any more than he "needs" art. To say that religion fulfills a "need" for a sense of order, of cosmos, of reality, is like saying that art fulfills a "need" for beauty. Similarly, to reduce religion or art to psychic trauma, infantile behavior, glandular disorder, or historical "causes" is finally to have said nothing—except, perhaps, that both the religious and the aesthetic experience are conditioned by the person to whom and the historical place and time in which they take place. Still, no matter what the context and conditions that may prompt or prevent such experiences may be, they are not in themselves the source of the experiences. The truth is that the religious experience, like the aesthetic experience, is "spontaneous, creative, free."[39]

In its insistence upon the irreducible nature of religious experience and expression, however, the history of religions has to watch that it does not become isolated from the re-

[38] Eliade, "History of Religions and a New Humanism," 5.

[39] Wach, *The Comparative Study of Religions*, 57. See also his insistence that "Wherever expressions [of religious experience] are genuine, they are meant not to serve external, that is, social, political, economic, aesthetic, or personal aims and purposes but to formulate and perpetuate man's deepest experience, his communion with God." *Sociology of Religion* (Chicago: University of Chicago Press, 1951), 371.

searches of the social sciences. This precaution again relates to the need for the history of religions to take history seriously. The important studies by anthropologists, historians, psychologists, and sociologists (of the social and cultural incorporations of religion, of individual and collective religious behavior, of social change and historical movement) all provide the historian of religion with a valuable understanding of the dynamics of religious life, both individual and collective, in the contexts of human society and culture. Thus, important as it is to know the history of the *bhakti* (devotional) Vaishnava sect as a *religious* movement in Hinduism, it is equally important to see the social-cultural dynamics of the movement in Indian society as, for example, among the Radha-Krishna Bhajans of Madras.[40] The historian of religions can scarcely ignore such studies produced by social scientists if he is to achieve a total and integrated understanding of the religious phenomenon in all its aspects.

Of particular significance for the history of religions has been the research of anthropologists and ethnographers on the question of the origins of religion and the nature of so-called primitive religion, matters which directly affect our image of man, including his "spiritual" nature.[41] Over the past one hundred years the study of religion has witnessed the promulgation of a number of hypotheses concerning the "origins" of religion, advanced largely under the influence of evolutionist and positivistic theories of human development. In 1852 Auguste Comte published

[40] See the excellent anthropological study by Milton Singer, "The Radha-Krishna Bhajanas of Madras City," in *Krishna: Myths, Rites, and Attitudes*, ed. Milton Singer (Honolulu: East-West Center Press, 1966), 90-138.

[41] E.g., the work of Adolf E. Jensen, *Myth and Cult Among Primitive Peoples*, tr. Marianna Tax Choldin and Wolfgang Weissleder (Chicago: University of Chicago Press, 1963). As Jensen remarks (2-3), "the science of religion, more than any other, stands to gain from ethnology, if only because of the preservation in primitive populations of forms of religious expression that antedate the archaic high cultures. Because the contemporary manifestations of primitive religion are usually mere petrifactions, they can be understood only with the help of insights offered by ethnology."

Catéchisme positiviste, which was followed seven years later by Darwin's *On the Origin of Species.* In 1871 Edward Tylor in his *Primitive Culture* put forth a brilliant reconstruction of the origins and evolution of religion from the earliest stage of "animism" through polytheism to monotheism. Tylor's views provided many subsequent scholars with a convenient framework within which to classify and categorize varieties of religious phenomena. By the turn of the century, however, Tylor's "animism" was giving way to "pre-animistic" hypotheses. R. G. Marett claimed that the beginnings of religion were to be found in the "pre-animistic" experience of an impersonal power (*mana*), whereas J. G. Frazer in *The Golden Bough* asserted that magic preceded any form of religion. The search for the earliest, the most elementary form of religious life attracted the interest and participation of a variety of investigators—psychologists, sociologists, ethnologists. Basic to the quest for many investigators were the assumptions that, on the one hand, the *simplest* societies (and thus the religious forms in these societies) were the earliest ones and that, on the other hand, to discover the "origin" of a thing (such as religion) was to discover also its essence. Durkheim, Fr. Schmidt, Freud, Jung, and others offered theories which in many respects illumined aspects of man's religious experiences and expressions but which never provided a final answer to the question of the genesis of religion.[42]

As it has turned out, all these researches and conflicting hypotheses have only pointed up the impossibility of ever finally determining *the* earliest form of religious experience and expression (if, indeed, there ever was *one* primordial mode) or of clearly fixing any universal evolution or development of religion. In the first place, the question of the origins of religion is not really a historical one. We simply cannot by historical research get back to the beginnings of human existence or fully decipher, in what material

[42] For excellent résumés and criticism of these theories, see Mircea Eliade, "The Quest for the 'Origins' of Religion," *History of Religions* IV (Summer 1964), 154-169; and "The History of Religions in Retrospect: 1912-1962."

remains we have, the totality of human experience behind them. It is true that archaeology and pre-historical investigations have revealed the impressive quality of early man's "spiritual" life and that we can speak with some confidence now about *evidence* of religion from at least middle Paleolithic times.[43] Yet, no amount of archaeological study and historical reconstruction will ever lay bare *the* primordial form of religion. Likewise, ethnological examinations of contemporary primitive societies can really do no more than disclose the varieties of religious structures which coexist in these societies; it cannot with certainty assign an ultimate priority to any one form. Moreover, a sociological or psychological analysis fares no better. An "explanation" of religion in terms of corporate or individual sentiments or "needs," of whatever sort, is, as has already been stated in this essay, really a description of conditions and not an explanation of causes. To say, as some have, that the religious experience is a psychological experience is to utter a truism, for all human experience is "psychological"; still, the *religious* element in that experience is simply not reducible to *nonreligious* factors. In the last analysis, the question of "origins" is not a matter for empirical inquiry, but for philosophy or theology. In any case, it is beyond the competence of the history of religions.[44]

Related to the question of the "origins" of religion has been the whole very complicated matter of "primitiveness." For Durkheim and others, "primitive" and "simple" were synonymous terms. Any society exhibiting the simplest possible social structure and a general absence of technology was classified as a "primitive society," and the religion of such a society accordingly was designated a "primitive religion." There are a number of errors in this assumption. First of all, as recent anthropological studies have demonstrated, the social structure of "primitive" societies is

[43] See, e.g., Karl J. Narr, "Approaches to the Religion of Early Palaeolithic Man," *History of Religions* IV/1 (Summer 1964), 1-22; and J. Marringer, *The Gods of Prehistoric Man* tr. Mary Ilford (London: Weidenfeld and Nicolson, 1960).

[44] Wach, "Religionswissenschaft," 1957.

usually far from simple, and there is no general absence of technological interests and skills. Besides, even in societies with a comparatively simple social organization or technology, it does not necessarily follow that religion is "simple." Indeed, ethnological studies again show that religion throughout so-called primitive societies is really quite complex.

For decades the field researches as well as the theories of ethnographers and sociologists were deeply influenced by an image of early man which in its more positive aspect portrayed him as somewhat of a child but which at worst regarded him as somewhat less than human. "In consequence," remarks Adolf Jensen, "the data on which ethnology must rely are fundamentally distorted and falsified or, at best, are not presented in the form of purely phenomenological reports."[45] It was until fairly recent times the conviction of most students of culture that in the matter of intellectual life (not to mention morality and aesthetic taste) a great gulf separated early man (including contemporary primitives) from civilized, modern man. It was asserted by a number of investigators, applying the yardstick of European culture and rationality, that early man simply was not capable of—or at least did not exercise—rationality, that his mental nature was, as one extreme position stated it, a "primal stupidity" (*Urdummheit*),[46] from which arose the initial forms of religion and culture. In one manner or another nearly all the important ethno-religious theories disparaged early man's mental capacity and his spiritual attainments. Any expression of the primitive mind which was not immediately comprehensible to the investigator—especially where religion was the expression in question—received a negative valuation as being, for example, a product of pre-logical mentality, incorrect thinking, intellectual deficiency, fear, superstition, or whatever. (It is regrettable that, having found their way into the textbooks

[45] Jensen, *Myth and Cult Among Primitive Peoples*, 2.

[46] *Ibid.* The characterization is that of K. T. Preuss in his "Der Ursprung der Religion und Kunst," *Globus* LXXXVI (Braunschweig, 1904-1905), 419.

on "man's religions," these characterizations of early man and his religious life have persisted, so that the present generation of teachers and students simply repeats them.) supporting this image of early man were certain biogenetic theories, particularly that of E. Haeckel, which stated that "ontogenesis is a recapitulation of phylogenesis."[47] Applied to man's intellectual life, this became the psychogenetic principle that human development from infancy to maturity reflects the intellectual development of the race. This view, coupled with the discovery that in their anatomy apes and human beings are strikingly similar, meant that poor early man had little chance of being accorded much human dignity. These ideas of his subhuman nature and intellectual infancy were simply applied *a priori* to paleontological and archaeological matters with totally predictable conclusions.

Increasingly, however, it is being recognized that the distance between primitive-archaic man and modern man is not as great as was formerly thought—that at least it is not one of fundamental intellectual equipment and activities. As one example, pre-historians Johannes Maringer and V. Gordon Childe in studying the stone tools of early man have seen implements which were intended to be "not only serviceable but also beautiful."[48] Maringer observes, in articulating an elevated view of early man:

> Boucher de Perthes, one of the earliest champions of this view, wrote that the man who first struck one flint against the other was also, so to speak, the first to chisel the marble of the Parthenon. In the same vein, Kraft declared that certain crudely-fashioned stones he was examining, with all their imperfections, offered as effective testimony to man's existence as the whole Louvre.[49]

[47] Karl J. Narr, "Approaches to the Religion of Early Palaeolithic Man," 3. Narr gives an excellent summary of the consequences of this theory in the study of early man.

[48] V. Gordon Childe, *What Happened in History* (Harmondsworth: Penguin, 1950), 15.

[49] Maringer, *The Gods of Prehistoric Man*, 7.

Recent anthropological studies of contemporary primitive peoples have also contributed to this new understanding of early man in terms of the fundamental unity of human nature. Claude Levi-Strauss, for example, has demonstrated that, unlike the "pre-logical mentality" with which Levy-Bruhl had credited the primitive, the "savage mind" is entirely capable of its own systems of logic and abstract thought.[50] In examining the mythic and ritual structures of primitive societies, Jensen sees them as expressive of the specifically *human* attitude assumed by man in confrontation with reality throughout his long history.[51]

The old characterizations of "primitive religion" as being something fundamentally different from "higher religion," then, simply have no basis in fact. It seems abundantly clear, for instance, that myth and ritual are not exclusively features of "primitive" religion, as was formerly thought. Rather, they are, to one degree or another, constituent features of religion wherever it is found. The truth of the matter is that man is *homo symbolicus* precisely because he expresses the profound experiences of his life symbolically—in the modes of myth and ritual. As the studies of anthropologists and historians of religions show, the mythic-symbolic and the rational-scientific are not contradictory, but complementary modes of thought; they represent two different but equally valid ways of seeing and knowing reality—the one quantitative and analytical, the other qualitative and synthetic. Neither one is reducible to the other.[52] As Pettazzoni put it, "human thought is mythical and logical at the same time."[53] For a historian of religions, religious expression can be "demythologized" or myth "demythi-

[50] Claude Levi-Strauss, *The Savage Mind* (Chicago: University of Chicago Press, 1966).

[51] Jensen, *Myth and Cult Among Primitive Peoples.*

[52] "If we make the effort, then, to use the insights at the root of mythic statements as scientific judgments, we must be fully aware of the consequences of such abstraction. The true, essential, and vital content of the myth will be lost." *Ibid.*, 182.

[53] Raffaele Pettazzoni, "The Truth of Myth," *Essays on the History of Religions*, 20.

cized" only at the risk of denaturing religion itself, for, as Eliade well says, "the myth is the ground of religion."[54]

Again, the restriction of magic to religion in primitive societies is unfounded. Rather than constituting a stage prior to religion or a mode of behavior quite distinct from religious behavior, it now is clear that religion and magic coexist. In Levi-Strauss' words, "each implies the other. There is no religion without magic any more than there is magic without at least a trace of religion."[55] In fact, it is even difficult to make a sharp distinction between religion and magic using the familiar definitions of religion as the worship or adoration of the supernatural and of magic as the manipulation or control of it. Is, a "rain dance" of an American Indian tribe, for example, more magical or less religious than a Christian rite of unction for recovery from illness? Perhaps Jensen's assessment of the relationship between the two is correct: "Magic is related to the religious world view, as applied physics is related to theoretical physics; nothing prevents a great technician from being a great theoretician also."[56]

These and other researches of the social sciences are of immense value to the history of religions in its work, just as the discoveries of the history of religions are—or should be—to the social sciences. Inasmuch as there is a common goal—the understanding of man—it is to be hoped that collaboration and fruitful exchange will increase.

"The object of the study of the history of religions," wrote Wach, "is a 'historical' one: the objectification of the human spirit; its method is an investigation which begins with exposition and culminates in understanding."[57] In the last analysis, the history of religions is entirely a matter of hermeneutics—an understanding of man in terms of his

[54] Mircea Eliade, "Australian Religions: An Introduction," *History of Religions* vi/2 (Nov. 1966), 117.

[55] Levi-Strauss, *The Savage Mind*, 221.

[56] Jensen, *Myth and Cult Among Primitive Peoples*, 231-232.

[57] Wach, *Religionswissenschaft*, 130.

religious history.[58] Indeed, from the standpoint of the history of religions, it can be said with Max Mueller that "the real history of man is the history of religion." But the religious experiences man has had in the long course of his history are not simply restricted to the historico-cultural moment. They have something to say about man—the dimensions of human experience and human expressiveness—and about reality—its modes of manifestation and comprehensibility.

With all the techniques of his discipline as a science and an art, the historian of religions in our culture performs what Eliade has termed "creative hermeneutics,"[59] deciphering and making intelligible to Western man the mysterious spiritual universe he is encountering in his growing con-

[58] I have not gone specifically into the complex matter of the process of understanding. This has been dealt with brilliantly and at length by Wach in his *Das Verstehen*, 3 vols. (Tübingen: Siebeck, 1926-1932). (See also his "On Understanding.") As a historian of religions, I have assumed, of course, that an understanding of a religion other than one's own is possible. There are those, however, who would deny this possibility. They would say that, for example, only a Buddhist can understand Buddhism. Applying this principle wholesale to the academic enterprise would introduce chaos—thus only a Marxist can understand (and teach about) Marxism, only a Frenchman French history, etc. This would turn the university into a zoo, to use John Wilson's apt image ("Mr. Holbrook and the Humanities, or Mr. Schlatter's Dilemma," *Journal of Bible and Religion* xxxii/3 [July 1964], esp. 260-61). It must be insisted that there are canons which, if observed, can lead to understanding with "relative objectivity." The mistake made by those who deny the possibility of genuine understanding of other religions is, as Professor Paul Ramsey has noted, to confuse an "understanding *of* faith" with an "understanding *in* faith." (Cited in Paul Harrison, "Theology and the University," *The Church Review* xxii/2-3 (April-May 1964), 15-17.

The basis for understanding the human facts of religion is, as van der Leeuw stated it, "*homo sum, humani nil a me alienum puto*: this is no key to the deepest comprehension of the remotest experience but is nevertheless the triumphant assertion that the essentially human always remains essentially human, and is, as such, comprehensible—unless indeed he who comprehends has acquired too much of the professor and retained too little of the man!" *Religion in Essence and Manifestation*, 675.

[59] Mircea Eliade, "Crisis and Renewal in the History of Religions," *History of Religions* v/1 (Summer 1965), 8.

frontation with non-Western cultures. Such understanding will, of course, significantly assist in bringing about a dialogue between Western and non-Western religious faiths. But, even more than that, it will contribute to a greater knowledge of man himself—not simply a quantitative knowledge, but a knowledge in *depth*—a deeper awareness by Western man of his human nature. As Eliade rightly suggests, the present encounters with archaic and Asian cultures (if correctly understood) will inevitably effect in Western man a change of consciousness which, in turn, will mean changes in cultural values. Surely, such changes are already to be seen in certain subcultural movements in the West which are largely the product of an assimilation of Eastern values—for example, Zen. But more than this is to be realized. By its hermeneutics the history of religions can unveil to Western man existential situations presently unknown to him, opening new and stimulating perspectives to Western philosophy, religion, and art. "In the end," says Eliade, "the creative hermeneutics *changes* man; it is more than instruction, it is also a spiritual technique susceptible of modifying the quality of existence itself."[60]

Does not this sort of hermeneutics really amount to a change in the complexion of the history of religions, altering the "objective" and empirical character of its study and giving it a normative function? Although it is true that at this point the history of religions moves beyond the purely descriptive to the fulfillment of what Wach called the systematic task, yet the empirical nature of the discipline is not renounced. In its hermeneutical activity the history of religions still does not advocate one religious form or another; it does not even advocate religion. It does not prescribe religion; it describes it and, in so doing, illumines the rich variety of ways in which men have been religious and what it has meant to men to be religious. Of course, the historian of religions, if he has any commitment to his study, will have already made, as Wach noted, a

[60] Van der Leeuw, *Religion in Essence and Manifestation*, 674.

"metaphysical decision."[61] He will have decided that religion is not illusory, that it is a fundamental and significant fact of human existence and therefore worth knowing and understanding. In this sense, then, the history of religions has a normative edge, but so also has, for example, the history of art or of science: any activity of human understanding requires explicitly or implicitly the decision that the thing to be understood is worth understanding.

The "creative hermeneutics" proposed for the history of religions may be said to be but the proper outcome of its phenomenological investigations. For the historian of religions, phenomenology is, after all, as van der Leeuw put it, "the interpolation of the phenomenon into our own lives. This introduction, however, is no capricious act; we can do no otherwise. 'Reality' is always *my* reality, history *my* history, 'the retrogressive prolongation of man now living.' "[62]

Thus, in attempting to understand a religious phenomenon, such as an initiation rite or a Taoist text or a Yogic trance, the historian of religions has finally to decipher not only its historical and morphological significance but its specifically *human* meaning—not simply the meaning of the experience to those to whom it occurred but its significance as a human fact to man.

Obviously, this decipherment need not violate the canons of objectivity. The hermeneutical activity of the historian of religions should not be an expression of his prejudices. The interpretation which emerges in the course of his investigation ought not to be an *a priori* imposition upon the facts. In a sense, the meaning of a phenomenon forces itself upon the investigator; yet he should hold this meaning as tentative, always open to revision. As Eliade himself states, "From a certain point of view, one can compare the hermeneutics to a scientific or technological 'discovery.' Before the discovery, the reality that one came to discover

[61] "On Understanding," 230. The "normative" nature of the history of religions was, for Wach, that common to all the humanities.
[62] Van der Leeuw, *Religion in Essence and Manifestation*, 674.

was there, only one did not see it, or did not understand it, or did not know how to use it."[63] The same can be said of other sorts of discoveries. The remains of the Indus Valley civilization "existed" for about thirty-five hundred years before they were "discovered" by excavators, but once discovered and correctly interpreted, they radically extended our knowledge about and understanding of Indian prehistory. So, in his historical-phenomenological investigations, the historian of religions discovers or "unearths" religious meanings not previously seen or fully understood, the effect of which is an enrichment of knowledge and an opening of new perspectives for understanding man. In this respect he is at one with all critical investigators of matters pertaining to man's existence. What the sociologist, the zoologist, or the physicist discovers in the course of his study can have a humanizing effect upon men, can contribute to a more profound understanding of human existence and thus provide men with new existential orientations.

In commenting on Toynbee's *Civilization on Trial*, George Thomas wrote:

> He may exaggerate the extent to which East and West are or will be united in their culture, but nc one can deny that the modern western impact upon the East is already provoking a reaction of the East upon the West, a reaction that will become stronger in the years ahead. The period of western cultural domination of the world is over.[64]

Whether or not we shall ever have the *one* world culture Toynbee envisioned, it is clear that the old cultural separations of "West," "East," and "primitive" are fading and that we are moving toward a world of what W. C. Smith has well termed "cultural pluralism."[65] In this development the role of the history of religions is or should be consid-

[63] Eliade, "Crisis and Renewal in the History of Religions," 8.

[64] George F. Thomas, "The History of Religion in the Universities," 102-103.

[65] Wilfred Cantwell Smith, *The Faith of Other Men* (New York: New American Library, 1965).

erable. For at the center of this emerging "cultural pluralism" are spiritual values the meaning of which the history of religions can uniquely elucidate. In effect, it can be the contribution of the history of religions to bring to the awareness of modern man not only his often disguised and deeply hidden religious nature but also a unity of mankind which extends not just across cultures but back to the beginnings of human existence.

The Religious as it Appears in Art

A. RICHARD TURNER

THE RELIGIOUS and aesthetic impact of Michelangelo's famed "Pietà" at Saint Peter's in Rome is so direct as to seemingly preclude any need of critical commentary. For the very reason that the work is universally accessible, I have chosen it as the particular vehicle for the discussion of a general question: what are some fruitful ways to look at a work of art in the context of the study of religion?

In asking this question, I assume that the student of religion will be satisfied fully neither by a sensitive aesthetic appraisal nor by a rigorous historical examination of the sculpture. And though by selecting this particular work I have chosen to focus on Christianity among the religions, this choice is not central to the issue. What is at issue is what might be called the "appearance" of the religious in art. The word "appearance" should be understood to have an ambiguous meaning. Many works of art which have explicit subject matter drawn from a particular religious tradition seem not to partake of any meaning beyond the simple, narrative, surface import of their subject matter. Although they are, by definition, examples of religious art, they fail to move us and may be said to yield merely the appearance of the religious. Other works, though in subject not a part of the imagery of a given religious tradition, reach out to touch on basic issues of the value and purpose of life. In them one discerns the appearance of the religious, even if their subject matter be wholly secular.

If this distinction is to be useful, I must immediately clarify what I mean by "religious." Out of the plethora of possible definitions, two should be emphasized, for the interaction between them underlies the subject of my essay. First, "religious" may denote the various aspects of religion as a part of culture. A religion with its myths, holy men, scripture, liturgy, and institutions is a complex historical phenomenon which may be described objectively. We may speak of religious tracts, religious art, religious relics, and so forth, confident that we mean no more than that the subject matter of these things is religion as a part of society and culture. Religious art, then, will convey the subject matter or symbols of a particular historical religion.

The possibility that works of art which are secular in subject might touch on issues of ultimate significance suggests a second meaning of "religious," a meaning stressed in such phrases as "religious concern," "religious commitment," and the like. Here we speak of private experiences, of the will of the individual to grapple with questions of belief and behavior which he considers to be of ultimate importance. This sort of experience is intensely personal and may have little to do with the objective phenomena of religion as a part of culture. Presumably, as I have indicated, a work of art may play a role in a man's quest to shape a life worth living, and though that work be secular in subject matter, its life-affirming resonance may be such that its meaning falls within the realm of the religious.

These two diverse meanings of "religious" throw light on a basic tension which confronts man today. He lives in an age where the forms and ritual of religion as a part of culture are on the wane, yet his need to pursue questions of ultimate concern is no less pressing than that of his forebears. Because institutionalized religion is losing its hold, the individual must assume greater risks and summon greater courage.

The religious quality of a work of art is a function of religion in both of these senses—religion as culture and religion as personal quest. When considering a work of art, the student of religion must have both meanings in mind. He will then find himself pondering a complex set of relationships: between subject matter and style, between the explicit facts of a physical object and the subjective qualities of the intelligence and temperament which experience that object, between the aesthetic and religious experience, and so forth. How, given these complexities, should a stu-

PHOTO—ALINARI

dent of religion approach the work of art? Are the customary modes of inquiry of the art historian and the theologian adequate, or should he add to them? In the pages that follow, I shall offer some tentative answers.

Instead of beginning with generalizations, we had best look closely at the physical object before us. Michelangelo's sculpture occupies the first chapel to the right as one enters Saint Peter's.[1] In spite of the vastness of the church, the roughly life-size marble group projects a mood of contemplative quietude. The subject is clear to even the untutored: the Virgin Mother laments over the limp body of her dead Son. There is a calm and simplicity about her grieving which is ineffable but immediate. The flesh is beautiful, and death not cruel, but rather the occasion for the contemplation of higher things. Beauty of form offers tangible assurance of the peace which passeth all understanding.

My impressions are subjective, but perhaps would be shared by most who experience the piece, whether or not they choose to meditate on the deeper meanings of the Atonement. The pervasive mood results from a number of conscious choices which Michelangelo made in matters of form. The group presents a rather low triangular silhouette, which suggests qualities of repose and stability. In order to achieve this unified form, the sculptor had to reduce slightly the size of Christ's body in relation to that of the Virgin, but this logical discrepancy is absolved by the aesthetic rightness of his decision. Lines are smooth-flowing, rather than angular, and so affirm the sense of repose. The outline of the piece moves slowly, and its very core is a loose spiral which begins its ascent on the left side of the base.

[1] Michelangelo in general and the "Pietà" in particular have been the subject of an enormous body of literature. The basic facts about the work and the artist's life presented in this essay are common knowledge. The fullest account in English of the artist and his works is contained in the five volumes by Charles de Tolnay, *Michelangelo* (Princeton: Princeton University Press, 1943-1960). An excellent source of bibliography is contained in the annotations to Vasari's life made by Paola Barocchi (*La vita di Michelangelo nelle redazioni del 1550 e del 1568*, 5 vols., Milan, 1962).

This line rises gradually from left to right, curving back toward the feet of Christ. From here it flows upward and toward the back of the piece, passing through the languid body of Christ and into the shoulders and head of Mary. Finally, the line moves forward through her left arm and finds release in a stoical gesture.

The drapery is disposed to echo the feeling evoked by the major compositional lines of the sculpture. The very abundance of the Virgin's drapery is necessary so that the nude body of Christ will stand out in contrast to her, and the sweeping, pendulous folds of the lower garment mirror the soft curves of the body which lies upon them. The limpness of the dead Christ is suggested not so much by the form of the body as by the weighty folds of drapery below. In a certain sense, Christ still seems to live, for his lassitude betokens not so much death as an eternal sleep, the meaning of which I shall discuss presently.

The poignancy of the group lies in the paradoxical juxtaposition of death and beautiful youth. The Christ is a young Grecian God, perfect of proportion and visage, the Virgin a maiden barely old enough to be a sister of her fallen Son. By their poses they seem united in a state of contemplation where the line between life and death is blurred.

Although other observations could be made about the piece, we now possess a basis for an exploration of some ideas suggested by its physical appearance. Remembering that our goal is an evaluation of the sculpture as an expression of ultimate concern, we should consider carefully the proper questions to ask. The first step might be to reflect upon the most basic ways in which any work of art may be discussed.

A work of art may be approached from at least two diverse points of view. The first is the disciplined, empirical approach taken by the art historian. The work of art is seen as the product of various forces—stylistic, intellectual, social, and so forth. These forces are to some extent susceptible of characterization, and so the genesis of the work and its meaning in historical context may be described.

This much is obvious, but the limitations of the method are not so clearly recognized. Too often art historians regard the work of art as an effect produced by various causes, and the scholar's attention is absorbed by the causes instead of by the work in front of him. The unique qualities of the work, precisely because they are unique, are considered less interesting than those qualities for which historical antecedents can be found. Further, like the scientist, the art historian tries to view his data as objectively as possible. The subject (the historian) views the object (the work of art) at a safe remove, and his inquiry is posed in terms of problems. And problems, of course, contain the conditions which lead to reasoned solutions, or else they are bad problems and must be posed anew. Art history, on the whole dominated by ways of thinking borrowed from the sciences, has solved many major problems and moved on to a narrower focus. This problem-solving has often been accomplished with brilliance and excellence, yet one should remember that fundamental features of man's experience of art remain largely untouched, precisely because they are not susceptible of formulation in terms of problems.

These very features neglected by the art historian constitute the primary concern of the second distinct approach to the work of art. More than an approach, it is the simple recognition that before all else, the experience of a work of an art is an existential encounter. By "existential encounter" I mean simply the meeting of the whole, not just cerebral, man with a work of art in a moment in time. This meeting involves an openness on the part of the subject, a recognition of a closing of the divide between subject and object. Whatever is ultimately true or beautiful about that work of art is, in Gabriel Marcel's sense of the term, in a realm of "mystery," approachable through reflection and intuition, but not through the rational channels of the scientifically oriented mind.

Although the student of art history may be satisfied with the first approach to the work of art, the student of religion cannot possibly be so. The essence of his inquiry must be speculation upon the import of the image to the whole man, the function of the image in worship and spiritual growth. Put more simply, religion and religious objects must be responded to fully and directly by the student if he is to perceive them correctly. It is on this fundamental point that rigorous methodology must come to grief, as we shall see.

In the spectrum of Christian thought between the celebration of the Incarnation in art and the fear of idolatry, it is clear where the "Pietà" is located. Though knowing nothing of the intellectual and spiritual background from which the work comes, one would still be able to say that its form bears witness to the immanence of the holy, to faith in a God who stands with, and not against, creation. But if one is to pass beyond this obvious intuition, one must support it with whatever historical assistance is available. Like the art historian, the student of religion should gather comparative materials and written documents in his attempt to discover what the work once meant. Unfortunately, the historical record is thinner than one might hope.

Although much is known about Michelangelo's life, the "Pietà" comes from a period of it which is not well documented. We know that Michelangelo spent the last four years of the century in Rome, but the time seems to have been unmarked by unusual occurrences. The artist frequented the circle of the antiquarian Jacopo Galli, but just what these men thought and cared deeply about cannot be recovered. Through Galli he received the commission for the "Pietà" from a French cardinal on August 27, 1498, and completed the work within two years. We know little of this man and little of Michelangelo's own thoughts during these early years. Our only intelligent course, then, is to return to the work itself, and examine its subject matter and style in the context of Italian art around 1500.

The iconography of the Virgin holding her dead Son was found in the fourteenth century both in Italy and in the North, the most familiar form being the tortured imagery of the German *Andachtsbild.* The iconography was generally less common in Italy during the fifteenth century, though it flourished in Florentine painting at the end of the century in an expanded version, which depicted Saint John and the Magdalene as helping to support the body of Christ.

As with the iconography of the "Pietà," so the style presents no unusual problems of interpretation. The classical calm of the piece complements the lively paganism of the contemporaneous "Bacchus," and both sculptures taken together prefigure the immediate future of Michelangelo's art, a combination of forms in noble repose and classic forms fraught with extreme tension. The stylistic principles of the "Pietà" accord with the artistic trends around 1500, as Heinrich Wölfflin made clear in his *Classic Art* many years ago. He who understands the principles of the "Pietà" will understand Leonardo's "Last Supper," and vice versa.

Of course, far more may be, and has been, said about the iconography and style of the sculpture. Anyone studying either the evolution of artistic style during these years or the history of this particular subject matter will no doubt object to my abbreviated account. My purpose here, however, is to speculate about the symbol which style and subject matter unite to form. And by "symbol" I mean not simply the narrative fact of the Passion here represented but the participation or reaching out of the subject toward the greater theological truth of the Atonement.

This last sentence will not sit comfortably with an empiricist, for how does one speculate about a symbol which points the way to an intangible truth? I think such speculation is possible if one begins with a question which, because of its vagueness, the art historian is likely to avoid. This question concerns what, in a Christian context, might be described as the mood of the piece. Mood is surely an elusive quality, as much a characteristic of the experiencing subject as of the object itself. Yet one need not fall back solely on personal reactions, for the "Pietà" may be compared to other objects of the same approximate date, and some consensus thereby reached regarding the sort of mood they possess. Difficult as mood is to define, one has to conclude that the quality of mood in a work of art has much to do with its efficacy as a religious image.

We have already seen that the sculpture through its quiet beauty invites contemplation of a death devoid of horror. The human body is glorified in the prime of life, and the artist's formal choices have all been directed toward a feeling of lassitude and calm. The artist who most approximates this mood in his own work is the Umbrian Pietro Perugino, the leading master of religious art in Florence in the 1490's. His Christs, Virgins, and Saints are all of a youthful, idealized type, unmarred by imperfections or psychological ambiguities. They inhabit an equally ideal world, either a simple and clean architecture or a benign Umbrian landscape whose feathery trees and blue hills know neither storm nor winter. Although the young Michelangelo may have found Perugino's artistic intelligence to be uninspired, he surely was attracted by the contemplative peace of his art.

This contemplative peace seems almost to be the pervasive mood not only of Florentine art but of much of European art at the turn of the century. One thinks above all of French *détente* sculpture, of the Master of Moulins, Giovanni Bellini, Hans Memling, Gerard David. All these men cultivated an art wherein the will of the the protagonists is suspended in reverie and quietude. These few years seem a quiet interlude between the strenuous formal investigations carried out earlier in the fifteenth century and the Grand Manner conceived by the High Renaissance masters in Italy and then exported to other parts of Europe.

At this point it would be natural to try to evaluate this mood of pensive calm, to seek out other expressions in the culture which seem to confirm the essentially optimistic affirmation made by the "Pietà" and Perugino's religious paintings. But quite possibly the student will stop short of this inquiry, finding himself beset by doubts about the sincerity of Michelangelo's work. What could it be that gives him cause for such doubts? Perhaps it is that the "Pietà" tends ever so slightly toward the sweet and sentimental, a characteristic offensive to the taste of our day. Or possibly he has misgivings because the work is so patently a technical tour de force, the facile and brilliant product of a young genius. More probably, however, he is suspicious of the "Pietà" because it lacks those qualities of tension and anxiety which are central to so much of twentieth-century experience. The proper way to dispel these doubts is to place Michelangelo's serene work in juxtaposition with the most contrasting sort of visual statement that one can find in Florentine art of the 1490's.

The painter who supplies this contrast, and who is generally taken as the surest reflection of the religious and social cataclysm of the times, is Sandro Botticelli. Famed for those mythologies which so well exemplify Laurentian Florence, he turned in the 1490's to a more highly abstracted art of almost mystical intensity. The "Pietà," or more properly Lamentation, in Munich (often dated after the death of Savonarola in 1498, but more probably a picture of the early 1490's) is a tortured counterpart to Michelangelo's sculpture. The strident colors fairly tear at one's eyes, and the horizontal compression of the figures is exceedingly uncomfortable. The lintel of the cave threatens to collapse and crush the gaunt, elongated figures, whose sunken and frozen faces bear witness to implacable tragedy.

The Botticelli and the Michelangelo could not be more different in mood and style, the one a tortured outcry, the other an expression of stoical contemplation. But which work, one wonders, more truly represents the religious temper of the times? The anxiety of these times is too well known and complex to describe here: the end of an era with the death of Lorenzo il Magnifico in 1492, the French invasions, the killing of Savonarola in 1498—just to mention some of the outward signs of this turmoil. The natural supposition would be that an art fully attuned to society would have mirrored this anguish, and so Botticelli is often regarded as the most faithful reflection of his distraught society. This evaluation is based on the assumption that an expressionistic style issues more from the depths of being than does an idealizing style. In our day Paul Tillich has put forward this point of view and has gone on to say that the reappearance of expressionism in twentieth-century art has made an authentic religious art possible once again.[2]

But both of the ideas—that authentic religious art must reflect the turmoil of the times and that expressionistic art most profoundly probes the ground of our being—are surely fallacious. In the first place, the artist may attempt to project through his art the very serenity and sense of order which his society so painfully lacks. And in so doing, he may consciously reject the expression of personal emotion in favor of an abstraction which he feels to possess a suprapersonal, or even universal, validity. In short, the question whether the "Pietà" (and the works of Perugino) or the late works of Botticelli more authentically convey the religious sensibility of their age is a question largely without meaning. Though diverse expressions, they are but opposite sides of the same coin. The one is an anguished affirmation in the face of a threat of nonbeing, the other a celebrative confirmation of the beauty and essential order of creation.

How can we account for this celebration of existence that Michelangelo conveys in this sculpture? As we know, he received no extensive formal education and, but for a remarkable circumstance, might have remained largely unlettered. This circumstance was the opportunity to enter the household of Lorenzo de' Medici in 1490-1491, where the young artist came into contact with a brilliant literary circle. In this environment he may well have acquired a taste for letters and knowledge of the prevailing Neo-Platonic philosophy. It must be admitted, however, that the extent of Michelangelo's contact with these men and the manner in which their frequently complicated ideas were digested by a sixteen-year-old remain strictly a matter of

[2] "Protestantism and the Arts," in *The Theology of Culture*, ed. R. C. Kimball (New York: Oxford University Press, 1964), 68ff.

surmise. The artist's taste for letters is mentioned, though, by the earliest biographers, who narrate that he spent time in Bologna (1494) studying the early Italian poets.

Notwithstanding the paucity of our knowledge, scholars have presented Neo-Platonic interpretations of Michelangelo's earlier works, notably the project for the tomb of Pope Julius II and the Sistine Ceiling.[3] The weakness of such interpretations, particularly of the Sistine Ceiling, is that they tend to assume the thought behind each work to be complicated, rather than simple. Neo-Platonism as expounded by Ficino is a nonvisual pedant's delight: it is at once abstruse, detailed, and pseudo-systematic. The tendency of the modern-day scholar who, like Ficino, is endowed with a mind which prefers complexity to simplicity is to bring the full weight of Ficino's pseudo-system to bear on any interpretation.

Yet is it reasonable to take the whole cloth of a philosophy in one hand, a work of art in the other, and juxtapose them? The answer of common sense must surely be "no," for what an artist understands and values in a given set of ideas may well be quite different from what the academic mind sees in them. So with Michelangelo, the poet, one must ask what Neo-Platonism meant to him. To explore this question, one need not resort to intuition alone, for there exists a quantity of letters and poems to which one may refer. The former are surprisingly devoid of discourse on ideas, whereas the latter embody a few simple and recurrent ideas.[4]

Matter is viewed in a paradoxical fashion. It is, on the one hand the earthly prison of the soul (*carcere terreno*), the bondage which prevents the desired reunion of the soul with God (*ritorno a dio*). On the other hand, seen in particular manifestations, matter reflects the purpose, splendor, and beauty of the divine order. Thus through love of an-

[3] Notably Charles de Tolnay, in the volumes cited above.

[4] The best translation of Michelangelo's poetry, with a good selection of the letters, may be found in *Complete Poems and Selected Letters of Michelangelo* ed. C. Gilbert and R. Linscott (New York: Random House, 1963).

other human being the lover may contemplate God, and the artist may look upon a beautiful human body as a mirror of God's goodness. So, while the world in one way appears to be only a shadow of reality, it may also be taken as an analogy for ultimate goodness and truth.

Assuming that Michelangelo was imbued with these ideas in 1498, do we find they help to illuminate the meaning of the "Pietà"? In any specific way, where events or exact texts might be brought forward, obviously they do not. It is at this point that the empirically oriented historian must throw up his hands, for the evidence is lacking. And yet the "Pietà" and the thought of Ficino may be juxtaposed in a most general way:

> There is born a particular love for a particular beauty, and so we are attracted to some man, a part of the world order, especially when in him a spark of the divine clearly shines. Love of this kind springs from two causes: first, the image of the Father's countenance pleases us, and second, the appearance and shape of a well-proportioned man agrees most clearly with that concept of mankind which our soul catches and retains from the author of everything.[5]

The harmonious quietude of the "Pietà" echoes the belief that the discord and dissonance within the soul are resolved only upon reunion with the One, a reunion achieved through love, and fully only when death affords release from the earthly prison.

I have already suggested that stylistically the "Pietà" is a coherent part of a group of works by Michelangelo, Leonardo, Raphael, and others which is described as High Renaissance in style. The question therefore arises whether Neo-Platonism does not offer an equally good philosophical grounding for the works of these other men. It might be objected that Leonardo's entire cast of mind would seem antipathetic to Neo-Platonism, and yet his art (the "Virgin

[5] *Philosophies of Art and Beauty*, ed. A. Hofstadter and R. Kuhns (New York: Modern Library, 1964), 224.

and Saint Anne" cartoon, for instance) at times is close to the style and mood of the "Pietà."

There are two ways out of this dilemma. One is to deny the validity of trying to explain or clarify a style by referring to the intellectual and social setting in which it arises. According to this argument, style develops largely through its own workings, and the ideas which bring about change are visual, not verbal.[6] The other possibility is to admit the connection between, in this case, art and Neo-Platonism but to emphasize that the connection is neither specific nor causal. By this method art and philosophy are laid side by side for the purpose of revealing whatever illuminating parallels they may display. This is far different from saying that Leonardo was a Neo-Platonist, or that he embraced any considerable portion of the system.

Historically speaking, aside from the inferences that Michelangelo was sympathetic to Neo-Platonism and Leonardo was not, Neo-Platonism is an equally good (or bad, depending on how one looks at it) point of reference for their respective works. What a student should understand is that the juxtaposition is better described as critical than as historical. It has little to do with the probability of the contact of a specific man with specific ideas at a given place and moment. Rather, the juxtaposition is made in the belief that common underlying characteristics of an age are more than an intellectual abstraction. In the particular case before us, the basic question is: how authentic is a work of Christian art which extols the beauty of the flesh and denies the corporeal finality of death? Although Neo-Platonism does not provide a full answer, it does suggest that Michelangelo's "Pietà" may be imbued with ideals other than those of pure form.

Much the same sort of critical use may be made of the alleged fact that Michelangelo was familiar with Dante's works before he did the "Pietà." Again, just what ideas

[6] The recent work of Professor Sydney J. Freedberg is an example of this. *Painting of the High Renaissance in Florence and Rome*, 2 vols. (Cambridge: Harvard University Press, 1961).

Michelangelo absorbed from the rich fabric of Dante's prose and poetry is uncertain. But anyone sympathetic to Neo-Platonism would find nothing but support in his reading of Dante. The fusion of Dante and Neo-Platonism in Michelangelo's day is attested to by Cristoforo Landino's commentary on the *Divine Comedy*, published in 1481.

Vasari, in his life of the artist, includes a madrigal composed at mid-century which refers to the "Pietà." Its concluding lines read:

> Bridegroom, son and father
> Your sole bride, daughter and mother.

The paradox of roles occupied by Christ and the Virgin is embodied in Michelangelo's piece by the only means possible, namely, the elimination of the difference in age between the two figures. It is sound theology, and one wonders whether both Michelangelo and the author of the madrigal had not reflected on the beautiful opening line of the final canto of the *Divine Comedy*, where Saint Bernard addresses his prayer to the Virgin:

> Vergine madre, figlia del tuo figlio
> (Virgin Mother, daughter of thy Son)

The simple yet profound concept seems echoed in the "Pietà," where all formal means are joined to effect a spiritual unity between two persons.

In brief summary of the discussion thus far, it may be said that a work of art, which stands largely in isolation when examined by a judicious empiricist, assumes rich meanings when associated critically with intellectual currents of its day. What I have done, essentially, is to try to characterize the mood of the piece and then to draw selectively upon its intellectual setting for supportive literary and philosophical parallels. This procedure, to repeat, is critical and not historical, for I ask for no proof, no cause and effect, no demonstrable ties between texts and visual objects. Does it matter whether Michelangelo actually thought of Saint Bernard's prayer to the Virgin while conceiving the "Pietà," or whether the death of Beatrice influenced his conception of death in the sculpture? Even if, as I suspect, neither supposition is correct, the validity of juxtaposing the works of the two men is hardly affected, for the truth of the meaning of what is expressed in the "Pietà" is not necessarily reducible to the facts of chronological sequence of cause and effect in the genesis of the work. If the theology of Dante helps to elucidate what with our own eyes we judge to be the theology of Michelangelo's sculpture, then our understanding of the work has been enriched, even if sound scholarly procedure has been violated. The point which must be brought home to students is that they should and must violate such procedure if they are to perceive the work of art as a religious object. This recognition constitutes acceptance of the fact that the recovery of what once really mattered can never be complete and only can be approached by a strong tempering of empirical reason by reflective intuition.

Clearly, then, a student today cannot afford to enjoy a comfortable, unproblematical relationship with a work of art, even if that work dates from a remote historical period. The work simply cannot be seen at a safe historical remove if one is to grasp its human significance. The "now" experience of the work must color any self-conscious attempts at scholarly objectivity. The "Pietà" will be a living presence for the student, though he may well wonder whether its vitality is a question of its Christian content, its form alone, or both. Many works of Christian art, once living symbols of another age, have lost their thrust and speak, even to the believer, in the language of museums. The work of art meant one thing to the artist who made it and to his contemporaries; the same work means something quite different to us.

Should a student wish to follow the vissicitudes of taste concerning the "Pietà," down to our own day, he will surely be frustrated. Although the work is mentioned fairly frequently in various sorts of literature, rarely do the passages amount to more than passing references. Only in the later eighteenth century did writers in quantity begin to question the status of the "Pietà" as a masterpiece. Their comments, grounded in a purely aesthetic point of view, were symptomatic of a fundamental change in European sensibility which provided the first obstacle to our ability today to see the "Pietà" as a work of Christian art. This change of sensibility, put most simply, was marked by the rise of the history of art as a discipline, with the German Winckelmann, and the foundation of aesthetics as a separate branch of philosophy, notably with Baumgarten and Immanuel Kant. Exactly why modern attitudes toward art should have been formulated by the 1760's is uncertain. But what is certain is that, for the literati of the Enlightenment, works of art had been largely drained of their sacral content. The work of art could be considered independently of the place and function for which it was intended, and instead of being seen in the context of Christian thought, it might be seen in the context of the Beautiful. Indeed, one might go so far as to suggest that the waning of Christian thought was a prerequisite for the rise of aesthetics as an autonomous field of inquiry.

Athough by the late nineteenth century the "Pietà" had already become "museum art," this status was to be reinforced by a further stage in the estrangement of the viewer from the work of art as a Christian phenomenon—the rise of the attitude of "art for art's sake." At the turn of the century Leo Tolstoy might lament that art was no longer a purveyor of religious values, but his old-fashioned words seemed only to be a quaint foil to Oscar Wilde's view that aesthetics was higher than ethics, that a good sense of color was more important than a sense of right and wrong. The work of art had become sacred in its own right, and, if anything, it was nature that copied art, rather than vice versa. The one sure result of such thinking (even if some of it were tongue-in-cheek) was further to assert the autonomy of the work of art, to assure that it would be regarded as a problem in form, and not as the medium through which to comment upon verbal ideas or dogmas.

That a work was Christian in subject was merely of historical interest and quite subservient to the matter of what formal problems and pleasures the work offered. Try as we may to compensate for this divorce of art from any sort of intellectual context, we partially fail. Our sensibility is attuned to works whose conundrums are wholly visual, and we resent both the illustrative and the didactic in the work of art. Even though Michelanelo's "Pietà" is still to be experienced in a sacral space, it no longer points to a reality beyond itself in the way it once did. The symbol has become Art.

This consideration raises the question whether all works of Christian art created in earlier ages may not now be simply museum pieces—indeed, whether today it is still possible to make a significant Christian statement in the visual arts. Obviously, the questions grow out of a double prejudice. First, one may have the feeling that the iconography of Christian myth and liturgy per se conveys no compelling message. The photograph of a dying soldier may stir more reflection upon the Atonement than a good painting of the Crucifixion. Second, in an age marked by abstraction in art, the artist finds it difficult to express himself through the human figure. The narrative and verbal associations provided by representational art disappear in favor of the moving but unspecific symbols of a nonobjective formal vocabulary.

If one defines religious art by our first definition—namely, as that art which draws its subject matter from the scripture and myths of a particular historical religion—then it can be argued that religious art is dying throughout the world and that Christian art, in particular, is nearly dead. Yet this possibility is not alarming, unless one goes further and says that art no longer has a place in man's personal quest for ultimate meaning. If art has such a place—and I have no doubt that it does—then our second definition of "religious" is applicable to art and would seem to be the most relevant use of the word in a thoroughly secular world.

So we may turn to the "Pietà" for the last time and try

to broaden our inquiry. As I have already suggested, the work has become "museum art," and to many viewers today it is moving only because it is a poignant statement about death in the prime of life, not because the viewer is disposed to meditate upon the uniqueness of this death or upon the universal significance of the Atonement. Let us suppose that a nonbeliever confronts the work, a man open to artistic experience, yet one for whom the subject is but one among many in a secular world. In what way, for this man, is this sculpture conducive to reflection upon values which are, in the broadest sense, religious? And this is simply a specific way of posing a more general question: how in a secular society may a work of art, be it historical or contemporary, help a man come to terms with issues of ultimate importance?

The "Pietà," like any serious work of art, is a religious affirmation when seen from the point of view of its creator. This simple idea should be stressed, for it is easy to forget that there are few, if any, more celebrative acts in human experience than the creation of a work of art. The nature of the celebration varies widely. The "Pietà," and many works of art non-Christian in subject, affirm and magnify the order everywhere present in God's creation. Other works, seemingly cries of anguish and despair, are in fact creative affirmations in the face of nonbeing. Their creators, failing to discover order in the world, make the ultimate affirmative step of imposing order on a seemingly formless world.

Through a fusion of form and subject, the content of any work of art evokes a mood which falls somewhere between poles of ecstatic immediacy and studied order. (In our day Jackson Pollock's art might represent the one, Josef Albers' the other—to take exaggerated examples both of life-styles and art.) Since religion is becoming ever less a question of explaining a world order and ever more the quest to compose a life worth living, these qualities of the work of art are significant for the good life. Any such life will be a blend of ecstatic immediacy and studied order—

hence is it not reasonable that works of art, which possess these qualities in a magnified degree, may in a certain sense function as models for the composition of an ordered life? So while an adherent of a particular religion might find the "Pietà" offensive for its specific subject, he would need be unreceptive not to recognize the aesthetic qualities of graceful order which on reflection are relevant to the profoundest issues of a man's life.

The drift of my observations suggests that, whatever the style of a given work of art, whether or not it is explicitly Christian in subject matter has little to do with its quality as an expression of ultimate concern. The double role of subject matter and style in communicating this concern might be clarified by a comparison of two twentieth-century paintings, one Christian and the other secular in subject.

Georges Rouault's "Christ Mocked" (1942) is a typical example of the Frenchman's Catholic art. The figure of Christ is drawn in simple, heavy outlines, his face and anatomy reduced to interlocked areas which are separated by bands reminiscent of the leaded strips of stained glass windows. The smouldering quality of deep reds and blues is intensified by the thick viscous pigment in which they are imbedded. These sonorous colors and the heavy drawing convey the emotional strength of the image, for, as is usual with Rouault, the strong stylizations preclude any psychological complexities based upon gesture or facial expression. The passion of Rouault's Catholicism and the bite of his social criticism are beyond question. But, in terms of twentieth-century modes of thought and feeling, how relevant is the image which he offers to us? How moving is a consciously unchanging art which both in subject and in certain formal characteristics recalls the art of the cathedrals?

Even granting the authenticity of Rouault's vision and its meaning to a devout Catholic, one suspects that for a wider Christian audience it is not truly viable as a contemporary Christian expression. My feeling about Rouault's work is the sort of feeling which Van Gogh experienced earlier about traditional Christian art. Though a religious man, Van Gogh chided his young friend Emile Bernard for painting Christian subjects, saying that such practice was no more than a delusion. Indeed, Van Gogh could not bring himself to paint traditional Christian subjects. The only exceptions are free copies after old masters, and even here, in one of these, he had to give life to old forms by endowing the suffering Christ with his own features. Van Gogh's passion and ultimate concern were limned, rather, in those convulsed landscapes of southern France. "When I have a need of—dare I say the word—religion, I go out and paint the stars." And so the cosmic landscape of "Starry Night" plumbs a meaning which the explicit symbols of Christianity could no longer touch. After Van Gogh, who speaks so clearly to the modern condition, a traditional Christian painter such as Rouault had to run the risk of irrelevance.

In the essay mentioned earlier, Paul Tillich singles out Picasso's "Guernica" as a great Protestant painting, an image which mirrors the anxiety and despair of modern man. I agree with Tillich's judgment, and at the same time I have no doubt that this secular subject is a far greater religious image than any of the Christian pictures which Rouault painted. The mural depicts the Basque town of Guernica, which was destroyed in 1937 by the Luftwaffe in the service of Franco—the first case of saturation bombing of a civilian target. In Picasso's mural we discover no antagonists in battle, only suffering victims amidst fire and death. There are no conquerors and conquered, and no distinctions of right and wrong. The specific event is universalized so that we may realize the fragmented and anguished fate of humanity is to suffer perpetually because of its own folly.

The flattened and sharp-edged planes of a belated Synthetic Cubism express forcefully the idea of a world become unhinged. The blacks, grays, and whites in the mural give an uncompromising starkness to this world, and the suggestion of newsprint by the dappling of certain surfaces bespeaks the anonymity of tragic events in the twentieth century. Yet amidst all the starkness and destruction there is the artistic affirmation in the face of the demoniac. Shattered bodies are nobly ordered in a triangular composition which, as has been suggested, is reminiscent of the pediment of a Greek temple.

The comparison of Rouault and Picasso, then, is a simple question neither of subject matter nor of form. It does help strengthen our conviction that confining the concept of religious art to art having explicitly Christian subject matter is indeed nonsensical. And it further suggests that the style of a work of art plays a powerful role in determining its religious relevance. Guernica as a subject could, after all, have inspired the most literalistic and dreary sort of narrative.

To take these thoughts one step further, does it matter, in the context of religion as a personal quest, whether a painting has a subject at all? May not the nonobjective paintings of an early Kandinsky or a Mondrian be seen as images which bear witness to an ultimate concern? Surely, the former produced pictures which celebrate qualities of the ecstatic and spontaneous, while the latter expressed the dynamic equilibrium of existence with a clarity which few artists have achieved. But although these observations seem right, they do not answer the question. The normal viewer can absorb both Kandinsky and Mondrian into his intellectual-cultural framework, but usually the acceptance will be cerebral rather than total. The artists will be familiar cultural landmarks, but in most instances the existential encounter of viewer and work of art simply will not take place. On the other hand, undeniably an elite minority has had its fundamental religious perception of the world reinforced by communion with such images.

This consideration brings us to the vital question of receptivity and participation as the *sine qua non* of religious imagery. It is a fact that not all persons are equally receptive to visual images. Part of their receptivity (or lack of it) may be innate, but much of it is a matter of experience. Ultimately the religious efficacy of a work of art depends not only upon its own quality but also upon the quality of participation on the part of the viewer. Openness to a work of art, particularly if it is not contemporary, unquestionably is enhanced by some knowledge of the historical situation out of which the work arose. This, joined to a self-conscious, reflective awareness of one's spontaneous reaction to the work of art, should lead to the maximum participation in the work. And this participation may well involve a religious experience.

Michelangelo's "Pietà," then, may be experienced either as a historical document or as the vibrant object of an existential encounter. I would suggest, however, that an either/or experience is not valuable. The student of religion interested in ascertaining the meaning of the "Pietà" as a Christian symbol at the time of its creation must overstep the judicious rules of historical scholarship and, with a recognized risk, indulge in intuition. Likewise, if he will approach the "Pietà" in a direct encounter, his perception cannot help but be enlarged by considering those bare facts of history which cast light upon the work. Unless he chooses to function solely as historian or solely as spontaneous participant, his approach will be an intuitive fusion of reason and feeling which has the courage to risk the vital but unscholarly quality of inconsistency.

Where, then, are we left in assessing the study of religion in the context of art? I have argued that, while we may analyze Michelangelo's "Pietà" in terms of mood and bring to bear relevant parallels in philosophy and literature, the essential perception of the "Pietà" as a religious object on the part of an observer in 1500 cannot be satisfactorily ascertained by applying scholarly method. I have also tried to show that our attempts to perceive intuitively the "Pietà" as a religious object may actually be more useful in understanding it than efforts to subject it to objective methodological procedures. Further, I have indicated by references to the art of our own time that it may be quite possible for a secular work to have greater religious import than a nominally religious one and that this religious import may have much to do with formal and stylistic choices made by the artist.

The whole tenor of this paper would seem to suggest that any profoundly embraced personal belief is religious, that any work of art motivated by such a belief is religious, and that open participation based upon such beliefs by an observer is religious. Such a conclusion is in part intended, though it is frustratingly vacuous in terms of any acceptable ground rules for scholarly procedure. The fact of the matter is that a work of Christian art possesses a degree of magic and potency, that it points to and participates in something beyond itself. And as I have already said, if the work is to be perceived rightly, it must be responded to directly as a religious object.

Where, we may now ask, should the student of art and religion go from here? Surely not to theology, which will use art to illustrate its categories, nor to art history, which is interested, but minimally so, in the direct encounter between the observer and the work of art. While traditional means will serve us to explore the role of historical art in historical religion, perhaps only a deepened understanding of the psychology of art will help elucidate some of the matters discussed in this paper. For this purpose we must seek increased knowledge in the psychology of art in juxtaposition to the psychological study of religion. The former is as yet in a rather rudimentary stage of development. How do we respond to a work of art, and how does this response relate to what we hold to be ultimately important? Perhaps the further advances of this scientific discipline will yield some answers. Until such time we shall have to put up with arid methodology or the perilously subjective sort of approach which I have dealt with here. For the time being, the latter may be the lesser of two evils, for it raises, if it does not begin to solve, the broader basic issue concerning the correct perception of religious objects.

The Study of Religion and Literature: Siblings in the Academic House

TOM F. DRIVER

In the early part of our century in America, theology was taught almost exclusively in seminaries. Most of these were under direct denominational control; a few were independent schools, and a few were part of universities such as Harvard and Yale. In undergraduate colleges instruction in "religion" was frequently given by persons not particularly trained for the task, whose work was usually thought to promote the "moral development" of the students rather than their academic knowledge. This situation began to change in the 1930's, with the result that the period since World War II has been marked by a vast proliferation of courses in religion, improvement of academic standards through the appointment of qualified teachers, the development of large departments in many institutions, and the gradual erosion of the difference in approach between church-related colleges and secular institutions.

The invigoration of the teaching of religion, especially from 1945 on, has led to a certain conceptual "expansion" of religion courses toward the concerns of other disciplines, a movement often spoken of as an attempt to establish or make evident the "relevance" of religion for the whole of human life. At its best the outward drive of the religion curriculum has involved an effort to engage other disciplines in dialogue about their basic assumptions regarding man and also regarding the nature of the knowledge that the several disciplines aim to produce. For obvious reasons, it has seemed more natural and feasible to initiate this dialogue with the subjects called "humanities" than with others, and among them a most productive encounter has already been achieved with the study of literature.

That religionists should be particularly interested in

literature is not surprising. To begin with, there exists, or used to exist, a strong tradition in theological education directing attention to *belles lettres* because of their bearing upon problems of rhetoric. In this tradition literature was conceived as being most relevant to homiletics. More fundamental matters were also at stake, however, and these began to surface again in recent times as religionists and teachers of literature encountered one another in academic rather than ecclesiastical surroundings. It became clear that both fields came separately upon problems of an interdisciplinary nature. There is, for instance, the problem of how to gain a right understanding of symbols and myths in a scientific and secular age; reflection on this problem leads to another called "hermeneutics," or the science of interpretive principles; and so on. These are ancient problems that have received a new importance in modern times, owing partly to developments endemic to theology and philosophy, partly to the vast increase in studies of comparative literature, and partly to the encounter between religion and literature that is our subject.

The encounter did not come about, be it noted, solely because of the outward push of rejuvenated departments of religion. It was prepared also by a certain tendency in modern literary criticism that was specifically Christian. The so-called New Criticism that was born in the 1930's and that came to dominate the field for about twenty-five years was in large measure informed by Christian or crypto-Christian assumptions. Although it is true that some of the New Criticism's most important mentors (I. A. Richards, for instance) were anything but Christian, it is also true that it was given impetus and the most useful interpretation by men who either professed Christian faith or drew much of their inspiration from its ways of thinking. Among them were T. S. Eliot, L. C. Knights, John Crowe Ransom, Allen Tate, Cleanth Brooks, and William Wimsatt. The New Criticism was radically "incarnationalist" in its interpretation of literature, making of the Christian doctrine of Incarnation an analogous literary doctrine that stood at the core of its enterprise. This provided in the field of literature a receptive ground for the invitation many religionists offered for dialogue and interdisciplinary teaching, even in the many instances where "incarnational" thought did not explicitly constitute the working agenda.

At the present time, then, there is no need to advocate the study of religion and literature as if it were a new experiment. It is already under way among undergraduates in the colleges, where new listings continually appear and where the courses are remarkably popular. It is also under way among graduate students in the seminaries and university religion departments, where the offerings again are multiplying, partly in response to the demand for undergraduate teachers and partly because of the inherent benefit that such work is assumed to have for both theology and literature. Although no thorough study has been made, it is probably safe to say that "religion and literature" courses are offered in most undergraduate colleges in the United States and in most seminaries and university graduate departments, too, even in those that do not at present provide for degree programs combining work in the two fields.

The task of this essay is to try to suggest the sort of understanding that ought to guide work already in progress, Toward this end I shall offer some theoretical reflections.

To GET THE best purchase on our subject, it is necessary to construe the topic "religion and literature" to mean "theology and literary criticism." The reason is that the fields we refer to as "religion" and "literature" are both essentially interpretive. In both of these disciplines "research" into factual matters previously unknown is subordinate to interpretation and reinterpretation of known data. Chronologically, of course, the student must begin his study by becoming informed about matters of which he was previously ignorant, but the intention of giving him such information is that he shall become able to interpret it, not that he shall be able to "use" it either for some technical end or for the purpose of engendering further research. In this sense, we are dealing with subjects in which the act of interpretation is its own end, rather than a means toward some other end. Let us consider this point first with respect to literature and then with respect to religion.

The study of literature, properly conceived, requires not only that one become familiar with a certain body of literary works and with the history of their composition but also, and primarily, that one become able to understand and evaluate those works wisely. That is, one must become able to state coherently and with power something of the literature's human meaning, so as to make it clear why the works do or do not deserve the sustained attention of men living in the present. The name for this activity is "literary criticism."

We usually reserve the phrase "literary criticism" to refer to writing done by people who have achieved a reputation as critics. This linguistic convenience, resting on a tautology, obscures a basic fact: the act of interpretation and evaluation, the literary critical act, is part and parcel of what we mean by *reading* literature. Without interpretation and evaluation a work of literature cannot be read at all, in any intelligent meaning of the word, though perhaps certain names, situations, and elements of plot may be picked out of the document for the purpose of passing an examination. By the same token, the act of literary criticism is required in order to make any sense of the history of literature. To be sure, knowledge of the history of literature aids the task of interpretation and evaluation of any particular work within that history, past or present. But unless the act of critical reading has come first, no history of literature can exist, nor can one have any notion of the relation of the particular work to the historical whole. So true is this that some critics have argued that the history of literature is a pernicious subject, that the work truly exists only in the present, without reference to historical location, held to be "extraneous" to its meaning. That is a vast oversimplification, of course, but it is true that historical perspective is ancillary, not basic, to the act of critical interpretation.

If we speak of the study of literature, then, we mean growth, through study, in the ability to perform acts of literary criticism. This in turn means that the literary criticism that already exists in the form of books and essays becomes part of our study. Right knowledge of literature, being interpretive, includes the knowledge of prior interpretations. The study of literature means study *in* and study *of* literary criticism.

The study of religion is analogous. Right knowledge of this subject requires, above all else, continued interpretation and reinterpretation of known data, without which no history of religions can exist and apart from which that history has no justification.

As there are several modes of interpreting literature, so are there various methods of interpreting religious data: historical, comparative, sociological, anthropological, psychological, and still others. These are all valid, but their use in the study of "religion and literature" is indirect rather than direct and can easily become misleading. Instead of helping to define what is meant by "religion and literature," they tend to deflect attention toward religion and *other* disciplines, those suggested by the names of the several methods mentioned.

There is, however, a kind of interpretation of religion that I have not yet named. The methods called historical, sociological, psychological, and so on, all imply a transitive approach in which the categories of one field are applied *to* another. There remains, however, a reflexive approach, born of religion itself. Call it the religious interpretation of religion, or the interpretation of religious data from a religious point of view. The proper name for this is "theology."

Theology is the rational self-interpretation and self-criticism of religion. It grows from the religious mentality itself, from religious practice, and from the need to defend and transmit a religious community's faith. To be sure, theology employs non- or quasi-religious categories part of the time, primarily drawn from philosophy. Nevertheless, the aim and norm of theology is not to achieve an extra-religious interpretation of religion, but instead an understanding consonant with and emerging from the religious phenomena themselves. This intention is expressed in Paul Tillich's dictum that the theologian, insofar as he is a theologian rather than a philosopher, operates "within the theological circle."[1]

There are many reasons why institutions of higher learning (let us refer to them collectively as "academia") are suspicious of any claim that theology should be part of the academic curriculum. The suspicion is the greater in those institutions supported by public funds, but it exists everywhere that academia is self-conscious about its devotion to criteria derived from the twin goals of disinterested research and the free exercise of reason. Thus in many quarters the term "theology" is eschewed in favor of the apparently more neutral term "religion," for religion may be regarded simply as one among many human phenomena, whereas theology carries a connotation of special pleading. In theology academia recognizes an inherent apologetic element. No amount of personal disavowal by theologians of an intent to proselytize or indoctrinate can overcome in principle the apologetic aspect of theology. Given the best and most liberal motives of theologians, they can avoid only the more crude, less intellectual, and less tolerant forms of apologetics, for there is an inexpugnable apologetic element in all that they do.

The choices available to academia with respect to the teaching of religion are thus three in number:

1. Academia may choose to avoid the study of religion altogether. To make this choice is not, at present, the trend among academic institutions, nor is there any reason why

[1] Paul Tillich, *Systematic Theology*, I (Chicago: University of Chicago Press, 1951), 8. Tillich notes: "Attempts to elaborate a theology as an empirical-inductive or a metaphysical-deductive 'science,' or as a combination of both, have given ample evidence that no such attempt can succeed."

it should be; for such a decision could be defended only on prejudiced grounds. Extended logically to the whole curriculum, it would eliminate virtually all subjects, since when they are allowed to develop methods of self-interpretation, they display an apologetic function every bit as clear as that of theology. The decision to study any field by methods peculiarly appropriate to that field carries with it the value judgment that the field exists as a "good." Otherwise, no insight can be gained, because insight is dependent upon a certain intellectual sympathy between subject and object. It is clear that literature cannot be long or well taught without the conviction that the literary imagination is "worthy" of attention and that it suggests, in large part, the criteria of interpretation that are proper to it. This condition of knowledge may be called "the apologetic situation" and is no different in religion from what it is in many other subjects, perhaps all. It appears different only because of our cultural history, wherein theological apologetics has been frequently intermixed with various forms of ecclesiastical, social, and political authority.

2. Academia may choose to insist that religion be interpreted in the curriculum only from nonreligious points of view, that is to say, from the "secular" or "neutral" perspectives of history, psychology, sociology, and so on. If such a strategy were in the long run to prove successful, the religious material would be assimilated totally into the categories of the various disciplines through which it was approached. As an autonomous realm of inquiry, religion would disappear. The failure of the strategy, on the other hand, would signify that the religious data had ultimately resisted such absorption. By success or by failure, then, this option would tend to cancel itself. To be sure, there is no *a priori* reason why it should not be tried, but there is good reason why religionists should oppose it as the *only* approach, for their acquiescence would be tantamount to an admission that religion has no integrity requiring a *sui generis* mode of interpretation. It would be to acknowledge

that religious phenomena, insofar as they *are* religious, are illusory—that is to say, epiphenomena to be accounted for by nonreligious categories.

3. Finally, academia may choose to allow the religious phenomena studied in the curriculum to suggest their own categories of interpretation, provided only that these categories, like those of other subjects, are from time to time checked against categories of interpretation arising in other fields, to the end of avoiding intellectual solipsism. This provision is consonant with the very idea of a university, which implies a concert of learning rather than a mere collection of totally independent intellectual endeavors. At the same time, it also belongs to the idea of a university, especially in the present age when neither theology nor philosophy nor any other discipline can lay claim to the title of queen of the sciences, that the correction and refinement of categories of interpretation in different fields shall be *mutual*. Lacking a regnant metaphysics, the modern university has no final court of appeal, no ultimate principle by which to adjudicate disputes that inevitably arise whenever cross-disciplinary confrontation of categories occurs. Nevertheless, the community of scholarship, supported by both public and private monies, is and must be predicated upon the provision that the work of scholars be subject to improvement by being criticized on occasion by other scholars. Within a given field this is taken for granted and is the primary reason for the requirement that scholars publish their views. It also accounts for the existence of learned societies. By the same token, cross-disciplinary critique, though it occurs less frequently, is also necessary and should be encouraged wherever the means for it are practical. Its aim is not to eliminate but to refine those categories that are peculiarly suited to the phenomena studied by the several fields.

If academia chooses to allow the third of the three alternatives here set forth, the result in the field of religion will be theological. Of course, this says nothing whatever about the orthodoxy of the theology that may emerge. Indeed, this approach, free from the constraints of orthodox opinion, would be academia's way of rendering theology a most useful service, thoroughly consistent with academia's own nature and general purpose. It would promote a theological inquiry unhampered by ecclesiastical authority, limited only by the nature of the subject matter, which could have great benefit not only for academia but also for society and the Church. Tendencies toward heterodox opinions, always dampened in church-supported seminaries (where even orthodoxy is not always welcome if it challenges entrenched practice), may be allowed open play in academia. (Witness Emory University's recent defense of Thomas Altizer, made possible largely because he was not in the seminary.) In time the Church may absorb from this source what is beneficial to it, rejecting what is not. The chances for liberalization of the Church's views are greater under this arrangement than when the Church enjoys a virtual monopoly of theological thinking.

The requirement, however, is that theology be considered as the reflective interpretation of religious faith and practice (including religious literature), rather than as an enterprise rooted primarily in abstract speculation on first principles. Only so can it claim a rightful place in the academic curriculum, and only so can it remain in fruitful interplay with its extra-academic sources.

I HAVE digressed from my main subject. I have wandered into the relation between academia and theology, and for a good reason: to show why, even in the university, the phrase "religion and literature" must be rephrased to incorporate the term "theology." Only if we use this term can we indicate what is properly involved on the religious side in any academic approach to "religion and literature." I have already suggested that on the literary side the term we need is "literary criticism." These matters may now be summarized in the following formula: theology is to religion as literary criticism is to literature.

In the academic encounter between religion and literature, both subjects need spokesmen. In themselves the subjects are facts, data, and phenomena that exist in their own right and are essentially mute with respect to their bearing upon realities outside themselves. Their spokesmen are theologians and literary critics, representing the discrete disciplines of theology and literary criticism. Thus a mediating structure is suggested. Only if such a structure is acknowledged and employed can the encounter between religion and literature prove enlightening rather than obfuscating.

This desideratum might seem quite obvious, but the principle of it is more honored in the breach than the observance. The breach has a less as well as a more sophisticated form.

The less sophisticated form is found in the tendency of some preachers and teachers to raid literature for homiletic quotations without regard for the formal properties of the literary work. In this way arise serious misinterpretations which in the long run cause the homily to backfire, since increased familiarity with the literature referred to will cause the hearer to recognize that the context of the citation has been violated. Sometimes, however, an opposite reaction occurs: the hearer takes the faulty literary reference at face value, in which case his own ability as a reader and interpreter of literature is impaired.

A more sophisticated form of bypassing the mediating structure that theology and literary criticism afford is to be found in the work of some theological interpreters of literature who assume that there are in theology certain doctrines, or categories, that can be made to yield canons of literary criticism. This way of approaching the relation of theology to literature has become very widespread. I am inclined to think that it serves as the rationale of most religion-and-literature teaching that now goes on at both the graduate and undergraduate levels. The position, which takes several different forms, is documented in a collection of essays entitled *The New Orpheus: Essays Toward A Christian Poetic*, edited by Nathan A. Scott, Jr.[2]

In the early 1930's T. S. Eliot wrote that "literary criticism should be completed by criticism from a definite ethical and theological standpoint" and that Christian readers should "scrutinize their reading, especially works of imagination, with explicit ethical and theological standards."[3] The statement seems plain enough in its apparent claim that theology should provide the capstone for such structures as literary criticism may build, yet a great deal will hinge on the way one construes the word "completed." Did Eliot intend to say that literary criticism remains incomplete without the addition of theological standards? And if so, did he mean further that the addition of such standards is the *only* way that literary criticism *can* be completed? If he meant the latter, I believe he went too far. That would be to say that theology is the queen of the science of literary criticism. If that were so, there would seem to be no reason why it should not be considered the queen of the other sciences as well—a claim that no one, I think, should be willing to defend today.

Eliot immediately added: "The 'greatness' of literature cannot be determined solely by literary standards; though we must remember that whether it is literature or not can be determined only by literary standards."

The first part of this sentence is surely true if taken in a general sense. That is, the "greatness" of literature will finally be determined by the totality of judgments about the good, the true, and the beautiful that a society shares. In the best possible world these might all be ordered by a right understanding of God and thus be theological; in a fallen world it is not likely that they will be so arranged. Yet it is only in a fallen world that the problem of the relation of theology to literary criticism emerges. The most we can now say is that literary criticism will indeed tend to be "completed" by much that is, properly speaking, out-

[2] (New York: Sheed & Ward, 1964).
[3] "Religion and Literature," in *The New Orpheus*, 223.

side its own sphere but that a clear definition of this "much" is not to be had, let alone obtained by theological imperialism.

The second part of Eliot's sentence I hold to be fatuous. The question whether a given piece of writing is or is not literature is of the same order as the question of literary greatness. The judgments we make in the one instance are different in degree but not in kind from those we make in the other. This truth is evident in a time such as ours when work that is praised by some critics is considered by others to be trash. Some writers are praised for the inclusion of elements (for instance, Jean Genet's fascination with perversity) that a number of critics hold to be inadmissible in literature.

This pluralism does not mean that there is no such thing as literary criticism. Insofar as it is analytic, literary criticism obviously exists and has an indispensable labor to perform. This is its beginning. Its "completion," which is synthetic, requires the making of value judgments and is open—that is, never quite complete. In a pluralistic culture we cannot speak of the "completion" of literary criticism by any specific program, whether theological, philosophical, psychological, or what-have-you. We may, however, invite the several disciplines to make their contribution to criticism's ideal, yet not realizable, completion; and it is on that basis that the dialogue between criticism and theology ought to proceed.

Eliot's call for a theologically oriented criticism has not gone unanswered. Professor Scott's useful volume includes a fair sampling of the response, which for the most part takes the form of trying to find in doctrine those canons by which literary creativity may be judged. Dorothy Sayers, for instance, puts forth the proposition that literary creativity is to be assessed according to a trinitarian scheme.[4] As God, in Christian doctrine, is a creator who makes himself visible and knowable through his Second Person and communicates himself in power through his Third Person,

[4] "Towards A Christian Aesthetic," *ibid.*, 3-20.

all the while remaining unfathomable and unimaginable in his First Person, so the artist, out of the unfathomable depth of himself, fashions expressive images that we may know and understand through a communicative power analogous to the action of the Spirit.

This tantalizing suggestion (more so to the theologian, I suspect, than to the literary critic because, aside from the emphasis laid on the idea of *expression* borrowed from Collingwood, it is hard to see how the scheme would help a critic to discriminate between any given works of literature) has been picked up by Denis de Rougemont.[5] He notes that, since the roots of our modern understanding of the work of artists are Romantic, we commonly say that the artist *creates*, that he *incarnates* in his works certain realities, and that he is *inspired*. These verbs, he remarks, "irresistibly evoke the attributes of the Holy Trinity." Warning against synergistic tendencies in this line of thought, he nevertheless goes on to declare that "Christian meditation will find in the vocabulary and dialectical arguments employed for nearly twenty centuries by trinitarian theologians the whole of a theory which introduces us better than any other to the human mysteries of the act of art."[6]

I have cited three of the more explicit attempts in Professor Scott's anthology to initiate a theory of art based on Christian theological premises.[7] A similar objective might be observed in the essays by David Jones, William Lynch, Preston Roberts, Walter Ong, and Professor Scott himself. Indeed, the editor tells us that the volume was compiled to illustrate the recent attempt "to discover wherein it is, if in any respect at all, that there may be said to exist the possibility of a Christian theory of literature."[8]

I maintain that the idea of "a Christian theory of literature," seductive as it may be for many theologians of cul-

[5] "Religion and the Mission of the Artist," *ibid.*, 59-73.

[6] *Ibid.*, 72.

[7] The reader should note that the idea of art takes precedence in this attempt over any specifically literary ideas.

[8] *The New Orpheus*, ix.

ture, is chimerical and dangerous. Fortunately, Professor Scott was generous and wise enough to include in his volume a notable essay by Vincent Buckley that explains what is wrong with trying to make Christian doctrine yield a literary critical theory.[9]

What is ultimately involved in criticism, Mr. Buckley writes, is "a full response—a kind of response which involves not only intelligence but the whole affective personality, and involves it even when the final judgment is a rejection of the values embodied in the work being assessed." If this is so, we may note, a Christian theory of literature, even if it existed, would fall short of that "completion" of literary criticism for which Eliot had asked. The point is that really valuable or "great" literature is of such a nature that one's most adequate response to it transcends all theory, Christian or otherwise, unless the theory be of such formality as to allow for literature's transtheoretical quality.

Miss Sayers might, of course, reply that this quality is just what she had in mind in invoking the trinity, especially in her reference to the unimaginable and unfathomable First Person. She would have touched there upon something similar to what Paul Tillich called the "depth dimension" of art, which is an inexhaustible dimension, whether taken to refer to God, the ultimate ground of all creativity, or to man, the inexhaustible perceiver of that which is created. But these reflections tend to turn us away from the literary work and our immediate response to it. They move us toward doctrines of God and man. In themselves they do not provide any criteria for distinguishing between the sort of response that is adequate to a poem and that which is adequate to a tree, because they are in fact doctrines of God (with corollary implications for man) employing aesthetic experience as analogy. Thus they have a certain theological use; but that benefit depends, in the last analysis, upon our keeping our artistic and literary response as open and as free from doctrine as possible, be-

[9] "Criticism and Theological Standards," *ibid.*, 172-186.

cause that is the only way that the analogate can retain its integrity and hence its pertinence for theology.

Mr. Buckley is right to insist:

> Of course, it is the whole person who responds to a poem or novel; and if that person is a believing Christian, then it is a believing Christian who judges; one can't, without great harm to oneself and to poetry, pretend to be something one is not. But it is not only as a believing Christian that one judges. If it were, then Christianity would be something exclusive; and all intellectual intercourse between Christians and non-Christians would become virtually impossible. But it is not. One's sensibility may be permeated with Christian values, one's vision of the world may be pervasively religious; but I see no reason why this should cut one off from full imaginative participation in the work of any artist, so long as that art has human significance and is complete within its chosen terms.[10]

To this may be added a recent remark of Professor Hyatt H. Waggoner in an article written to show that the "point of view" of a literary critic and scholar is and ought to be subordinate to his ability to see the literary work accurately and report truly what is in it: "Let the scholar-critic hold whatever point of view he chooses to, or has to, to live and work by, but let him hold it lightly enough when he is at work, so that he can entertain opposing insights, take seriously feelings which are not his own, do justice to meanings which he does not, in his nonprofessional capacity, believe in."[11]

Some theologians will object that it is wrong to regard Christian doctrine as "a point of view." They will hold it to be the expression of ultimate truth, therefore either to be rejected totally or accepted as having universal relevance.

[10] *Ibid.*, 176.

[11] " 'Point of view' in American Literary Scholarship and Criticism," in *Mansions of the Spirit: Essays in Literature and Religion*, ed. George A. Panichas (New York: Hawthorn Books, 1967), 57-58.

If the latter, they will say, then its extension into literary theory is appropriate and cannot do violence to whatever is authentic in literature.

Aside from the point that such a claim must be unwelcome in a modern university, there is the further objection that it proceeds from an improper understanding of theology. It rests upon a confusion between theology and religious faith, which is why earlier I called it a way of bypassing the structure of mediation that theology and literary criticism provide for the encounter between religion and literature. A religious faith, and perhaps especially Christian religious faith, *is* universal in its import. Christian faith is a trust that in the person and work of Christ there may be found all that is required for salvation. The theological interpretation of this faith is, however, another matter. It is by nature relative to changing times, places, education, and culture. As a man of faith, the believer will no doubt read all literature in the light of its approximation to the Incarnate One. As a theologian, however, he has to step back from personal faith (with which, in all likelihood, personal taste is mixed) to make judgments about the meanings of theological statements and systems that have emerged in history and are still emerging today. He is thus at one remove from the immediate claims of faith. Only with the aid of this reflective distance do statements of faith become theological, and only so do they become "negotiable" in human discourse.

In a similar way, the literary critic is at one remove from the immediacy of his reading of literature. He does not throw this immediate experience out the window, any more than the theologian throws out his immediacy of faith; but he holds it in reserve while he engages in reflection, analysis, and historical and sociological judgment. Finally, for the purpose of evaluation (always a treacherous business since, in principle, it ought to exclude nothing) he will readmit the immediacy of his reading experience, knowing that a literary evaluation always has about it something of a confession and a testimony.

It is when they are working at an appropriate intermediate distance from their materials that the theologian and the literary critic may receive a mutual benefit in confrontation. It is here that the theologian may discover the literary critic "unfolding" for him a literary work, *oeuvre*, or period in such a way that he can ascertain its relevance for those particular theological formulations (his own or others') on which he is working. It is here that the literary critic may find the theologian's explications relevant to his own labors of abstract or historical reflection. In short, it is while they are wrestling with "meanings" that the theologian and the critic enter upon territory common to them both, and there they may fruitfully learn from and correct each other. Finally, however, their objects are different, and therefore their ultimate conclusions will diverge. Even if, by chance, they end up saying very similar things, they will say them in quite different ways, corresponding to the different materials to which each is primarily responsible. There is no identity between theology and literary criticism, though in many formal respects they are similar and though they partly treat the same phenomenon—the human imagination expressing itself in words.

The distinction between theology and literary criticism obtains even if the theologian and the literary critic are the same person. Although this circumstance (which today is less rare than in some times past and will become more common as religion-and-literature teaching increases) produces a certain amount of ambiguity, it no more obliterates the line between the two disciplines than the theological use of philosophical reasoning obliterates the distinction between theology and philosophy. On any given occasion, the theologian-critic must decide whether he wants his final declaration to be more adequate to his theological work or to his literary critical work. The benefit that the one of his disciplines may bring to the other can and should be considerable, and I would argue that only if he is trained well in both fields can he do justice to the subtleties of thought that arise. He should be able to handle these subtleties better than any two persons can do in dialogue. Yet he will, at some point, experience a cleavage, which is the price he pays for living in human culture rather than in the Kingdom of Heaven. Then he must choose between the two fields. This is not necessarily a vocational choice to be made for the rest of his life, but rather the tactical one of where to come to rest on a given occasion. If he fails to make the choice, he will bring suspicion upon himself both as a critic and as a theologian. So will he also if he attempts to subordinate the one field to the other methodologically.

We are left, then, with a problem. Theology and literary criticism are mutually catalytic, but there is no general theory to explain this fact. The circumstance renders the teaching of religion-and-literature problematic. The subject is an area of interdisciplinary concern and not a "proper" academic field. What renders it improper is its lack of an indigenous method.

There are methods indigenous and proper to the study of theology and also to the study of literature. These methods, though always subject to improvement, are born of the material being studied and are designed to give maximum "insight" into them. Thus we may speak in a general, yet intelligible, way of theological method and literary method. But we may not speak of a theological-literary-critical method, for no such thing exists. If it did, it would be in the nature of a meta-method, incorporating and transcending the methods of the separate fields. No such meta-method has yet emerged, nor is one likely to do so.

A little reflection will show why. The achievement of a meta-method for theology and literary criticism would imply the solution of "the hermeneutical problem." That is, it would imply that we knew the interpretive principles by which all literature is to be understood, the imaginative kind we usually call "literature," the technical kind we call "theology," the less well-defined types called "liturgical," "devotional," "prophetic," and the like, and perhaps all other kinds as well. The hermeneutical problem, however, is not in the least solved. We are the heirs of classical, medieval, Far Eastern, and various modern European hermeneutics. These give us trouble enough *within* theology and literary criticism; they are far from telling us how to put the two fields together. Hermeneutical indecision is perhaps the prime symptom of the pluralism of our culture, and as long as that pluralism remains, the hermeneutical problem will not be put to rest.

Perhaps one can say, without being thought to be merely rationalizing the existing situation, that it is best that hermeneutical pluralism persist. At any rate, it cannot be overcome without a broad social agreement on first principles in philosophy, and the trouble with such agreement, even were we to reach it, is that it would be inimical to historical change. There is an asset (whatever be the liabilities) in philosophical pluralism—namely, the openness to historical and cultural change that such a condition requires. Where philosophical principles and their value correlates are fixed, society resists change. This is the reason why, if one digs deep enough into the call for a Christian theory of literature, one will find a strongly conservative social position, the most famous instance being T. S. Eliot's idea of a Christian society.

For the sake of historical growth it is necessary to abandon any attempt to construct a meta-method for the consolidation of theology and literary criticism. To be sure, this renunciation makes constructing a curriculum for their interdisciplinary study, especially at the graduate level, extremely difficult; in fact, it renders it theoretically impossible. Nevertheless, modern academia can afford the luxury of a type of training that is not theoretically justified. The social sciences and even many graduate programs in the natural sciences proceed in similar circumstances without embarrassment.

Actually, the relation to be proposed between theology and literary criticism is dialectical, though perhaps the dialectic here is an imperfect one, certainly not Hegelian, in that there is no synthesizing "third term." The two disciplines are capable of interacting with each other, stimulating, learning from, and correcting each other in numerous mutually profitable ways without our knowing, except in a most general sense, what is the overarching principle that makes their positive tension possible.

It may now be thought appropriate that I should offer some answer, however brief, to two questions that the foregoing analysis will have raised. First, into whose province in the university should the joint study of theology and literary criticism be given? Second, what positive results should come from it?

There can be no general answer to the first question. The answer must depend upon tactics and practical considerations within the university. There is no *a priori* reason why the organization of such joint study should be more the responsibility of a religion department or a seminary than of a department of English. Wherever possible, their joint responsibility should be made formal, since each has something to gain as well as many headaches to endure. At the undergraduate level, cross-listing of relevant courses and a limited amount of team teaching are usually possible and sufficient. An interdisciplinary major at the undergraduate level is not to be encouraged. At the graduate level, where a rigorous bidisciplinary Ph.D. *is* to be encouraged for a limited number of students, one department or another will probably have to assume final responsibility, though it should not do so without the strong support of the faculties in the other fields concerned.

The answer to the second question is more complicated, though it also is without an ultimate theoretical justification. Part of the answer has already been given, but a bit more may be said. Let us consider first theology's possible contribution to literary understanding.

Theological insight into human nature, into the encounter between self and world, and between self and "ultimate reality" can be of immense help to literary criticism in ascertaining and articulating the depth of human meaning in literature. In order to show just where in the work of criticism this help may be welcome, we may refer to Northrop Frye's analysis of the five phases of literary symbols—not to maintain that Professor Frye's system is everywhere accepted, but purely by way of illustration.[12]

The first two phases Frye identifies, the "descriptive" and "literal," point to characteristics of a literary work that must be analyzed primarily according to methods belonging almost exclusively to literary criticism, for these have to do with the mode of a work's description of setting, character, event, and such, and with the literary devices exploited to give the work style and unity. Insofar as these phases can be isolated for study, they present no problems to which theology is relevant, save only the incidental cases in which religious phenomena are described in literature, religious vocabulary employed, or religious forms such as liturgy put to use.

With the third phase, however, the focus begins to shift; for in the "formal" phase one is concerned with the capacity of the work's total form to suggest (Frye says by allegory) an interpretation of the world and man's relation to it. Here a clearly literary question—how adequately to describe the form of the given work—is compounded with matters philosophical and theological—how best to describe the "world" that is being spoken of indirectly and to compare it with the "real world" given to us by personal and social experience. To answer such questions apropos of *Oedipus Rex*, for instance, is to become involved willy-nilly with theological substance, and the trained religionist, provided he can appreciate the literary judgments that are here being made simultaneously, is at some advantage. His advantage is all the stronger with respect to the fourth and fifth phases.

The fourth phase, which Frye calls "mythical," requires literary knowledge insofar as the work is now to be considered in the context of comparative literature, its sym-

[12] Reference is to the "Second Essay" in Northrop Frye's *Anatomy of Criticism* (Princeton: Princeton University Press, 1957), 71-128.

bolic expressions compared and contrasted with those that recur in the history of the world's literature, where an astonishing amount of variation on common themes is encountered. But this phase of interpretation becomes to some degree extra-literary insofar as it has to do with the questions why the common themes and symbols recur in human history and what this recurrence tells us about human necessities. Inasmuch as many of these themes and symbols are also endemic to religious literature, the religionist has a positive contribution to make to their interpretation.

Frye's fifth phase, which he terms "anagogical," is clearly religious, or at least ontological, since it assumes that with certain works of literature we come to or near the center of "what all our literature is about." Certain great works (*The Divine Comedy*? *King Lear*?) tend to become in themselves symbols of the meaning of the whole of human literature. This gathering together of literature into certain points of supreme importance suggests a parallel with the way in which religious faith finds the whole of life concentrated at certain points of revelation.

These latter three phases of analysis clearly require of the critic philosophical, historical, and theological judgment. In this light we may rightly understand what Eliot meant, or should have meant, in calling for a theological "completion" of literary criticism. I think it most accurate to say that theology should not complete but rather *help* to complete the act of literary criticism. Theology is one of several extra-literary disciplines whose assistance the critic will need before he is through. Many, like myself, would hold the theological contribution to literary criticism to be especially great, but it would be wrong to say that theology alone has the key to what human imagination is all about. Faith perhaps, but not theology.

I think now of another service theology should render literary criticism: assistance in discriminating between better and worse trends in literary fashion. The literary imagination is not only individual but also social, with respect to its creation as well as its effect. Because it is partly a social phenomenon, literary creativity is stimulated more in some climates of opinion than in others, and its development is guided by the social response to it. For this reason literary criticism can itself be creative through the discernment and encouragement of new types of writing. In this aspect of its work, however, criticism once again passes into something other than "pure" criticism, and for its own health it requires supplementation by informed extra-literary opinion. Theological perspective on the human situation can therefore be of use to it. Like psychology, and unlike most other disciplines, theology is apt to be aware that the human imagination is potentially evil as well as good. It thus appreciates how great is the importance for the health of society of the guiding and shaping function that literary criticism exercises. It can participate in this function if its sensitivity to literary values is sufficiently acute.

These considerations point to the motivation for theology's interest in literary criticism. Insofar as such interest has to do with what theology gives to the dialogue, rather than with what it receives, we may say that it is ethical. My use of this word should not be interpreted to mean merely that theology will try to encourage literature that is ethically righteous and to discourage the rest. The wise theological critic will know that the important ethical issues reside, not in the didactic quality of literature (which is nevertheless real), but in its imaginative quality. Theological interest in literature, properly conceived, is ethical because it is concerned with the ethos of literary imagination, past, present, and future. Theology must attempt to be responsive to and partly responsible for a social ethos in which lively, authentic, and liberating literary creativity is fostered. Hence its concern for literature is analogous to its concern for politics and economics. As it eschews a Christian political theory and a Christian theory of economics, so also should it turn aside from the siren call of a Christian literary theory, that it may become more responsive to the positive human benefit in all theories and better able to see the errors in dogmatism, including its own.

From the side of literary criticism, we may also look for positive contributions made possible by the joint study of theology and literary criticism. First, although not most important, among these is to bring a needed measure of sophistication and learning to bear upon the apologetic use of literature by religion. I have mentioned above that such use is often heedless of good literary analysis and knowledge of literary context. The apologetic use of literature is perhaps not to be encouraged in any case, but since it has always existed and probably will continue to exist, it had best be done with more, rather than less, literary knowledge and taste. Literary criticism will enter the dialogue, therefore, partly in order to protect literature from abuse, a function thoroughly in keeping with criticism's calling.

Beyond this contribution, something more important in an academic way is to be expected. I refer to the potential benefit to be derived from analysis and critique of religious literature by literary methods. In Old and New Testament studies today the hermeneutical problem (referred to above) is acute. It cries for clarification both at a theoretical level and in every specific case of exegesis. The problem also exists in literary studies, to be sure, but there is reason to think that at present those who study religious texts have more to learn about interpretation from literary critics than vice versa. One reason may be that literary critics have for the most part had the good sense not to get themselves embroiled in discussions of hermeneutics! If biblical scholars in the past century had taken as many cues from American, British, and French literary critics as they took from German philosophers, biblical study would be far ahead of where it is today.

The full impact of literary criticism upon biblical theology has yet to be felt. The method of biblical study known as form criticism has never yet benefited as it might from a sufficiently literary understanding of form. Much biblical theology has been hampered by a rather wooden distinction between form and content. Biblical authority has been invalidly understood to mean the authority of the content of Scripture (usually conceived as doctrine) and not at all a type of authority resident in the unity of form and content in the Scriptural text. To pursue this line of thought would, of course, require that the concept of authority be reconsidered, for it would have to become less a concept of the authority of "teaching" and more a concept of authority in the imaginative life, where form and content are indissoluble. Yet the potential importance of such a reconsideration can hardly be exaggerated.[13]

Yet another contribution literary criticism may make to theology is to assist it to a deeper understanding of religious myths and symbols, aided by the critics' familiarity with the occurrence of these in world literature. Another still is to help bring to light the influences that literature has had upon the history of theology and the shaping of theological vocabulary.[14]

Finally, one may speak with some hope of the favorable influence that literary criticism may have upon the work of purifying and renewing the rhetoric of religion. *Aggiornamento* has nowhere had a more noticeable effect upon religious life than in the efforts of many religious communities, not only Roman Catholicism, to bring the language of religious expression into a natural and powerful employment of modern idiom. This movement, now more pervasive than at any time since the Protestant Reformation, is a sure sign of spiritual life. It runs the risk, however, of achieving the opposite of what it intends: it may not, in fact, strengthen but rather weaken religious language, by incorporating language robbed of conviction by advertising and mass media. The literary critical sensibility, combined

[13] A small, yet notable, start along these lines has been made by Amos N. Wilder in *The Language of the Gospel* (New York: Harper & Row, 1966).

[14] See my lecture "The Latent Image: Literary Sources of Theological Understanding," in *The Union Theological Seminary Quarterly Review*, Jan. 1968.

with theological insight, is needed here in a task of discrimination.

In summary, let me remind the reader once more that the study of religion-and-literature is not to be justified on theoretical grounds. Its strategies and its fruits will, to the extent that they are good, be practical. They will have to do with judgments, not deduced from principles, but born of the interplay among overlapping yet discrete categories, methods, and sensibilities. To avoid gross errors of oversimplification, the encounter between religion and literature is to be mediated through an encounter between theology and literary criticism. Unless this mediation is carried out, no significant progress can be made. But this mediating structure does not solve the theoretical problems thrown up by the encounter's interdisciplinary nature. The desired, though unrealizable, overarching principle of harmony between the disciplines is to be found neither by making literary theory over in the image of theology, nor by reducing theology to a species of literary criticism, nor by constructing a meta-theory to embrace them both. Nevertheless, the encounter is to be encouraged within academia because its practical benefits are considerable and because academia exists not only to deduce conclusions from established theories but also to move, by such discipline as it already possesses, from *praxis* to *theoria.* In this particular instance the theory is not likely to be found, but the search for it is valuable as an exercise of mind and a means of entrance into the wisdom of culture.

Meanwhile, those who embark upon this way, if they are willing to undertake severe labors, will find their knowledge of theology or literature, perhaps both, immeasurably increased. In academia are many mansions. Most people live in one. It is not possible to live in all, but some can and should maintain residence in two.

The Study of Religion in Colleges and Universities: A Practical Commentary[1]

JAMES M. GUSTAFSON

During recent decades there has been rapid growth in the provisions for the formal study of religion in colleges and universities. Interesting changes in emphasis have occurred, and perhaps a turning point has been reached in the claims for legitimacy of the field within the arts and sciences. I shall focus on the changing criteria for legitimation in an attempt to give some interpretation of what has occurred. I shall also examine some issues which the field does and will face.

The Legitimacy of Religious Studies

Very few, if any other, fields are as preoccupied with their legitimacy and as introspective about their self-understanding as religious studies. There are many reasons it has taken on this self-conscious posture. In religious studies we have a special burden from the past to bear. The scholarly study of religion has historically been bound up with the propagation of faith and with the apologetic interests of religious institutions in such a way that our colleagues in other fields are, even now, suspicious of the presence of covert evangelical intentions. As an integral part of the professional education of the clergy, it has been carried on in seminaries and in ecclesiastically sponsored colleges and universities. Often there has been warrant for our colleagues' suspicions. The intention underlying some instruc-

[1] Editors' note: Professor Gustafson addressed the banquet which was held during the Conference, offering some reflections on the present condition and future development of the study of religion. Although his discussion is not strictly comparable to the foregoing essays, the editors judged that it should be included in this volume because it reviews practical matters and immediate issues not examined in other chapters.

tion in religion has sometimes been directed toward saving students' religious faith while it is undergoing the challenge of critical discourse in other fields. Provocative and dramatic classroom performances have been staged for the purpose of evoking their religious interests. When the teaching has had the very proper aim of liberalizing the minds and spirits of students, it has often not been accompanied by the kinds of research and scholarly writing that accompany liberal teaching in other fields. No one would deny the legitimacy of having "religiously musical" persons teach religion, just as one would want teachers of Shakespeare who have an "ear" for drama, or teachers of the history of art who are gifted with aesthetic sensitivity. But other fields have not had quite the same kinds of extra-academic institutional sponsorship making the truth claims that religious institutions have often put forth. And, of course, prejudice is fairly evenly distributed in colleges and universities; it exists in both the critics and the defenders of religious studies. Other reasons for the attention given to the legitimacy of the study of religion need not be rehearsed; they are widely known to readers of this volume.

This quest for legitimacy is often accompanied by a lack of self-confidence on the part of the designers and proponents of studies in religion. I note this particularly because it points to a factor that is significant in the politics of higher education, although its intrinsic importance is not great. Timidity and self-criticism often attend certain forms of religious belief and practice. But while humility may be a virtue in religious life, it hardly makes for success in pursuing the claims of a field in colleges and universities. "Nice guys come in last" is an appropriate warning to all departmental architects and chairmen, including those in the field of religious studies. Perhaps this lack of self-confidence on the part of some who teach in the field is a reflection of the uncertainties of the religious enterprise in the contemporary world. If it is, it constitutes a failure to distinguish sufficiently between scholarly teaching and study, on the one hand, and vital practice of religion, on the other. Of course, it is easier to feel confident if one is working in a field that enjoys wide public acclaim and is the recipient of vast funds on the grounds of some immediate cash value that is anticipated from the research. Covetous glances toward other fields, however, will not resolve the problems that are internal to the spirit and work of a particular subject.

Insofar as religious studies has earned legitimacy in colleges and universities, there are grounds for confidence. How has the legitimacy been earned, and what are the grounds? In my observation, several developments are worth noting.

First, the process of differentiating between several types of concern with religion has proceeded rapidly. The study of religion within the framework of arts and sciences has been increasingly distinguished from (a) the professional education of religious leadership and (b) the religious, pastoral, and moral care of students. Two symbols of this change are salient. One is the institutional separation of professional theological education from undergraduate and graduate studies which the establishment of the Departments of Religious Studies at Yale University and at Duke University represents. The second is the separation of the office of chaplain in many colleges and universities from the department of religion. It is certainly my impression that there are now fewer chaplain-teachers than there have been in the past.

I believe that different fundamental intentions can be distinguished in these three enterprises, though often they are best stated in negative terms and often there is a considerable amount of overlap remaining between them. Departments of religion are not training men to serve as pastors in congregations, and they are not developing creative forms of religious ministries; seminaries are. Although there are distinguished universities which continue to keep Ph.D. studies and professional studies under the auspices of divinity schools, and although there are distinguished seminaries which also have graduate programs (and more seminaries that are developing cooperative arrangements to establish such programs), each has some awareness that professional education and scholarly research and teaching cannot be collapsed into one another. Undergraduate departments do not undertake to stimulate the devotional life of students; they are not agents to bring about religious conversions; they do not seek to be pulpits for gifted preachers. And they have no special vocation to instigate social reforms, though personal religious life and social conscience may be indirectly enhanced through exposure to their offerings. There are, of course, exceptions: even in some state universities one observes departments that make their primary appeal, not to the subject matter of religion, but to the spiritual, religious, and moral concerns of undergraduate students.

The open questions that remain after this differentiation of intentions has been noted pertain not only to areas of overlap but also to matters for which members of departments of religion might continue to have personal (though perhaps not official) responsibilities. Most scholars in the field of religion would be unhappy, for example, if professional theological education were modeled on technical or trade school training and oriented by the whimsies and fickleness, as well as by the defensible concerns, of religious communities. Certainly, high-quality research and instruction is necessary in theological schools as well as in departments of religion. What, then, does constitute professional education for religious leadership in a time when the arts and sciences provide much of the academic orientation in religion and when the purpose of religious leadership in our society is itself uncertain?

Those who now hold appointments in departments of religion have the comfort of greater certitude of purpose than do teachers in seminaries; they would be at least ungrateful and perhaps even irresponsible if they did not assist in the clarification of the distinction between professional education and their own work.

A second open question is the significance of the religious

and moral interests and concerns of undergraduate and graduate students. Clearly, the departments have no official responsibility to nourish these interests, though they are their beneficiaries insofar as study of religion is motivated by them. Some would assert that whatever significance the departments have for these interests is to be "caught" and not "taught." Others would make room in the kinds of studies students do, the kinds of papers they write and questions they are asked to answer, for expression of these concerns. My observation is that the work of a department can be more plainly and easily oriented around its peculiar academic intention where there are very intelligent and sensitive chaplains or other religious leaders on the campus. When such staffs are not very competent, more burden falls on the teachers in the field to meet these needs in extracurricular (if not curricular) ways. In this respect members of departments of religion are probably less unlike members of other departments than is sometimes perceived. Political scientists and sociologists, for example, are frequently called upon to be leaders of action projects or counselors to those in voluntary student groups who wish not only to learn about politics and society but to develop and act on their own political beliefs.

A third open question pertains to the diversity of opinion regarding the positive delineation of the intention of the work in a department of religion. With some ease we can draw the outside lines to mark off what the purpose of a department is *not*, but within these perimeters there remains extensive difference of opinion. The differences concern issues some of which are substantial, some peripheral. The disciplines and methods of research, for instance, are frequently subjects of debate. Religious studies is most often seen as belonging to the family of the humanities; this view of it raises questions about the place of sociology and psychology of religion in departments and programs. Within the disciplines of the humanities, there are preferences for historical study over philosophical study and for study of texts over studies of religious institutions in relationship to culture, to cite two examples. Personally I would plead for pluralism in such matters and for the avoidance of ideological purity in the delineation of approaches to the study of religion. The qualitative judgments of the research and teaching done, whether as philosophy, sociology, history, or psychology of religion, are more important in establishing a consensus on standards than is formal agreement on a discipline or approach to the study.

A second achievement in religious studies over the past decades is the establishment of legitimacy in the arts and sciences through the development of a posture of analytical rigor, of disinterested objectivity, and sometimes of disinterested irreverence. I use the word "posture" quite deliberately to refer to the stance toward the material that has been adopted. Persons working in religious studies are not likely to wince at the profanation that seems to take place when the procedures of various disciplines are applied to religious subject matter—though they will continue to encounter colleagues who will attempt to shock them with remarks that are designed to be irreverent. They are not put on the defensive because they have learned that personal detachment is a requirement of academic discourse about any subject matter and that no sanctuary from criticism is properly granted within liberal education. Disinterested objectivity and irreverence might appear to be too strong to be commendable; analytical rigor seems more balanced and proper. These terms have been added precisely to twist the comments toward the more problematic. They suggest that there may be some overreaction to the demands for rigor on the part of some teachers in the field, that a legitimate posture turns into dramatic posturing for the sake of proving oneself or for the sake of shocking naive students. Such dramatic posturing, even as a pedagogical device, hardly sustains the legitimacy of scholarship and teaching in religious studies any more than it would elsewhere, though it may create momentary excitement.

More substantial than a posture (even in the best sense) is the achievement of scholarly competence. It is my personal judgment that nothing legitimates religious studies more than the demonstrated competence in scholarship of those who work in the field. Since one may say the same for every other field as well, this may appear to be an inane comment. Yet it is worthy of reiteration. Scholarly competence is demonstrated both in the quality of teaching and in the value of publications that come from research. Again, what is obvious seems sometimes to be forgotten. In one lecture I heard on "good teaching" in religion, the speaker did not once mention mastery of subject matter but dwelled instead on many points which, in my judgment, are far more trivial. Mastery of the subject matter, of the critical issues in it, of the methods by which it can be explored and developed, of alternative possibilities for interpretation and explanation, of how to make a cogent argument—these are all necessary in any field. As work in religious studies proves itself capable of fulfilling these and other criteria of scholarly competence, it wins respect in the colleges and universities. Without this proficiency teaching becomes clever or superficial.

The publication of competent and significant scholarly work is a third achievement which has contributed to the legitimacy of the field. This is of greatest importance in developing not only the reputation of a given department in a specific university but the intellectual vigor of the field of religious studies as a whole. In this area there are considerable differences in performance among subdisciplines within the field of religion, and the waters are often muddied by the multiple roles played by scholars in the field. The technical rigor of scholarship in biblical studies and in the history of Christianity, for example, is often more impressive than what one finds in the studies of religious ethics and religious thought. Work in the history and thought of non-Western religions, which comes from linguistic and historical competence, earns its way more than imaginative leaps from thought to thought which titillate the curiosities of students seeking to save their souls or to find their identities. Respect for the field, in my judgment, is gained faster by publication that can win the esteem of persons in other disciplines and fields than it is by any other single factor.

The roles of persons in the field continue to be multiple: there are religious communities which turn to scholars for guidance in the formulation of their ideas, for literature which assists in the propagation of the faith, for speaking and lecturing to the religious masses. No other department in the humanities is placed in quite the same sociological situation as religious studies, since seminaries are not sufficient in themselves to fulfill all the services required by religious communities. My point can be made clear with the following observation. Some of the most newsworthy writers in the field of religious ideas during the past decade would be an academic embarrassment to many of the most respectable departments of religion in our universities. Some might use this observation as a platform from which to criticize the work of such departments: they would be accused of irrelevance, unimaginative thinking, pedantry and general dullness. Others might suggest that there are different vocations in the production of literary work in religion and that the same persons might well exercise alternative ones on different occasions. After all, some scholars in other fields as well are publicists and activists. Still others would wish that an individual's vocation be kept fixed and that any effort to combine several vocations in one person's career be eschewed. The issue is not the denial of anyone's right to be a public figure who "makes" the news magazines. Rather, it is the recognition that judgments about competence in scholarship have their own criteria and that the reputation of a department or a field in the universities is properly measured by these criteria and not extrinsic ones. Under "scholarly writings" by some professors in religious studies one can, unfortunately, still find listed sets of church school lessons they have written or articles for denominational magazines.

A fourth achievement during recent decades which has also worked toward increased legitimacy is that departments of religion are overcoming their Protestant Christian myopia. There are ready historical explanations for the existence of this myopia: many departments, for example, were established in Protestant colleges, and the teachers were trained in seminaries. (Certainly, the theology departments of Catholic colleges and universities were at least as restricted in their vision as the Protestant ones were.) Further, it is clear that departments of religion are not the only ones in the humanities which have suffered from shortsightedness: departments of history have not attended to Asian and African and Latin American history nearly as much in the past as they have to European and American history. At present I know of no department with a Protestant past that does not intend to extend its work in Buddhism, Hinduism, Islam, primitive religions, and the history of Hellenistic and other "dead" religions, as well as in Judaism and in Christianity (to include Catholicism and Orthodoxy). Departments with Catholic histories are engaged in the same kind of extension. Limitations upon such development are those of financial resources and adequately trained personnel in the non-Western fields. No doubt there are a number of explanations for this broadening of intention; the ecumenical movement, the interest in area studies, the wider popular knowledge of other cultures, and the like have all contributed to it. But I believe that, in addition to these, there is a growing recognition among scholars in religion that the field itself requires that justice be done to the wide variety of religious life and thought in human history.

A fifth achievement is one in which the Princeton University Department of Religion especially took the lead. That was to conceive of graduate studies in religion in such a way that the necessity for (or expectation of) an intermediate professional degree could be eliminated. There seems to be no really persuasive reasons why a person with a solid bachelor of arts major in religion or in history and other fields cannot embark upon the graduate study of religion without spending time in a seminary. In practice, the importance of seminary study for graduate work has been twofold. For the seminary provided both a general education in Christianity or in Judaism upon which more specialized graduate study could be built (I would include language study in the biblical languages as part of that general education) and also a kind of maturation period, in which students could become familiar with certain concepts and certain ways of thinking which could then be assumed at the Ph.D. level of studies. Although these contributions continue to be beneficial, they are not necessary for several reasons. First, as the departments extend their reach beyond the traditional Christian curriculum, undergraduates are gaining a broader understanding of religions than seminaries can offer them. Second, as the departments upgrade the quality of their teaching and research (as they have with marked rapidity) and as good departments (rather than the seminaries) become the most desirable places for good scholars and teachers to engage in their work, the level of preparation reached in undergraduate study will come to match that attained in even the best seminaries. Third, if broad general education in religion is deemed to be a necessity (a debatable point), the graduate student without a professional degree can spend a year or so longer in his studies to overcome what are judged to be deficiencies. Fourth, there are many areas of specialized study in religion which do not require the general background that seminaries have presumably provided, such as Asian religions, historical studies of Western and non-Western religions, philosophy of religion, and others. Relevant to this point is the speculation that, increasingly, scholarly research and teaching in religion will be carried on in larger departments in various universities. These locations will allow scholars the room for more specialized teaching and demand performance in more specialized research. While the small department in the small liberal arts college may continue to require more generalized teaching, I believe the proportion of instruction in religion done in such departments will decrease. And fifth, as seminaries are properly forced to clarify the significance of professional theological education, they may well become less able than are many good departments to provide the background work for Ph.D. studies.

The final achievement I note is the disruption of the oligopoly status that a few centers of religious studies enjoyed for so many decades in American academic life. The growth of the departments in state universities and elsewhere itself points to the acceptance of the legitimacy of religious studies in the university; but, even more, the quality of work being done in many of these experiments enhances the legitimacy of the field in the wider culture of higher education. There are many effects of this change. One is the increasingly wider distribution of major talent in the field. To teach in a seminary is becoming almost a special vocation; to be able to explore religions in the context of the arts and sciences has become for many persons the more demanding and more interesting task. A second effect is the expansion of the number of points of view, methodologies, areas of interest, and so on, in religious studies. In the past the academic genealogies of religion scholars and teachers in the United States have displayed too much inbreeding for the good of the field as a whole. A small number of clans has dominated the field, with occasional invitations to others, primarily from Europe, to join the kinship system. With the institutional spread of departments, each one developing characteristic ways of working over the next generations, I believe we shall have a healthier diversity and more creative approaches to scholarly research and to teaching. The benefits from this changed situation will be forced even on the established grandfather institutions which have enjoyed a status in the academic market almost as dominant as that of General Motors, Chrysler, and Ford in the automobile industry.

Potential Stresses and Strains

Although I am no seer, there are some indications of stresses, strains, conflicts, and problems in the field of religious studies that are fairly apparent and worthy of notice. These circumstances should provide possibilities for development in positive ways; I deliberately avoid dramatizing them as crises. Some of them are general matters of concern throughout the humanities and are not exclusively issues in the field of religion.

The first is one to which I have already alluded, namely, that the interests of students in studying religion often run counter to the interests of scholars and teachers in the field. Many students are motivated to take up the study of religion, at least in part, by personal religious, moral, and spiritual uncertainties; many persons teaching religion believe that to address these personal motives would be to compromise their newly acquired scholarly postures. This issue, in its most generalized form, is not peculiar to our field; the charges of irrelevance to the situations of students and the problems of our society are made with reference to many fields in both the humanities and the social sciences. But I believe that the historical circumstances of religious studies place the same problem in a different setting. That is, religious studies has recently achieved legitimacy in part by denying "relevance" as the ground for its inclusion in arts and sciences, by avoiding "preaching," by distinguishing its aim from the functions that religious advisors and professional training serve. Yet it is precisely at this time that the pressures for more attention to the needs and interests of students and to the utility of the work for the problems of society are mounting. Students are requesting more personal judgments about ideas, more proposals for constructive alternatives, at the very time when many persons in religious studies are assuming a more disinterested posture, particularly if they work in universities and colleges where the charge of "preaching" has had some validity in the immediate past. Scholars in religion are finding a sense of departmental identity just when students are pressing for more interdisciplinary work. They are judging themselves by criteria of specialization and precision at the same time that students are questioning these values and are responding to daring and imaginative classroom rhetoric.

I have previously indicated some alternative responses to this set of circumstances: at one extreme, what is relevant to the students' needs is to be "caught" and not "taught"; at the other, the fulfillment of these needs becomes the primary orientation of teaching. Certainly, there will be work done in departments that will explore other options. Ways of teaching will be found that, while allowing for an honest response to the existential interests and motives of students, will at the same time lead them toward more careful and precise studies of critical and historical sorts. For example, in my own field of religious ethics, one can readily begin with a moral issue that students feel deeply about and then proceed to explore the religious principles which have been brought to bear on that issue or similar ones and the methods by which thinkers in the various traditions have proceeded to practical moral judgments about the issue.

The second constellation of issues pertains to the relation of religious studies to other fields. There has been some tendency to develop courses which explore the "religious dimensions" of many more areas of human life than would be covered within a commonsense understanding of religion. Indeed, there are programs in religious studies which have made this extended conception of religion central in their work. In such a perspective, resting as it does on a particular understanding of religion, almost anything in the college curriculum is fair game for religious analysis. For both reasons of conviction and practical reasons, I regard this as a misplaced direction for development of religious studies. It makes almost impossible the delineation of proper responsibilities, and it opens the way for religious analysis to play the servant of all the disciplines. Although that may be a less presumptuous role to assume than queen, it nevertheless tempts persons in religious studies to violate the integrity of other fields.

But even if religions are operationally defined in more

commonsense terms as texts, institutions, ideas, practices, and so on, which emerge from history and cultures as phenomena that can be differentiated from primarily political, economic, and other aspects of experience, we still find other departments engaged in research concerning religion: history of art, philosophy, history, sociology, psychology, and others. The possibilities of these confluences of material and interest—as well as accompanying strains—will grow in importance in the future. They will enrich religious studies but render it more complex. Joint or cross-listed courses at the undergraduate level are already being offered in many institutions. The procedure of joint appointments (with different degrees of responsibility and participation in the departments involved) is useful, but not without its burdens for those whose obligations are proliferated. At the level of doctoral research one foresees the possibility of having dissertations jointly directed by persons from different departments; one also can imagine the difficulties of such joint direction, owing to the differences in training and interest on the part of faculty members involved and to the degree of competence that will be expected in the field which is more minor than major in the research.

A different sort of relation to other fields and departments might well emerge in the near future. As the policy sciences and professional schools become even more embroiled in actual matters of public action and public policy, departments of religion may also be asked to engage in a normative task which for good reasons they have heretofore officially eschewed. "Field experience" is beginning to become a part of undergraduate work in some of the social sciences, both as a way of learning about the subject matter involved and as a way of relating the subject matter to students' personal moral interests. Institutes and centers which concern themselves with policy problems in an interdepartmental way already exist in many universities; the participation of personnel from religious studies may well be increasingly requested if they have the competence and the interest to make a positive contribution. Under these circumstances the posture of disinterestedness so recently cultivated would probably undergo revision as at least some colleges and universities redefine their roles with reference to matters of public well-being.

A third area that will require further development and exploration is the relation of undergraduate preparation to graduate studies in religion. It is too early to tell whether there will be any growth in the number of religion majors, and there are vast differences between colleges and universities in the proportion of students now taking courses or majoring in the field. But as graduate schools prepare themselves to accept students who have done no work beyond the bachelor of art level, undergraduate programs will have to be examined in the light of their strengths and weaknesses as preparatory for doctoral studies. We are turning a corner in the field; religious studies is becoming less important as a part of a general liberalizing education and more important as a potential field of research leading to a professional academic career. One focus ought not replace the other, but thus far not enough attention has been given to the latter aspect. For example, what programs in language training should be made available to the undergraduate student who will go on to work in Buddhist studies, in biblical studies, and so on? What courses on methods and procedures of research are needed to prepare students? Are the seminars that are offered specialized enough? Or do we want more general seminars? Should we open various undergraduate tracks for students who intend to specialize in various aspects of religious studies at the graduate level?

The proliferation of graduate programs, which I have lauded previously, also brings problems of many sorts. This is another area of concern for the future. The economy or present distribution of personnel and library resources, among other things, is not as healthy as it ought to be for the rapid growth that many persons contemplate. It is regrettable, but nonetheless a fact, that library collections with the great depth needed for graduate research are usually located where there are strong seminaries. Language training and other rudimentary areas of competence essential for specialized research in various religions require the presence of cognate areas in the university and good working relations with them. In the long run, expansion of graduate programs without due regard for qualitative assessment of various resources will debilitate, rather than promote, the field of religious studies as a whole. Experimental cooperative use of resources is already under way in certain urban centers where there are clusters of universities and seminaries. Other efforts will have to be made—for example, to rotate students among centers where special work is best offered.

Persons in this field hardly need to be reminded of another area in which problems have a special urgency—namely, the availability of funds for research. As part of the humanities, religious studies shares in the general and comparative scarcity of available financial resources. Further, as a field which evokes ghosts in closets—such as church-state relations, interests in propagation of religion, and so on—religious studies suffers under a special handicap. Here, as elsewhere, when the posture of objectivity is fulfilled by a growing body of competent research, I believe some persuasive evidence will be in hand to make the case for more research funds from various sources.

Finally, I would observe that the existence of strong professional societies plays an important role in the maintenance of vitality in any field and in the sustenance of high standards of scholarship. I know of no field of American education which suffers from the proliferation of learned societies in the way that religious studies does. There are historical explanations for this situation, to be sure. Societies primarily concerned with professional education of religious leaders have their own right to exist. But the state of societies in the field is chaotic at the present time, and, unfortunately, new ones seem to emerge annually around different clusters of interests. Consolidation would be difficult at best, for historians and social scientists concerned with religion, for example, probably prefer to meet with persons who share their disciplined methods and procedures rather than with persons who share their interests in a broad, if common, subject matter. But the exploration of ways of cooperation, if not consolidation, is imperative for the sake of the field itself and for the sake of its members' access to research funds as well as other benefits.

These observations and comments are the expression of one person's reflections on the field of religious studies as a whole. Underlying them, however, is a central plea. That is, religious studies will settle its legitimacy in the arts and sciences (and its teachers and students will gain in confidence) as performance in research and teaching increasingly meets the expectations and promises developed out of our introspective self-examination. There is no substitute for competence—for intelligence, imagination, hard work, productivity, rigor, and clarity. To stress specialized professional competence is not to leave behind the concerns for the study of religion as part of an overall liberalizing education. A unity of mastery over the subject with interest in the students is possible. But emphasis does need to be placed on specialized professional competence. The bearings we take and our achievements in following them will, I hope and believe, make unnecessary the publication of many more volumes such as this. Perhaps this volume and the Conference out of which it came will make a turning point from introspective searches for legitimacy to an acknowledged legitimacy based upon proved performance in the context of the arts and sciences.

Selected Bibliography

A REMARKABLE volume of literature bears directly on the study of religion in colleges and universities. Numerous books and articles place the subject in a variety of frameworks which are essentially external to it. (Whether or not they are more comprehensive is an open question.) One example is provided by the literature concerned with "religious education" in which the study of religion is frequently discussed under the categories of "faith" and "nurture." Another example of an "external framework" would be the perspective of those who emphasize the "presence" of religion on campuses and for whom student volunteer work, chapel programs, and academic inquiry into beliefs and practices form a necessary and interrelated continuum. This selected bibliography undertakes to present the variety of relevant literature while placing emphasis upon the type of material most immediately concerned with appropriate definition of the academic study of religion.

The general relationship of religion to higher education was considered between the two world wars in a conference held at Princeton in February 1928. A report of the proceedings was published as *Religion in the Colleges*, edited by Galen M. Fisher (New York: Association Press, 1928). See also the volume based on a conference held at Chicago two years later, *Religion in Higher Education*, edited by Milton C. Towner (Chicago: University of Chicago Press, 1931). More recently assumptions and practices of the period were extensively and carefully reviewed by Merrimon Cuninggim in *The College Seeks Religion* (New Haven: Yale University Press, 1947), which developed out of a doctoral dissertation submitted to Yale University in 1941. The author undertook to canvass the variety of institutional attitudes toward and arrangements for religion, focusing more upon extracurricular matters than upon specifically academic provisions for the study of religion. Yet more recent publications in the same genre (although not as broadly gauged) are represented by the following. As part of the centennial commemoration of student religious activity at the University of Michigan, Seymour A. Smith wrote "an historical sketch" called *Religious Cooperation in State Universities* (Ann Arbor: University of Michigan, 1957), which concentrated primarily upon extracurricular developments in the major public institutions. A companion monograph by C. Grey Austin entitled *A Century of Religion at the University of Michigan* (Ann Arbor: University of Michigan, 1957) was intended as "A Case Study in Religion and the State University." An earlier "case study" charted united religious work at Cornell University between 1919 and 1939: Richard H. Edwards' *Cooperative Religion at Cornell University* (Ithaca, N.Y.: Cornell Cooperative Society, 1939).

Impetus for the development of religion study in colleges and universities has been consistently expressed in and through the National Council on Religion and Higher Education (recently renamed the Society for Religion in Higher Education), which was founded in 1922 under the leadership of Charles F. Kent, Woolsey Professor of Biblical Literature at Yale University. As the Second World War came to a close, for example, it joined with other interested groups to sponsor a Program of Faculty Consultations designed to assist an institution in clarifying the appropriate place of religion in its overall program. (See John W. Nason, "Religion and Higher Education," *The Educational Record* xxvii/4 [Oct. 1946], 422-432.) In recognition of twenty-five years of annual conferences held by the Council, there was eventually published a series of papers (by distinguished members of the organization) which reviewed the place of religion in higher education, entitled *Liberal Learning and Religion,* edited by Amos N. Wilder (New York, Harper, 1951). More recently the Society sponsored two publications by Robert Michaelsen as expression of its continuing concern with the subject: "The Scholarly Study of Religion in College and University" (New Haven: Society for Religion in Higher Education, [1964]) is a programmatic essay-pamphlet, while *The Study of Religion in American Uni-*

versities (New Haven: Society for Religion in Higher Education, 1965) brings together ten case studies "with special reference to state universities." See also Michaelsen's "Religion as an Academic Discipline," *Liberal Education* XLVII/1 (March 1961), 72-83.

The place of religion study in state universities has been frequently reviewed during recent years, and many of the following references include discussions of the ramifications of this issue, in terms of legal questions, policy matters, and so on. The most widely known literature on this particular subject became available as a result of the centennial celebrations at the University of Michigan, noted above. *Religion and the State University*, edited by Erich A. Walter (Ann Arbor: University of Michigan Press, 1958), has had extensive use and has been made available in a paperback edition (Ann Arbor Books). While the chapters in this book range over questions regarding the nature of a religiously plural society and include reflections on the quality of campus and community life, a substantial series of essays is devoted to "Religion and University Education" (Section II). In addition, William K. Frankena's "Concluding Statement" (295-309) warrants special attention. (A direct report of this First National Consultative Conference, held on November 16-19, 1958, may be found in *Religious Education* LIV/2 [March-April 1959], 83-137. In that issue there were also appraisals of "The Outlook for Religion in the State Universities" [139-148], independent of the Conference.) *The Teaching of Religion in State Universities*, edited by Milton D. McLean and Harry H. Kimber (Ann Arbor: University of Michigan Press, 1960), was originally prepared as a background paper for the Conference and subsequently was made available for wider use. Seymour A. Smith's article "Religious Instruction in State Universities," *Religious Education* LIII/3 (May-June 1958), 290-294, is a useful summary discussion of trends. The Society for Religion in Higher Education published the proceedings of a conference held in October 1964 at Indiana University Medical Center in Indianapolis in *A Re-*

port On An Invitational Conference On The Study Of Religion In The State University (New Haven: Society for Religion in Higher Education [1965]). Major essays on "Sociology and the Study of Religion," "Systematic Theology," and the religious approach to "Non-Western Studies" are included in this volume. Two panel discussions embodying significant opening statements are also represented. One panel concerned policy regarding, and the implementation of, the scholarly study of religion; the other covered additional matters, such as student interest, legal issues, and educational concerns. The report of a subsequent conference on the same topic, held in November 1965 at Southern Illinois University, was published as *Religious Studies in Public Universities*, edited by Milton D. McLean (Carbondale, Ill.: Southern Illinois University, 1967). This book included a substantial directory of "Courses and Programs in Religion in 135 Public and 11 Private Colleges and Universities, 1965-66" (61-266). One distinctive pattern of providing for the study of religion in the context of state university education has been the establishment of "schools of religion" adjacent to campuses but privately funded. This pattern has been most prominently developed at the State University of Iowa. Marcus Bach wrote a "popular presentation of [its] history and influence" in *Of Faith and Learning* (Iowa City: School of Religion, State University of Iowa, 1952). A historical pamphlet on the program was written by M. Willard Lampe: "The Story of An Idea" (State University of Iowa Extension Bulletin Number 704, March 1, 1955).

Numerous symposia have been published during recent years, in addition to the many invitational conferences which have been arranged, on the topic of religion and its study within higher education. See, as one example of the former, the collection of essays printed in *Religious Education* LIII/6 (Nov.-Dec. 1958), 483-520, under the title "The Humanities and Religious Education." *The Journal of General Education* devoted its issue of October 1961 (XIII/3) to the question of religious studies and included six relevant essays on different aspects of the matter. Another symposium was presented in *Religious Education* in 1964 entitled "Religion and Higher Education" (LIX/5 [Sept.-Oct. 1964], 405-421). The Association of American Colleges took the lead (through a commission) in organizing a conference on the teaching of religion at the State University of New York at Stony Brook, Long Island, in January 1966. Selected papers from the gathering were published as *The Study of Religion on the Campus of Today*, edited by Karl D. Hartzell and Harrison Sasscer (Washington, D.C.: Association of American Colleges, 1967). In December of the same year the Commission on Religion in Higher Education of the Association issued a brochure, "Religion as an Academic Discipline," which "unreservedly" recommended that specific steps be taken toward incorporating the "scholarly study of religion [as] part of the liberal arts curriculum in all colleges and universities, public as well as private." Another such conference was one sponsored by the Department of Higher Education of the National Council of Churches as a consultation in New York City in January 1967. It was reported in *The Study of Religion in College and University* (New York: National Council of Churches, 1967).

Finally, a substantial literature has been directed toward specification of the content of religious study in conjunction with clarification of the intent underlying it. Shortly after the Second World War the Edward W. Hazen Foundation joined with the Committee on Religion and Education of the American Council on Education in sponsoring *College Reading and Religion* (New Haven: Yale University Press, 1948), a review of that subject in various established disciplines. A subsequent series of related pamphlets was collectively published in bound form under the title *Religious Perspectives in College Teaching*, edited by Hoxie N. Fairchild (New York: Ronald Press, 1952). Alexander Miller brought a self-consciously Christian concern to his discussion of higher education in a twentieth-century perspective; see especially his "Teaching Religion and Teaching the Christian Faith" (Chap. V) in *Faith and Learning* (New York: Association Press, 1960). Probably the most significant volumes on this topic during recent decades were a part of the Princeton Studies in Humanistic Scholarship in America. In one study strictly comparable to the others in the series, each of seven authors reviewed and assessed the scholarship in his own field. The essays included "The History of Religions" by Philip H. Ashby, "Old Testament Studies" by Harry M. Orlinsky, "The Study of Early Christianity" by Robert M. Grant, "The History of Christianity" by James H. Nichols, "Theology" by Claude Welch, "Christian Ethics" by James M. Gustafson, and "Philosophy of Religion" by John E. Smith. (*Religion*, edited by Paul Ramsey [Englewood Cliffs, N.J.: Prentice-Hall, 1965].) The second book in this series concerned with religion was specifically commissioned to define in a careful manner the terms in which the study of religion is properly a part of American humanistic scholarship. Clyde Holbrook's *Religion, A Humanistic Field* (Englewood Cliffs, N.J.: Prentice-Hall, 1963) makes an important contribution to clarification of the status of religion study within colleges and universities at the present time, though it does not seek to examine religious scholarship except in an incidental manner. A critical discussion of his assumptions, together with his rejoinder, may be found in "Mr. Holbrook and the Humanities, or Mr. Schlatter's Dilemma" by John F. Wilson (*The Journal of Bible and Religion* XXXII/3 [July 1964], 252-266). A recent essay by the reviewer, "Developing the Study of Religion in American Colleges and Universities," appears in *The Journal of General Education* XX/3 (Oct. 1968), 190-208.

The Study of Religion in Colleges and Universities has attempted to move beyond the special pleading and apologetics which characterizes so much of the literature of the field, some of which is cited above. Assuming that the study of religion is appropriate to colleges and universities, the essays in this volume have reviewed established as well as projected fields within the whole and sought to suggest their probable futures.

Contributors

William A. Clebsch is Professor of Religion and Humanities, Stanford University

Malcolm L. Diamond is Professor of Religion, Princeton University

Tom F. Driver is Professor of Theology and Literature, Union Theological Seminary, New York

James M. Gustafson is Professor of Christian Ethics, Department of Religious Studies and the Divinity School, Yale University

Paul M. Harrison is Professor of Religious Studies, The Pennsylvania State University

David Little is Associate Professor of Christian Ethics, the Divinity School, Yale University

Arthur C. McGill is Professor of Theology, the Divinity School, Harvard University

Jacob Neusner is Professor of Religious Studies, Brown University

Victor Preller is Associate Professor of Religion, Princeton University

Paul Ramsey is Harrington Spear Paine Professor of Religion, Princeton University

Krister Stendahl is Dean of the Divinity School, Harvard University

H. P. Sullivan is Professor of Religion, Vassar College

A. Richard Turner is Professor of Art, Middlebury College

John F. Wilson is Associate Professor of Religion, Princeton University